BREWING

❧ CLASSIC ❧

STYLES

80 Winning Recipes Anyone Can Brew

Jamil Zainasheff and John J. Palmer

**A Division of the
Brewers Association
Boulder, Colorado**

Brewers Publications
A Division of the Brewers Association
PO Box 1679, Boulder, Colorado 80306-1679
www.beertown.org

Printed in the United States of America.

10 9 8 7 6 5 4 3 2

ISBN: 0-937-381-92-6
ISBN-13: 978-0-937381-92-2

Library of Congress Cataloging-in-Publication Data
Zainasheff, Jamil, 1961-
  Brewing classic styles : 80 winning recipes anyone can brew
/ by Jamil Zainasheff and John Palmer.
     p. cm.
  ISBN 978-0-937381-92-2
  1. Brewing. I. Palmer, John J., 1963- II. Title.

TP570.Z35 2007
641.8'73--dc22

2007029472

Publisher: Ray Daniels
Copy Editing and Index: Daria Labinsky
Production & Design Management: Stephanie Johnson
Cover and Interior Design: Julie Lawrason
Production: Michael Blotz
Cover Photo: Rick Souders, Souders Studios, www.soudersstudios.com
Interior Photos: Jamil Zainasheff and John Palmer unless otherwise noted

BREWING CLASSIC STYLES
80 WINNING RECIPES ANYONE CAN BREW

ACKNOWLEDGEMENTS

No work of this sort is created in a vacuum. In my case it was the kindness, generosity, sharing, and love of my family, friends, and the community of brewers that made this possible.

My incredible wife, Liz, and two wonderful daughters, Anisa and Karina, have been very understanding of why Dad spends so much time on his "beer stuff." They are always willing to help with odd brewing tasks and travel with me to out-of-the-way places just so I can taste a unique beer. I do love them more than beer, but they never ask me to prove it.

Thanks to Ray Daniels for his landmark book, *Designing Great Beers*. More than any other book on brewing, it was this book that taught me how to make my own recipes. I never could have written this book without first learning from Ray.

Thanks to those who had the faith in me to speak or write about beer styles. My tremendous fear of saying something wrong on air or in print made me relearn a lot of things about brewing that I only had a passing knowledge of before.

And my friends, my brewing brothers and sisters, you have shared your beers, your homes, your knowledge, and most important to me, your friendship. Thank you for being there for me. If you were the only friends I knew, I would consider myself very lucky.

–Jamil Zainasheff

First, I need to thank my wife, Naomi, for suggesting that I write another book. It seemed like a crazy idea at the time, having just finished the previous one, but she knows that I love doing this stuff.

Second, I want to thank Ray Daniels and all my other friends at the American Homebrewers Association and Brewers Publications for all their support and enthusiasm. Being treated like a famous author has its merits, but being accepted as a friend is better.

Finally, thanks to Gordon Strong and the rest of the Beer Judge Certification Program organization for letting us write on their coat-tails like this. As Jamil and I discussed the concept for the book, we said, "Wouldn't it be great if they let us use the current organization and descriptions of the styles, so that we would all be consistent?" And they did.

–John Palmer

The BJCP Style Guidelines were used in creating the "Style at a Glance" for each recipe. The BJCP style information is used with permission of the copyright holder, Beer Judge Certification Program Inc. The current version of the style guidelines can be found at the BJCP website, www.bjcp.org.

INTRODUCTION

John: I have been wanting to write a book called *How to Brew With Extract* for many years, because I feel that extract brewing doesn't get the respect it deserves. I also wanted this book to have some killer recipes for lots of different beers styles, and while my recipes are OK, I wasn't fooling myself into thinking they were stellar. I thought that my friend Jamil could probably help me there, since he is one of the best brewers I know.

Jamil: I hadn't seen John in quite some time when I ran into him at the Great American Beer Festival^{SM}. As we talked, John mentioned he was preparing to write a book on how to brew great beer with extract. He said he needed a handful of good recipes to include in the book, and I offered to help. Well, even the best laid plans tend to evolve, and this book quickly turned from a book on extract with a few recipes into a recipe book with advice on brewing, applicable to all brewers.

John: At some point in our conversation at the GABF (I think we were over by the Brooklyn Brewery at this point, or maybe it was Dogfish Head), Jamil mentioned, "I have a recipe for every style. …" Even though I didn't realize it then, this was the turning point of the whole project. I took another sip of beer and said, "Cool."

But as we started working on the book, outlining the content and discussing the theme, I quickly realized that great recipes were much more marketable than extract brewing tips, which I had covered fairly well in *How to Brew*. The more I thought about it, the more I liked the idea of a book that described how to brew a specific recipe for every style in the Beer Judge Certification Program Style Guidelines. I am good at describing the mechanics of brewing, but I am not good at describing the art, the intuition that can be applied to it. From listening to "The Jamil Show" podcast on The Brewing Network, I knew that Jamil could.

Jamil: Recently someone asked me how long we have been working on this book, and I started thinking back to my first conversations with John. Before I could answer, someone else said, "He's been working on it since he started brewing." Ah yes, that is so true. The recipes in this book are the product of dozens of countries visited, hundreds of batches brewed, and thousands of beers tasted. When I started home-brewing, I set myself the goal of being able to brew a good example of every recognized style in the BJCP. To check on my progress, I entered my beers in a number of competitions. I methodically tweaked and tested each recipe until the beers began to win awards. In fact, every recipe in this book has won a number of awards, some more than others, but all are proven recipes.

Many people wonder why I would be willing to "give away my award-winning recipes." Those who taught me to brew all shared a core ethic: If you know something about brewing, you share it with others. It seems to me that all of the best brewers I know are willing to share their recipes and techniques. They hold nothing back. Brewers who feel the need to hide a recipe or other information often only have one or two beers that they can brew well and are afraid to let it go for fear of not finding more good recipes.

Our hope is that you will look at this book as much more than just a collection of recipes, and once you learn from it, you will build upon that knowledge and share it with others. This book is intended as a guide to help you successfully brew the most recognized beer styles in the world. Too many brewers focus on just a handful of their favorite styles and miss out on some really wonderful beer styles. Don't let that happen to you. Please make an effort to brew every style in this book well.

Some people ask how to become a better brewer. Becoming a great brewer is like becoming a great chef. Foremost, it takes a great deal of practice to master the fundamentals. You don't become a great chef without mastering the basic cooking techniques and the most common menu items. Once you have mastered the basics, then you can stretch your wings and create some new and unusual dish. It is the same for brewing. You must master the basics of sanitation, fermentation, and ingredients. You must understand how to brew to style before you can soar and create something entirely new. It is not unusual for someone to claim they have created a beer that doesn't fit in any of the style categories, yet when a person with enough experience tastes it, they can easily identify it as being a good example of one style or another. Become a better brewer by making a commitment to brewing all of the BJCP-recognized styles. If you're not sure of how well you are doing, enter your beer in several competitions to get feedback. (You can find a list of competitions at www.bjcp.org.) Get yourself a copy of John Palmer's *How to Brew* and read it cover to cover. Read all the brewing literature you can. Check off the styles you complete, and once you've brewed them all successfully, you will have earned quite an education.

No matter what happens in your brewing education, don't get discouraged and don't let fear of failure stop you. Brew, brew, brew. After all, it's just beer.

Publisher's note: Beyond this introduction, the chapters were prepared by one or the other of the authors. John Palmer wrote chapters 1 through 4 and Appendices B, C, and D. Jamil Zainasheff wrote recipe style chapters and Appendix A. In the recipe chapters the first-person singular pronoun "I" refers to Jamil.

1 | BREWING WITH STYLE

All beers started out in someone's home. Beer was brewed with local water, local ingredients, and local methods. Thus the beer brewed in London was different from the beer brewed in Flanders and different from the local beer in Munich. All of these factors come together to define the beer, and that definition, that description, is its style.

Some styles are similar and only differ by the relative quantity of a single ingredient. English bitter and extra-special bitter have similar ingredients but differ primarily by having more or less of them. Similarly, India pale ale will often have the same malt body but twice as much hop bitterness as American pale ale. Dortmunder export differs from Munich helles because it is brewed with a higher-sulfate water, so the export's hop bitterness is more assertive and balanced to the malt than that in the helles, which has a softer, slightly sweeter finish.

Some styles are very similar in ingredients and amounts but will differ by the type of yeast or merely by the local fermentation conditions. These beers are often grouped together when judged in competition because of the similarity of the styles. For example, in the Amber Hybrid category, California common beer has ingredients and fermentation similar to those of a Düsseldorf altbier, but the overall character is different largely due to the yeast strain.

Other beers from the same region can differ greatly in flavor and style and depend on the brewer's art to craft equally superb beers from the same fermentation conditions. Munich dunkel is the beer that grew from the local conditions, but the good brewers at the Spaten brewery learned to remove calcium carbonate from the water in 1895, enabling them to brew the lighter helles to compete with Pilsener-style beers.

But why should you brew according to a style? Shouldn't we celebrate individuality and creativity within the art as much or more so than those who routinely produce a standard beer? Yes, and we do. Look at some of the brewing superstars: Vinnie Cilurzo of Russian River Brewing Company, Randy Thiel of Brewery Ommegang, and Sam Calagione of Dogfish Head Brewery. These brewers are renowned for creating unique beers, beers that don't fit a standard style. But they know and understand the styles and use their skill to successfully reach outside of the style to brew a beer that is wonderful, rather than just being weird. You learn the fundamentals, and then you test your understanding by making a known standard. Musicians work the same way. The performance is judged not only on technical merit but also on artistic merit—the interpretation, the sense of passion that they bring to that performance. To brew an award-winning beer, you will need to do the same.

Do you have to compete? No, but there are two reasons to enter competitions—to compete, and to get feedback. When each of us first entered competitions, it was for feedback—to learn how we were progressing as brewers. In one competition John entered the Porter category with an extract-and-specialty-grain clone of Sierra Nevada Porter, and it won. But the judge's feedback encouraged him to try some changes in his brewing process and ingredients. He became a better brewer as a result. And when you feel you have earned your chops as a brewer, then it's fun to compete!

Choosing Your Style

The purpose of this book is to provide you with the recipes and brewing techniques to brew any one of the more than eighty classic beer styles in the world today. What would you like to brew? Do you like light, easy-drinking, thirst-quenching beers? Then you may want to try the Light Lager, Pilsener, and Light Hybrid Beer categories. Do you want an easy-drinking beer with a bit more malt? Try Scottish and Irish ale. Do you want a darker malt character but without bitterness? Try European dark lager or English brown ale. Do you want bitterness? Then American Ale is probably your category. More bitterness? The kind of beer that would make Popeye give up spinach? Then India pale ale is your beer.

Are you looking for a beer to serve with a special dinner? Belgian, French ale, and sour ale make the perfect accent for many rich foods. How about a beer for after dinner, one to relax with around the table? Belgian strong ale, or English old ale and barley wine are perfect. We could go on and on, but you get the idea. There is a beer for every occasion and every taste, and once you have brewed them all, you will know where in this spectrum to create your own.

To help you decide what to brew, the following table has the styles sorted according to the brewing process and the type of brewing equipment required.

The next chapter is all about the flavors of beer and where they come from.

Table 1—Styles Categorized According to Level of Effort to Brew Them.

Beginner	Intermediate	Advanced
These styles are easily brewed with extract and steeped grain and basic equipment	These styles are often high gravity and may include tricky yeasts, odd ingredients, and extra steps. The brewing process requires more attention to fermentation temperature.	These styles may include partial mash, bacteria cultures, and extended fermentation. The lager styles require active temperature control for fermentation.
American Amber Ale	American Barley Wine	Baltic Porter
American Brown Ale	American Stout	Berliner Weisse
American IPA	Belgian Blonde Ale	Bohemian Pilsener
American Pale Ale	Belgian Dark Strong Ale	Classic American Pilsener
American Wheat or Rye Beer	Belgian Dubbel	Classic Rauchbier
Belgian Pale Ale	Belgian Golden Strong Ale	Dark American Lager
Blonde Ale	Belgian Specialty Ale	Doppelbock
Brown Porter	Belgian Tripel	Dortmunder Export
Dunkelweizen	Bière de Garde	Dry Stout
English IPA	California Common Beer	Eisbock
Extra-Special/Strong Bitter (English Pale Ale)	Christmas/Winter Specialty Spiced Beer	Flanders Brown Ale/Oud Bruin
Irish Red Ale	Cream Ale	Flanders Red Ale
Mild	Düsseldorf Altbier	Fruit Lambic
Northern English Brown Ale	English Barley Wine	German Pilsener (Pils)
Oatmeal Stout	Foreign Extra Stout	Gueuze
Robust Porter	Fruit Beer	Imperial IPA
Scottish Export 80/-	Kölsch	Imperial Stout
Scottish Heavy 70/-	Northern German Altbier	Lite American Lager
Scottish Light 60/-	Old Ale	Maibock/Helles Bock
Southern English Brown Ale	Other Smoked Beer	Munich Dunkel
Special/Best/Premium Bitter	Saison	Munich Helles
Standard/Ordinary Bitter	Specialty Beer	Oktoberfest/Märzen
Sweet Stout	Spice, Herb, or Vegetable Beer	Premium American Lager
Weizen/Weissbier	Strong Scotch Ale	Roggenbier (German Rye Beer)
	Weizenbock	Schwarzbier
	Witbier	Standard American Lager
	Wood-Aged Beer	Straight (Unblended) Lambic
		Traditional Bock
		Vienna Lager

2 | CHOOSING YOUR INGREDIENTS

To build your beer of choice, you need to start with the malt. Most beer styles were probably built from the malt up. Consider that hundreds of years ago, breweries usually had their own maltings and brewed from what they made. If the beer turned out bland, they would increase the kilning temperature. If the beer turned out acrid and burnt tasting, they would lower the kiln temperature. If they didn't get the conversion they wanted in the mash, they would cook the grain to help it along. Once they had the malt character where they wanted it, they would season it to taste with hops. Local ingredients and local conditions combined to create local styles. Other, similar styles were often created when neighboring areas tried to copy a tasty beer. Perhaps they couldn't get the same hop variety, or perhaps their water had a different mineral character. Ingredient substitution is as common today as it was then, as brewers adapt recipes to meet local conditions. This chapter will examine the characteristic flavors and aromas of the ingredients to help you make appropriate substitutions.

Malt Flavors
Maltsters usually divide the malt world into four types: base malts, kilned malts (including highly kilned), roasted, and kilned-and-roasted. Varying the moisture level, time, and temperature develops the characteristic flavors and colors of each specialty malt. Caramelization and Maillard reactions both play a role in the development of the wide variety of flavors in these malts and the beers made from them.

Caramelization is a sugar-to-sugar reaction that occurs at high temperatures and low moisture. (It does not happen during normal wort boiling.) Maillard reactions occur over a range of temperatures and moisture levels and will always occur during normal wort boiling. Maillard reactions produce volatile, low-molecular-weight flavor

compounds, reductones, and melanoidins. Reductones bind oxygen to improve flavor stability, and melanoidins are the browning aspect of the Maillard reaction.

Both types of reactions can generate some of the same flavors, like toffee, molasses, and raisin, but in general, caramelization reactions are responsible for the toffee-sweet caramel flavors in malt, while Maillard reactions are responsible for the malty, toasty, biscuity flavors often associated with baking. The low-temperature, high-moisture Maillard reactions produce malty and fresh bread flavors, and the high-temperature, low-moisture Maillard reactions produce the toasty and biscuit flavors. Roasted flavors like chocolate and coffee are produced by the highest temperature Maillards and the actual charring of sugars.

The kilned malts, like pale ale malt and Vienna malt, are heated dry at low temperature and low moisture to retain their diastatic enzymes. The flavors expressed are lightly grainy with hints of toast and warmth. Aromatic and Munich malt are kilned at higher temperatures to produce rich fresh bread and bread crust flavors. Only Maillard reactions are involved. These malts must be mashed to yield soluble extract but can be steeped to impart some characteristic flavors.

Specialty malts like caramel and chocolate are roasted at high temperatures to produce caramelization and Maillard reactions for distinctive flavors. (*photo courtesy of Briess Malting Company*)

The caramel malts, such as caramel 60 °L and caramel 120 °L, are produced by roasting green malt—i.e., malt that was not dried by kilning after germination. These malts are put into a roaster and heated to starch conversion range, effectively mashing them in the hull. After conversion, these malts are roasted at various temperatures, depending on the degree of color wanted. Roasting causes the sugars inside the kernels to caramelize, breaking them down and re-combining them into less-fermentable forms. Maillard reactions are also occurring and are responsible for darkening of the sugars, as well as some of the flavors. The lighter caramel malts have a light honey to caramel flavor, while the darker caramel malts have a richer caramel and toffee flavor with hints of burnt sugar and raisin at the darkest roasts. These malts are fully converted and can be steeped to release soluble extract.

The kilned-and-roasted malts are amber, brown, chocolate, and black malt. These malts start out green like the caramel malts above but are kilned to dry them before roasting. Amber malts are produced by roasting fully kilned pale ale malt at moderately high temperatures. These temperatures give the malt the characteristic toasty, biscuity, and nutty flavors. Brown malts are roasted longer than amber malts and achieve a very dry, dark toast flavor, with color similar to that of the caramel malts. These malts must be mashed to yield soluble extract but can be steeped to impart some characteristic flavors.

Chocolate malt goes into roasting with more moisture than brown malt, but less than caramel malt, to develop chocolatey flavors. Some degree of caramelization occurs, but the majority of the flavors are from Maillard reactions. Black (patent) malts are roasted at slightly higher temperatures to produce coffee-like flavors. Roasted barley is produced in a similar manner, except that it is never malted to begin with. Roasted malts can be steeped to release soluble extract.

To summarize, kilning produces bread-like flavors from the low-temperature, low-moisture Maillard reactions. Roasting dry malts increases the Maillard reactions and accentuates the malt flavors of biscuit and toast. Roasting green malt causes both Maillard and caramelization reactions that produce sweet toffee flavors. Kilning and roasting of green malt at high temperatures produces the chocolate and coffee-like flavors.

What Is Malty?

So if we tell you that Beer A is maltier than Beer B, what exactly do we mean? What is malty? Well, as we described above, the many flavors and aromas of malt that derive from Maillard reactions are the same as those from baking bread. Most malt flavors and aromas are associated with fresh bread and the crisp and toasty crust. The roasted flavors of malt are most often associated with other, more common foods, like chocolate and coffee, but they are malty flavors, too. Assembling all these flavors to build a picture of maltiness can take the form of a histogram, like the one shown below. The point is that "malty" is composed of a range of flavors, and the majority of perceived malt flavor consists of the flavors associated with fresh baked bread.

What about malt sweetness, you ask? Good question. Sweetness is largely separate from malty; a malty beer can be either sweet or dry. The attenuation of a beer can be manipulated by the mashing regimen, and two beers with the same grain bill can be equally malty yet have different final gravities and residual sweetness. You may perceive the sweeter beer as being "maltier," but our position is that the maltiness of the beers is the same—it's the balance of the final gravity to the hop bitterness that changes. The quick answer is that the perceived difference is maltiness, but the more accurate answer is that the balance of the two beers is different.

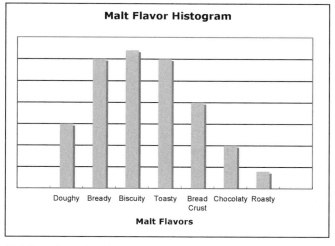

Malt Flavor Perception Histogram

The body of a beer is also commonly perceived as being part of maltiness, but again, it is more complicated than that. The body or mouthfeel of a beer is enhanced by unfermentable sugars (e.g., dextrins), soluble protein, and beta glucans from the malt. In general, a beer that contains more malt (i.e., higher original gravity) will have more of these body-enhancing components, but there are several beer styles like Oktoberfest, Scottish ale, and dry stout that pack the same intense malt flavor without the heavier body and higher OG of styles like India pale ale and bock.

Table 2—Malt Types. The following is a table of the malts used in the recipes sorted by type. If a specified malt in a recipe is not available, a malt of the same type and a similar color will often make an acceptable substitute. It won't be the same beer, but it will be close, and perhaps close enough.

Base Malts Need to be mashed	Kilned Malts Need to be mashed, but may be steeped	Roasted Malts Can be steeped or mashed	Kilned-and-Roasted Malts Can be steeped or mashed
American two-row American six-row Pilsener malt Continental Pilsener malt British pale ale malt Rye malt Wheat malt	Vienna malt Munich malt Aromatic malt (20 °L) Biscuit (25 °L) Victory (28 °L) Melanoidin (28 °L) Special Roast (50 °L) Brown malt (70 °L) German beech-wood- smoked rauch malt	CaraPils/dextrine malt Crystal (15 °L) Honey malt (18 °L) CaraVienna (20 °L) Crystal (40 °L) CaraMunich (60 °L) Crystal (60 °L) Crystal (80 °L) Crystal (120 °L) Special "B" (120 °L) Meussdoerffer Rost (200 °L)	Pale chocolate malt (200 °L) Light roasted barley (300 °L) Chocolate malt (350 °L) Chocolate malt (420 °L) Carafa Special II (430 °L) Chocolate malt (475 °L) Black barley (500 °L) Black patent (525 °L) Black malt (600 °L) Roasted barley (450 °L) Roasted barley (500 °L) Roasted barley (575 °L)

Hop Character

The primary use of hops is for bittering. Bittering hop additions are boiled for 45 to 90 minutes to isomerize the alpha acids; the most common interval is 1 hour. The aromatic oils of the hops used in the bittering additions tend to boil away, leaving little hop flavor or aroma. By adding the hops midway through the boil, a compromise between isomerization of the alpha acids and evaporation of the aromatics is achieved to yield moderate bitterness and characteristic flavors. These flavoring hop additions are added 20 to 40 minutes before the end of the boil, with the most common choice being 30 minutes. When hops are added during the final minutes of the boil, fewer of the aromatic oils are lost to evaporation and more hop aroma is retained. One or more varieties of hop may be used, depending on the character desired. Finishing hops are typically added 15 minutes or less before the end of the boil, or are added "at knockout" (when the heat is turned off) and allowed to steep for several minutes before the wort is cooled. Hops can also be added to the fermenter for increased hop aroma in the final beer. This is called "dry-hopping" and is best done late in the fermentation

cycle. If the hops are added to the fermenter during active fermentation, then a lot of the hop aroma will be carried away by the carbon dioxide. By adding different varieties of hops at different times during the brewing process, a more complex hop profile can be established that gives the beer a balance of hop bitterness, taste, and aroma.

The main bittering agents are the alpha acid humulone resins, which are insoluble in water and not particularly bitter until isomerized by boiling. The longer the boil, the greater the percentage of isomerization and the more bitter the beer gets. One humulone constituent, called co-humulone, is easier to isomerize than the others, but it is also commonly perceived to give a rougher bitterness to the beer. Even though this position is debatable, selection of low co-humulone character was encouraged as new hop varieties were developed. Many of today's high-alpha varieties, like Magnum and Horizon, have lower co-humulone than older, lower-alpha varieties of the past, such as Galena and Cluster.

While most of the bitterness comes from isomerization of the alpha acid resins, the characteristic flavor and aroma compounds come from the essential oils, which are typically 1 to 2 percent of the dry weight of the cone. These are volatile and are lost to a large degree during the boil. The light aromatic oils (myrcene, linalol, geraniol, limonene, terpineol, etc.), are responsible for the fresh hop aroma you smell when you open the bag, and are what you can impart to your beer by dry-hopping. Myrcene contributes a spicy character, linalol and geraniol contribute floral notes, pinene is evergreen, and citral, limonene, and cadinene contribute citrus and fruity character. The heavier aromatic oils (e.g., humulene, caryophyllene, farnesene) and their oxides/epoxides are what you smell from middle and late hop additions to the boil, and it is these aromas that are identified as "noble." The percentage of alpha acid resins and essential oils will vary somewhat from year to year, but the essential character of a hop variety will stay consistent.

The "noble hops" are considered to have the best aroma and are principally four varieties grown in Central Europe: Hallertauer Mittelfrüh, Tettnanger Tettnang, Spalter Spalt, and Czech Saaz. The location in which a hop is grown has a definite impact on the variety's character, so only a Tettnanger/Spalter hop grown in Tettnang/Spalt is truly noble. There are other varieties that are considered to be noble-type, such as Perle, Crystal, Mt. Hood, Liberty, and Santiam. These hops were bred from the noble types and have very similar aroma profiles, having high humulone oil content and low co-humulone alpha acids.

Table 3 – Hop Substitution Table. The hops are arranged according to principal origin and characters. Hops may be substituted (broadly) within a subgroup, and to some extent across the categories in the same row. See the Hop Character Wheel on page 20 for a more visual interpretation of each hop variety's character. This organization is very subjective and subject to differences of opinion.

Category	English Hop Varieties	European Hop Varieties	American Hop Varieties	Pacific Hop Varieties
General Character	Herbal, Earthy, Fruity	Floral, Spicy, Evergreen	Citrus, Herbal, Spicy	Fruity, Citrus, Floral
Substitution Group A	East Kent Goldings Fuggles Styrian Goldings Target	Hallertauer Mittelfruh Tettnang Spalt Saaz Hersbrucker	Crystal Mt. Hood Liberty Sterling Willamette Horizon Santiam	NZB Saaz NZD Saaz Pacific Hallertau NZ Hallertau Aroma
Substitution Group B	Challenger Northdown	Perle Northern Brewer Magnum	BC Goldings Glacier Chinook Cluster Simcoe	
Substitution Group C	West Goldings Variety Brewers Gold Progress		Amarillo Cascade Centennial	Nelson Sauvin Pacific Gem Pacific Jade
Substitution Group D			Columbus Warrior Nugget Galena	Super Alpha Green Bullet Southern Cross Pride of Ringwood

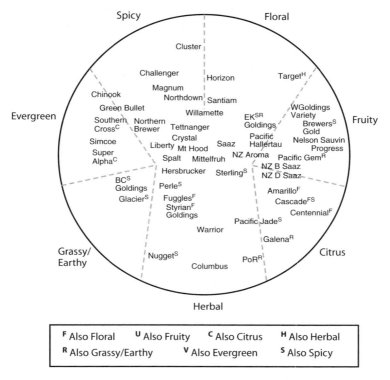

Hop Character Wheel

Hop Forms

It is rare for any group of brewers to agree on the best form of hops. Each of the common forms has its own advantages and disadvantages. The recipes in this book typically use hop pellets, which have slightly better utilization in the boil, but other hop forms can be used and may be specified depending on the style. For example, aged whole hops are used for brewing Belgian lambic.

Whichever form of hops you choose to use, freshness is important. Fresh hops smell fresh, herbal, and spicy and have a light green color like freshly mown hay. Old hops or hops that have been mishandled are often oxidized and smell like pungent cheese and may have turned brown. It helps if hop suppliers pack hops in oxygen barrier bags and keep them cold to preserve the freshness and potency. Hops that have been stored warm and/or in non-barrier (thin) plastic bags can easily lose 50 percent of their bitterness potential in a few months. Aged hops are not oxidized hops; the alpha acids and essential oils have gone beyond oxidized to "gone." Only the beta acids are left in aged hops and, lacking aroma, these hops are principally used for the sour beers of Belgium.

Table 4—Hop Forms and Merits

Form	Advantages	Disadvantages
Whole	Easy to strain from wort Best aroma if fresh Good for dry-hopping	Soak up wort, resulting in some wort loss after the boil Lupulin tends to fall out of the cones and accumulate in the bottom of the bag, making the bittering more variable Most easily oxidized, stability is problematic
Plug	Better stability than whole form Convenient half-ounce units Behave like whole hops in the wort	Can be difficult to break apart into smaller amounts Soak up wort just like whole hops
Pellets	Best stability and storability Easy to weigh Small increase in utilization due to shredding	Turns into hop sludge in bottom of kettle, which is difficult to strain Hard to contain when dry-hopping—creates floaters

Choosing Your Yeast

As you probably know, there are a multitude of yeast strains to choose from when you are trying to decide on which one to use for your brew. While we recommend a couple of different yeast cultivars for each of the recipes in this book, we also want you to understand the selection process. It is not simply matching the name of the yeast to the style (although, conveniently, this does seem to work in many cases). Think about the style of the beer you plan to brew. Is it a toasty, malty beer with some touches of fruity esters and some residual sweetness? Or is it a drier, crisper beer with a significant bitter edge and no esters? Or is it a complex medley of dried fruit and spicy, warm alcohol? These stylistic aspects tell you the kind of yeast you should be selecting.

Do you want a little bit of fruity esters? Then you want an ale yeast strain that is comfortable fermenting at relatively cool temperatures. Do you want a lot of fruity esters? Then you probably want one of the English or Belgian yeast strains that prefers warmer temperatures and throws a lot of esters. Do you want some residual sweetness and a fuller mouthfeel or a drier, more thirst-quenching beer? Look at the manufacturer's website for the apparent attenuation of the yeast; some strains (and cultivars) ferment more fully than others. Yeast that have

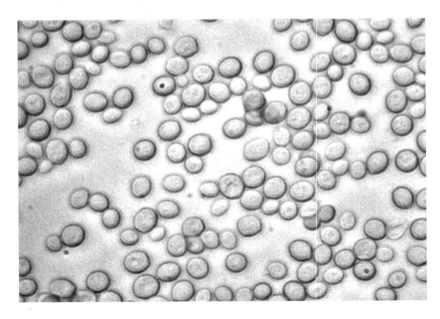

an apparent attenuation of 68 to 72 percent will leave a lot of residual sweetness in the beer. An apparent attenuation of 73 to 77 percent is more typical, having a lower residual sweetness, and a higher apparent attenuation of 78 percent or more will produce a drier beer with a lighter body.

Note: If you cannot get the yeast used in the recipe and must select another strain instead, check the apparent attenuation and adjust the fermentability of your wort to compensate. This will help keep the balance of the beer's flavor closer to the original recipe. To increase the fermentability of the wort, replace some of the base malt with a few weight percent of white table sugar, the same amount as the difference in the attenuation of the yeast. If you need to decrease the fermentability of the wort, use a less fermentable extract, add some maltodextrin powder, or increase the mash temperature if brewing all-grain.

There are many different strains of brewer's yeast available nowadays, and each strain produces a different flavor profile. Some Belgian strains produce fruity esters that smell like bananas and cherries, some German strains produce phenols that smell strongly of cloves. Those two examples are rather special; most yeasts are not that dominating. But it illustrates how much the choice of yeast can determine the taste of the beer. In fact, yeast strain is often the main difference between certain beer styles. Yeast companies have collected different strains from around the world and packaged them for homebrewers. It is always best to use the liquid yeasts if you can, as they tend to be truer to style. These are the same yeast strains sold to commercial breweries.

Dry yeast is convenient because the packets provide a lot of viable yeast cells, they can be stored for extended periods of time, and they can be prepared quickly on brewing day. It is common to use one or two packets (5 to 22 grams) of dried yeast for a typical 5-gallon batch. This amount of yeast, when properly rehydrated, provides enough active yeast cells to ensure a strong fermentation. Dry yeast can be stored for up to two years (preferably in the refrigerator), but the packets do degrade with time. Check the use-by date on the package. Some leading and reliable brands of dry yeast are Fermentis Yeast, Cooper's, DanStar (produced by Lallemand), Muntons, and Edme. Dry yeast should be rehydrated in de-aerated water before pitching. Do not just sprinkle it onto the wort, which some instructions suggest; this is a shortcut that usually works but it is not ideal. For best results, rehydrate the yeast in warm, preboiled water (95 to 105° F, 35 to 40° C).

Pitching Rate Effects

There are many factors that combine to determine just how much yeast you should pitch to your wort to produce a good fermentation, and thus, a good beer. The most obvious factors are wort gravity and fermentation temperature. If you intend to brew a low-gravity mild ale, you don't need a lot of yeast to do the job. With typical levels of nutrients and aeration, a relatively low number of yeast will easily reproduce enough cells to ferment that wort very well. On the other hand, if you are going to brew a high-gravity doppelbock, then you are going to need to pitch a lot more yeast, because the cooler fermentation temperature will decrease the activity level and reproduction rate, and more total yeast mass will be needed to ferment the higher-gravity wort adequately. As a general rule, you need to pitch more yeast for higher-gravity worts and you need to pitch more yeast for cooler fermentation temperatures.

The White Labs pitchable vials and the 125 milliliter Wyeast Activator pouches deliver about 100 billion viable cells per package. The number of active yeast cells in dry yeast packages is conservatively stated to be about 6 billion viable cells per gram, so you would get 50 to 70 billion cells in a single packet, which is good for 5 gallons of most of the common beer styles. Usually the viability is higher. The viabilities vary from lot to lot and from strain to strain. Dry lager yeasts usually have lower viabilities than ale yeasts, because lager strains are more difficult to dry, and they have larger cells and thus fewer cells per gram (probably 5 billion to 8 billion). If the yeast packet is relatively new and has been stored in a refrigerator, then the number for ale yeast is probably 10 billion to 20 billion per gram. (Your mileage may vary.)

To simplify things, the recommended pitching rate for each recipe in this book is given in terms of the number of yeast packages to use. Alternatively, you can use a yeast starter to build up the cell count from 1 to 2 packages to reduce your cost. Appendix A gives equivalent starter combinations for the number of liquid yeast packages given in the recipes. The pitching rate can have a large effect on the character of the beer. In the first few days of the fermentation cycle, when the yeast are rapidly reproducing, more diacetyl precursor, acetaldehyde, and fusel alcohols are being produced than at any other time. Low pitching rates mean more total cell growth, more amino acid synthesis, and therefore more by-products. High pitching rates mean less total cell growth and fewer by-products.

Diacetyl and acetaldehyde are removed by the yeast during the conditioning phase of fermentation, but esters and fusel alcohols are not. A diacetyl rest should be used if the lager beer is pitched warmer than the intended primary fermentation temperature; this will help the yeast to absorb these off-flavors before lagering.

Ideally, the starter wort temperature should be within 10° F (6° C) of the planned fermentation temperature. If the yeast is started warmer and then pitched to a cooler fermentation environment, it may be shocked or stunned by the change in temperature and may take a couple of days to regain normal activity.

The starter process may be repeated several times to provide more yeast to ensure an even stronger fermentation. When you are pitching a large starter, we recommend that you only pitch the yeast slurry and not the entire starter-beer. Chill the starter in the refrigerator to settle all the yeast. (This may take a couple of days.) Pour off the unpleasant tasting starter beer so only the yeast slurry will be pitched. This helps prevent the taste of the starter from influencing the taste of the final beer.

Water

Water is one of the most important ingredients in brewing, because it can make or break the flavors of the beer. Unfortunately, water chemistry can also be one of the most complicated topics in brewing. For the purposes of this book, we will focus on the basics: eliminating chlorine, understanding water hardness, and basic water adjustment. First, let's look at a couple of methods for eliminating chlorine and chloramine.

Removing Chlorine and Chloramine

Activated charcoal filtration. Charcoal filters are an easy way to remove most odors and bad tastes due to dissolved gases and organic substances like nitrates. These filters are often reasonably priced and can be attached in-line to the faucet or spigot. This is quite handy, since it provides a ready source of dechlorinated water whether you need 1 gallon or 100. Charcoal filtration alone will not affect dissolved minerals like iron, calcium, magnesium, copper, or bicarbonate, but there are ion exchange filters that will remove most of these ions if you need deionized water. Most carbon filters are highly effective at removing chlorine and chloramine, as long as you follow the manufacturer's instructions on temperatures and flow rates. Check the manufacturer's product information to find out what a particular product will or won't filter.

Campden tablets (potassium metabisulfite or sodium metabisulfite). Most city water supplies now use chloramine instead of chlorine to kill bacteria because it is more stable than chlorine. The trouble is, "more stable" means that you can't just let the water stand overnight to get rid of chloramines, which you could do with chlorine. However, a single Campden tablet is an inexpensive and effective method for removing chloramines. Crush 1 Campden tablet to a fine powder and add it to your water before the boil. Stir thoroughly to help it dissolve. One tablet will treat 20 gallons, although using 1 tablet for only 5 gallons won't hurt anything. Both chlorine and chloramine are reduced to insignificant levels of sulfate and chloride ions (<10 ppm) within a couple of minutes at room temperature. Campden tablets are commonly used in winemaking and should be available at your brew shop.

Other water. Bottled drinking water is available from most grocery stores and supermarkets and typically has low levels of alkalinity and other minerals. Bottled water works very well for extract brewing. Reverse osmosis and distilled water can be added to your tap water to reduce the mineral levels as necessary. Generally, adding RO or distilled water will reduce the minerals at the same ratio as the dilution. You can also use distilled water alone when you are brewing with malt extract, because the extract will provide all the necessary minerals for yeast health.

Water Hardness

Hard water contains significant amounts of calcium, magnesium, and other metal ions. The equivalent sum of all these metal ions is calculated as the "total hardness as calcium carbonate" ($CaCO_3$) and will be listed as such on your local water report. Water hardness is quantified according to the following ranges by the U.S. Geological Survey:

- Soft   0-60 ppm total hardness as calcium carbonate
- Moderate   61-120 ppm total hardness as calcium carbonate
- Hard   121-180 ppm total hardness as calcium carbonate
- Very Hard   >180 ppm total hardness as calcium carbonate

However, water hardness is not the problem; hard water is actually good for brewing. Calcium is an important biological co-factor for many brewing processes. Water alkalinity (carbonate/bicarbonate) is the parameter that brewers need to be concerned about. Water alkalinity can be quantified by the following ranges:

- Low   0-50 ppm total alkalinity as calcium carbonate
- Moderate   51-150 ppm total alkalinity as calcium carbonate
- High   151-250 ppm total alkalinity as calcium carbonate
- Very High   >250 ppm total alkalinity as calcium carbonate

Beer is an acidic beverage, and the pH of beer should typically be 3.8 to 4.6 pH when measured at room temperature, depending on style. If your water is highly alkaline, the beer pH may be too high, causing the beer to taste dull, soapy, or excessively bitter. Light-colored beers should be brewed with low-alkalinity water (which is typically "soft"), and dark-colored beers should be brewed with moderately to highly alkaline water. In this case, the water alkalinity balances the dark malt acidity and prevents the beer pH from being too low and tasting acrid.

Basic Water Adjustment

Burtonizing. A lot of people try to add brewing salts like gypsum or table salt to the boil to imitate the water of a famous brewing region, such as the Burton region of Britain. Most tap water supplies are fine for brewing with extract and don't need adjustment. The proper amount of a salt to add to your water depends on the mineral amounts already present, and the recipe author probably had entirely different water than you do. You may end up ruining the taste of the beer by adding too much. So if you are brewing a recipe that calls for the addition of gypsum or Burton salts, you need to get a mineral report for your water first, and then figure out how much to add to approach the target level.

Decarbonation. Several areas of the United States are cursed with highly alkaline water. Normally this would only be a concern for all-grain brewers, because alkalinity greatly affects the mash chemistry and beer flavor, but it can also affect the flavor of extract beers. If your water is high in alkalinity (i.e., bicarbonate ion concentrate >250 ppm or Total Alkalinity as $CaCO_3$ >200 ppm), highly hopped pale beers will often have a harsh, chalky bitterness.

Here is a procedure to remove some of the alkalinity from the water:

1. Add 1 teaspoon of calcium carbonate to 3 to 5 gallons of brewing water, and stir. This will create precipitation nucleation and growth sites, i.e., seed crystals, and help some of the alkalinity precipitate out.
2. Boil for 10 minutes and allow to cool.
3. Pour the decarbonated water off the chalk sediment into another pot.

Water softeners. Water softening systems can be used to remove bad-tasting minerals like iron, copper, and manganese, as well as the scale-causing minerals calcium and magnesium. Salt-based water softeners use ion exchange to replace these heavier metals with sodium. Softened water should never be used for all-grain brewing. The softening process leaves all the alkalinity in the water and takes out almost all of the balancing hardness, creating very alkaline water, which is always bad for mashing. If the alkalinity level in the source water is relatively low, the softened water will be fine for extract brewing, but if it's high, it will cause the beer to taste bitter and chalky.

Water Summary
Just remember these simple guidelines:
- Home water softeners are generally bad for brewing.
- Chlorine and chloramine can and should be removed from brewing water by Campden tablets or carbon filtration.
- Extract-based beers (all styles) can be brewed with confidence using distilled, deionized (reverse osmosis), or low-alkalinity bottled water.
- Partial-mash and all-grain brewers will have the best results from using low-alkalinity water for light-colored beer styles and medium-alkalinity water for dark-colored beer styles. (This is the complicated part.)
- Adding brewing salt additions for flavor enhancement requires that you know how much you are starting with from your water report.

Water chemistry is important for all-grain brewing. The mineral profile of the water has a large effect on the performance of the mash. Water reports, and brewing salts and their effects, are discussed more fully in the book *How to Brew* by John Palmer (Brewers Publications, 2006).

3 | BREWING GREAT BEER WITH EXTRACT

Brewhouse for production of malt extract
(*photo courtesy of Briess Malt & Ingredients Company*)

Malt extract starts out in the brewhouse just like beer. To make malt extract, the wort is transferred to evaporators after boiling instead of to a fermenter. Malt extract is simply concentrated wort. The malt extract may consist of a single malt or a combination of different types, depending on what style of beer is being made.

Manufacturers of malt extract boil the wort to coagulate the hot break proteins before running it to the evaporators. The wort is dehydrated to 80 percent solids to make a shelf-stable product without the use of preservatives. By boiling off the water under a partial vacuum, browning reactions are reduced, and the original flavor and color of the wort is preserved. To make a hopped extract, hops can be added to the initial boil, or hop iso-alpha acid extracts can be added to the extract later. Malt extract takes a lot of the work out of homebrewing.

Malt extract is sold in both liquid (syrup) and powdered forms. The syrups are about 20 percent water, so 4 pounds of dry malt extract is roughly equal to 5 pounds of liquid malt extract. LME weighs about 4 pounds per 1.5 quarts, or 1.28 kilograms per liter. Dry malt extract is produced by heating and spraying the liquid extract from an atomizer in a tall, heated chamber. The small droplets dry and cool rapidly as they settle to the floor. DME is identical to LME except for the additional dehydration to about 2 percent moisture. DME is typically not hopped.

Malt extract is commonly available in pale, amber, and dark varieties, in both liquid and dry forms. Specialty extracts are also available, including: wheat (typically 60/40 percent wheat/barley), Munich (100 percent Munich malt), and other extracts for specific styles like Vienna, Munich dunkel, porter, etc. The fermentability or degree of attenuation is typically 75 to 80 percent, with the darker varieties typically being less attenuable. A list of the malt extracts and adjuncts that are used in the recipes follows, and they should be available at your homebrew supply shop or by mail order. To brew the recipes as true to style as possible, use the malt extract that is from malt that is appropriate for the style, i.e., English pale ale malt extract for English pale ales, Pilsener malt extract for German and Czech Pilseners, etc. In addition, try to use an extract from the country that originated the style, i.e., use a German Pilsener lager malt to make a German Pils. It will add that extra bit of true character that an American Pilsener lager malt would lack (due to the malting barley variety and malting schedule). If you can't get the malt-specific extract for the style, a generic light/pale malt extract will suffice in most cases. However, generic light/pale malt extract should not be substituted for the wheat, Munich, or *rauch* extracts.

Extracts Used in This Book

- English Pale Ale LME
- Pilsener LME
- Munich LME
- Rauch LME
- Wheat LME
- Brewers Corn Syrup (high maltose)
- Rice Syrup (high maltose)
- Cane or Corn Sugar

Keys to Extract Brewing Excellence

To brew good beer, you need to have good, solid brewing practices; it doesn't matter whether you are brewing with malt extract or all grain. To brew award-winning beer, you need to have award-winning sanitation practices. Several of the recipes in this book use bacterial cultures to add sour character to the beer, but don't get the idea that you have to burn your equipment afterwards. Metal and glass equipment can easily be cleaned and sanitized after use. In the case of plastic and vinyl, it is probably best to get separate utensils, hoses, and buckets to reduce the possibility of cross-contamination.

Second, you need to be able to control the fermentation. Good fermentation controls consist of good yeast handling, wort handling, and temperature control. The key to successfully reproducing the award-winning beers in this book depends on pitching the right amount of fresh, healthy yeast and controlling the fermentation temperature(s) according to the recipe. A recipe is just a collection of ingredients without the proper procedure, and if you want to brew the beer that won the competition, you will need to brew it according to the stated procedure. On the other hand, you are the brewer, and this is going to be your beer. For all we know, your brew could be superior to the original. Recipes don't brew award-winning beers, brewers brew award-winning beers.

The third key is especially important to extract brewing, and that is the freshness of the ingredients. Liquid malt extract typically has a shelf life of about two years if stored at or below room temperature, during which time its color will approximately double. The Maillard reactions that are responsible for the color change can generate off-flavors like licorice, molasses, and ballpoint pen aroma. Beer brewed with old extract syrup may also have a dull, bitter, and/or soapy flavor to it. These flavors are caused by the oxidation of the phenols and fatty acid compounds in the malt. These off-flavors are part of a group that is collectively known as "extract twang." Homebrewers will often complain that they can't make good beer with extract, but it's usually just a matter of freshness. The bottom line to brewing great beer with liquid extract is to use the freshest extract possible by checking the "Use By" dates on the cans, or to buy from a shop that has a high stock turnover. Dry malt extract has a much better shelf life than liquid, because the extra dehydration slows the chemical reactions. If you can't get fresh liquid extract, use the dry.

Converting a Recipe to a Partial Boil

The recipes in this book were originally created as all-grain, full-volume boil recipes, but we have created malt extract versions to make them more accessible for new brewers. However, the ingredient quantities and hopping schedules are still based on a 7-gallon boil (26.5L), with 6

gallons (23L) at the end of the boil, 5.5 gallons (21L) going into the fermenter, and 5 gallons (19L) going into the bottles or keg. If you don't have a large pot and a propane burner, you can still brew these recipes by converting them to a partial boil (e.g., 3 gallons, 11 liters) that you can do on your kitchen stove. The basic method can be summarized like this: Boil all of your hops in half of your total malt extract, in half the recipe volume, add the remaining extract at the end of the boil to pasteurize it, and then dilute to the final recipe volume in the fermenter. Piece of cake, right? The goal is to design a partial-boil wort that has the same gravity, specialty malt flavors, and therefore the same flavor development from the boil as the full-sized wort. Sometimes it will be impractical to get the gravity and wort composition exactly the same, but close is good enough.

OK, let's break this down step-by-step.

Create the Wort. The first step to designing your boil is to determine the contribution of any steeping grains in the recipe and subtract that from the target boil gravity. The difference will determine the amount of extract you need to add to the steeping wort to create the target gravity of the partial boil. Ideally, the percentages of the malts in the partial wort should be the same as they are in the full-sized. However, it's usually not practical to split the specialty grain contributions in half; it is easier to steep or mash them all at once, and add your extract to that wort to create the boil. Likewise, even though it may be ideal to split or divide the specialty malt extracts, it may be more practical to just add them all up front if the percentage to the total extract is fairly small. The difference is fairly small, and it's one less thing to have to think about at the end of the boil.

Boil the Hops. Once you have created a partial-volume wort that has the same gravity and flavor profile as the original, you can boil your hops. And here is the nifty part: You can use the same hop quantities and boil times as the original recipe! The equation for calculating IBUs consists of estimating how much alpha acid is going to be dissolved and isomerized into the wort, and then dividing that amount by the final volume to arrive at the final isomerized alpha acid concentration. These alpha acids will be isomerized based on the boiling time and wort gravity. The physical size of the boiling pot doesn't really affect the utilization like the boil gravity does, because the amount of alpha acid dissolved into the wort is still relatively small compared to the total volume.

Add the Remaining Extract. At the end of the boil, turn off the heat and stir in the remaining extract. Let the wort sit for at least 1 full minute to pasteurize it, and then cool the wort to pitching temperature (preferably with a wort chiller). Don't let the wort sit hot for more than a couple of minutes before chilling, because that will promote the formation of dimethyl sulfide (DMS), a cooked-corn off-flavor common to pale malts.

Example: Hoppiness Is an IPA

Let's work through a complete example using one of the India pale ale recipes.

OG: 1.065 (15.9 °P)
FG: 1.012 (3.1 °P)
ADF: 81%
IBU: 64
Color: 7 SRM (13 EBC)
Alcohol: 7 percent ABV (5.5 percent ABW)
Boil: 60 minutes
Pre-Boil Volume: 7 gallons (26.5L)
Pre-Boil Gravity: 1.055 (13.6 °P)

Extract	Weight	Percent
Light LME (2.2 °L)	9.75 lbs. (4.42kg)	84.8
Munich LME (9 °L)	0.5 lb. (227g)	4.3

Steeping Grains		
Crystal (15 °L)	1 lb. (0.45 kg)	8.7
Crystal (40 °L)	0.25 lb. (113g)	2.2

Hops		IBU
Horizon 13% AA, 60 min.	1 oz. (28g)	49.7
Centennial 9% AA, 10 min.	1 oz. (28g)	6.9
Simcoe 12% AA, 5 min.	1 oz. (28g)	7.6
Amarillo 9% AA, 0 min.	1 oz. (28g)	0

Yeast

White Labs WLP001 California Ale, Wyeast 1056 American Ale, or Fermentis or Safale US-05

1. Estimate the yield from the steeping grain. In this case, 1.25 pounds of crystal malt will be steeped in 3 gallons of water. Assuming 70 percent yield, this equates to:
   1.25 lbs. x 24 ppg / 3 gal. = 10 gravity points or 1.010
   Subtract these 10 points from the boil gravity. 55 − 10 = 45

2. Calculate the amount of extract to use in the boil.
   From the gravity equation 45 = x lbs. x 36 ppg /3 gallons
   The lbs. of extract is 45 x 3/36 = 3.75 lbs. of LME

3. But what about the specialty extract—the Munich? Ideally, the wort composition in the partial boil should be the same as that in the full-sized boil. If the recipe had 50 percent light LME and 50 percent Munich LME, then you would want to do the same for the partial, and the 3.75 pounds needed in this example would be half light and half Munich. However, in this recipe the proportion of Munich is only 5 percent (i.e., 4/85), so it won't make a lot of difference whether you scale it, add it all at the beginning of the boil, or add it all at the end. We suggest adding it all at the beginning, which means that the 3 gallon boil consists of:
   1.25 lbs. of steeping grain
   0.5 lbs. of Munich LME
   3.25 lbs. of light LME

4. Steep the grains and add the extract. To get really technical, you would need to calculate exactly how much water the steeping grain will absorb and carry away (about 0.5 qt./lb. or 1L/kg), and balance that against the volume of the malt extract being added to get the right volume to steep the grains in to get the target gravity in the target volume.

   Don't bother. The yield from the steeping grain is also an estimate, close enough is good enough, and the simple calculations in Steps 1

Remember that the gravity/volume calculation is based on the total volume of the solution. In other words, to create a wort of 1.036, you start with 3 pounds of extract and dilute it to get 3 gallons total volume. You don't take 3 pounds of extract and add 3 gallons of water to it, because that would be more dilute. Liquid malt extract has a density of about 12 pounds per gallon (1.4 L/kg), although that number varies slightly with temperature and manufacturer. In other words, 3 pounds of liquid malt extract has a volume of 1 quart or 700ml/kg. The ppg concept can also be used with the metric units of liter degrees per kilogram, i.e., L/kg or pts./kg/L. The conversion factor between ppg and L/kg is 8.3454 x ppg = L/kg.

and 2 will get you firmly in the ballpark. If you feel it's really necessary, the tools to calculate the volume balance are given in the sidebar, but it is probably easier to just measure the gravity at the start of the boil and adjust the gravity with more extract or water.

5. Boil the hops according to the recipe (same amounts, same times).

6. Turn off the heat at the end of the boil and stir in the remaining extract. Let the high-gravity wort rest at high temperature for 1 full minute, and then chill and dilute to final volume in the fermenter.

4 | BREWING THESE RECIPES

You are about to embark on a unique opportunity: a Brewniversity education of more than eighty award-winning recipes for eighty of the world's classic beer styles. The recipes you are about to brew are not recipes that won competitions twenty years ago, they are up-to-date recipes that are winning BJCP-sanctioned competitions now. These recipes are being brewed almost annually and have evolved with the current interpretations of each style. No recipe is more than a few years old; they are truly classic examples of each style.

But before you start, we had better lay out all the baselines and assumptions so you will understand how the recipes were formulated and can make educated decisions if you need to adapt them to your equipment and procedures. Let's start at the beginning.

Ingredients

All of the recipes were formulated using Promash Brewing Software by the Sausalito Brewing Company, although any software or method of formulating recipes will work, if you use the following assumptions:

Malt extract. The yield for liquid malt extract in these recipes is baselined at 36 points per pound per gallon (300 L°/kg). The yield for dry malt extract is assumed to be 42 points per pound per gallon (350 L°/kg). Remember that these yields are based on the gravity and volume of the solution, so that if 1 pound of liquid malt extract is dissolved in enough water to make 1 gallon of wort, that wort will have a gravity of 1.036.

Malts. The malt yields are based on 70 percent efficiency of the maximum yield. The maximum yield is the fine grind, dry-basis number for "total soluble extract"* (a percentage of the dry weight of the sample) on the malt analysis sheet for each malt. The estimated yield for steeping of specialty grains is assumed to be the same as the mashing yield, 70 percent. If you determine that your steeping yield is less than 70 percent in your brewing system, then you will want to increase the grain amounts accordingly.

Hops. Except for lambics, all recipes assume the use of pellet hops for all hop additions, and International Bittering Units are calculated using the Rager formula. The alpha acid levels for each hop addition are listed in the recipe. If your hops have a different alpha level due to year-to-year variation or due to varietal substitution, adjust the quantities accordingly to obtain the same IBUs for the recipe.

Beer color. All of the recipes use the Morey model for calculation of beer color based on the usage weight and Lovibond color value of each malt or malt extract.

Processes

Mashing. All mashes are assumed to be single-temperature infusion mashes of 60 minutes' duration, unless stated otherwise. A specific mash temperature will be stated for each recipe, depending on the desired fermentability of the beer.

*R.M. Crumplen, Ed., *Laboratory Methods for Craft Brewers*, (St.Paul, Minn., The American Society of Brewing Chemists, 1997), pp. 7-10.

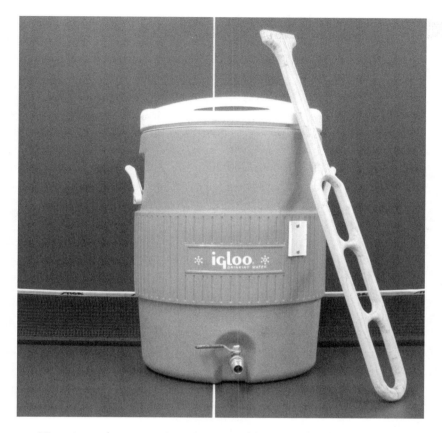

Note: A mashout step is not required but may be done at your discretion. Also, if you find your system needs a higher or lower mash temperature to get the desired results, that adjustment can often be applied across all recipes.

Wort Boiling. All of these recipes are designed to leave 6 gallons (22.7L) of wort in the kettle at the end of the boil. It is assumed 5.5 gallons (20.8L) are transferred to the fermenter and this will yield a full 5 gallons (18.9L) of beer into packaging after loss due to trub. For most recipes, the boil time is 60 minutes (except where noted) at an evaporation rate of 15% per hour.

Fermentation

Ales. The tried-and-true fermentation temperature and pitching rate for each beer are given in the recipe. As noted above, your system may require a shift from the recommendations, but the recipe as given should produce optimal results. In general, we recommend a single-vessel fermentation for a minimum of 1 week, and not more than 4 weeks, before packaging. Racking to a secondary fermenter is not recommended except for beers requiring a long maturation, such as lagers, or beers requiring a second fermentation, such as sour ales and fruit beers. Specific instructions for secondary fermentation will be given in the recipe.

Lagers. We recommend a method similar to a Narziss fermentation, where the first two-thirds of the fermentation is done cold and the final third is done warmer. This differs from the most commonly recommended procedure for lagers, where the yeast is pitched to a relatively warm wort (60 to 68° F, 15 to 20° C), cooled over the first two days of fermentation to the primary fermentation temperature, and then warmed back up to the initial temperature for a diacetyl rest before lagering. The idea behind the Narziss fermentation is to reduce the production of esters and other less desirable compounds during the most active phases of fermentation, and to increase the yeast activity near the end of fermentation, converting most of the undesirable compounds into less offensive substances. For example, diacetyl is a buttery-tasting compound that is a common flaw in warm-fermented lagers. The diacetyl precursor alpha-acetolactate is excreted by the yeast during the early phase of fermentation. Keeping the temperature low during that time keeps the amount of alpha-acetolactate low. Yeast will reduce diacetyl at the end of fermentation, when they are working on building their energy stores. Warming the yeast near the end of fermentation makes them more active and improves the reduction of diacetyl. The overall effect is a cleaner beer.

Assuming you have clean, healthy yeast, controlling the temperature of fermentation is the most important step. The preferred procedure for these recipes is a little different, in that we recommend chilling the wort down to 44° F (7° C) and racking the beer away from the bulk of the cold break material before oxygenating and pitching the yeast. The fermentation chamber should be set up to warm slowly over the first 36 to 48 hours to 50° F (10° C) and held at that temperature for the rest of fermentation. This results in a clean lager, with very little diacetyl. If your wort was warmer during the initial yeast growth, or your fermentation was warmer, you'll need to do a diacetyl rest during the last couple of days of fermentation, when the airlock activity noticeably slows. Generally this will be about the fifth or sixth day after pitching. To perform a diacetyl rest, warm your beer up about 10° F (6° C) above the fermentation temperature and hold it there until fermentation is complete. This keeps the yeast active and gives them a chance to eliminate the diacetyl. Then rack the beer to a 5-gallon carboy or Cornelius keg for lagering.

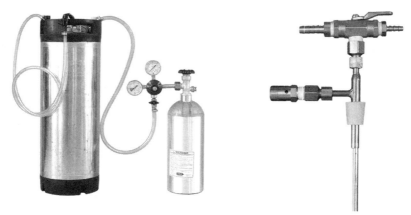

Photo courtesy of MoreFlavor.com

In any case, don't rush things. Good lagers take time, and they ferment more slowly than ales, especially when fermented cold. Once the beer has finished fermenting, a period of lagering for a month or more at near-freezing temperatures can improve the beer. Generally, the higher the alcohol content of the beer, the longer the lagering period should be. A 5 percent alcohol-by-volume Munich helles might be best after 4 to 6 weeks. An 8 percent doppelbock may need 6 months or more for some of the harsher aspects of the beer to mellow and for the melding of complex flavors to occur.

Packaging. Generally, we recommend transferring the beer to a Corny keg and force-carbonating, instead of priming and bottling, because it is more convenient and easier to control. Some beer styles undoubtedly benefit from bottle-conditioning, like strong ales and lambics, but in most cases it is just easier to keg it. There is little difference in the foam quality or head retention between bottle-conditioned and force-carbonated beers. Perhaps there is a spiritual difference, but otherwise dissolved CO_2 is dissolved CO_2.

To bottle your beers for competition, we recommend the use of a counter-pressure bottle filler. Again, the reasons are convenience and consistent results. If you have bottle-conditioned your beers, then you are ready to go. Beer judges do not mark down for bottle-conditioned beers, nor do they award points for it. Good Brewing!

5 | LIGHT LAGER

Light lager is a category with a wide range of substyles. They range from the low-calorie, light-flavored light American lager to the rich, flavorful, but balanced Dortmunder export style. What these beers have in common is that they are all fairly light-colored lager beers. If you are looking to make a clean American lager, similar to the beer from some very large American breweries, then you want to focus on the light, standard, and premium American lagers. The other two styles are more malt- or malt/hop-focused, German-style lager beers.

LITE AMERICAN LAGER

A clean, light, refreshing pale lager with very low malt and hop flavors. This is an advanced style that can be brewed by extract or all-grain methods. Ferments at 50° F (10° C).

OG	FG	IBU	Color	Alcohol
1.028–1.040	0.998–1.008	8–12	2–3 SRM	2.8–4.2% ABV
(7.1–10 °P)	(-0.5–2.1 °P)		4–6 EBC	2.2–3.3% ABW

Keys to Brewing Lite American Lager:
This is a light, refreshing, lower-alcohol beer style. It has very little malt character, very little hop character, and very little yeast-derived character. You might have read that brewing this clean and low-flavor beer style is difficult. It can be, but if you keep in mind two key points, you will have success.

First, you will need to avoid strongly flavored ingredients. The key is fresh, domestic (U.S.) two-row or six-row malt or a very light malt extract made from similar malts and plenty of adjuncts, such as rice or corn. Avoid using extracts or malts identified as continental Pilsener or pale ale malts. They have too much flavor for this style of beer. For all-grain brewers, it isn't necessary to use six-row malt (which can be hard to find), unless you are using a very high percentage (more than 25 percent) of rice or corn that needs to be converted. Two-row malt will do just fine, and at the worst, you will just need to allow some extra time for the conversion to complete. Alternatively, you can use rice syrup, in which case there is no conversion to worry about.

The second area to focus on is fermentation. It is important to have a clean, cool fermentation. The standard advice of pitching plenty of clean, healthy yeast and oxygenating your wort is fundamental to making a good lager, and it is critical on such a light lager beer. Make sure you can control the fermentation temperature and can keep it steady in the low 50° F (10° C) range.

RECIPE: ANDER-STONE LITE

One day I introduced a friend of mine to the world of craft beer. A lifelong American light lager drinker, he was wowed by the big bold character of the beers I poured for him. Instantly, he was hooked. Over the years his appreciation and knowledge of craft beer has grown tremendously. He has brewed with me, judged competitions, and regularly searches out new craft beer wherever he goes. Of course, he still loves his American light lager and finds it indispensable when he wants a few beers to while away a hot day. I crafted this recipe for him, and he enjoys it in place of the beer he spent most of his life drinking.

OG: 1.038 (9.5 °P)
FG: 1.007 (1.8 °P)
ADF: 81%
IBU: 10
Color: 2 SRM (5 EBC)
Alcohol: 4.1% ABV (3.2% ABW)
Boil: 60 minutes
Pre-Boil Volume: 7 gallons (26.5L)
Pre-Boil Gravity: 1.032 (8.1 °P)

Extract	Weight	Percent
Light LME (2.2 °L)	5.0 lbs. (2.26kg)	79.4
Rice Syrup (0 °L)	1.3 lbs. (0.59kg)	20.6

Hops		IBU
Hallertau 4.0% AA for 60 min.	0.61 oz. (17g)	10

Yeast

White Labs WLP840 American Lager, Wyeast 2007 Pilsen Lager, or Fermentis Saflager S-23

Fermentation and Conditioning

Use 15 grams of properly rehydrated dry yeast, 3 liquid yeast packages, or make an appropriate starter. Ferment at 50° F (10° C). Allow the beer to lager at least 4 weeks before bottling or serving. When finished, carbonate the beer from 2.5 to 3 volumes.

All-Grain Option

Replace the light extract with 6.8 lbs. (3.08kg) American two-row or six-row malt. Replace the rice syrup with 1.7 lbs. (0.77kg) flaked rice. Mash at 149° F (65° C). With the low mash temperature and the need to convert the flaked rice, most brewers will need to lengthen the rest to a minimum of 90 minutes to get full conversion. Also increase the pre-boil volume as needed to allow a 90-minute boil, which helps reduce DMS in the beer.

STANDARD AMERICAN LAGER

A clean, dry, refreshing pale lager with very low malt and hop flavors. This is an advanced style that can be brewed by extract or all-grain methods. Ferments at 50° F (10° C).

OG	FG	IBU	Color	Alcohol
1.040–1.050	1.004–1.010	8–15	2–4 SRM	4.2–5.3% ABV
(10.0–12.4 °P)	(1.0–2.6 °P)		4–8 EBC	3.3–4.2% ABW

Keys to Brewing Standard American Lager:
This beer is similar to the American style, but it is made a bit bigger, with more alcohol and a touch more character all around. It is crisp, dry, and refreshing with very little malt, hop, or yeast character.

The key to brewing this style of beer is essentially the same as brewing lite American lager: minimize strong malt and hop flavors through ingredient selection, and keep the fermentation clean through good temperature control.

RECIPE: WHAT MOST FOLKS CALL BEER

OG: 1.046 (11.5 °P)
FG: 1.008 (2.2 °P)
ADF: 81%
IBU: 12
Color: 3 SRM (5 EBC)
Alcohol: 5.0% ABV (3.9% ABW)
Boil: 60 minutes
Pre-Boil Volume: 7 gallons (26.5L)
Pre-Boil Gravity: 1.039 (9.9 °P)

Extract	Weight	Percent
Light LME (2.2 °L)	6.25 lbs. (2.83kg)	80.6
Rice Syrup (0 °L)	1.5 lbs. (0.68kg)	19.4

Hops		IBU
Hallertau 4.0% AA for 60 min.	0.72 oz. (20g)	12

Yeast

White Labs WLP840 American Lager, Wyeast 2007 Pilsen Lager, or Fermentis Saflager S-23

Fermentation and Conditioning

Use 18 grams of properly rehydrated dry yeast, 3.5 liquid yeast packages, or make an appropriate starter. Ferment at 50° F (10° C). Allow the beer to lager at least 4 weeks before bottling or serving. When finished, carbonate the beer from 2.5 to 3 volumes.

All-Grain Option

Replace the light extract with 8.3 lbs. (3.76kg) American two-row or six-row malt. Replace the rice syrup with 2 lbs. (0.9kg) flaked rice. Mash at 149° F (65° C). With the low mash temperature and the need to convert the flaked rice, most brewers will need to lengthen the rest time to a minimum of 90 minutes to get full conversion. Also increase the pre-boil volume as needed to allow a 90-minute boil, which helps reduce DMS in the beer.

PREMIUM AMERICAN LAGER

A clean, refreshing pale lager with very low malt and hop flavors. This is an advanced style that can be brewed by extract or all-grain methods. Ferments at 50° F (10° C).

OG	FG	IBU	Color	Alcohol
1.046–1.056	1.008–1.012	15–25	2–6 SRM	4.6–6% ABV
(11.4–13.8 °P)	(2.1–3.1 °P)		4–12 EBC	3.6–4.7% ABW

Keys to Brewing Premium American Lager:
This beer is bigger and has more malt character than the other American lager styles. The leading mass-market beers in most countries also fall under this style. This is a fuller, richer, higher-alcohol beer than the other two light American lager styles, but it is still a fairly crisp, dry, refreshing beer style with less malt-, hop-, and yeast-derived character than any other lager styles. This beer should not have bold or assertive flavors or aromas. If you are making an American version, stick with a light, low-flavor extract. If you want to brew something along the lines of a European version of this beer, replace the light extract with a Pilsener-type extract, or, if you're an all-grain brewer, use continental Pilsener malt.

RECIPE: JAMIL'S EXTRA YELLOW

OG: 1.053 (13.2 °P)
FG: 1.010 (2.6 °P)
ADF: 80%
IBU: 20
Color: 3 SRM (6 EBC)
Alcohol: 5.7% ABV (4.5% ABW)
Boil: 60 minutes
Pre-Boil Volume: 7 gallons (26.5L)
Pre-Boil Gravity: 1.045 (11.3 °P)

Extract	Weight	Percent
Light LME (2.2 °L)	8.0 lbs. (3.63kg)	88.9
Rice Syrup (0 °L)	1.0 lb. (0.45kg)	11.1

Hops

	IBU
Hallertau 4.0% AA for 60 min. 1.25 oz. (35g)	20

Yeast

White Labs WLP840 American Lager, Wyeast 2007 Pilsen Lager, or Fermentis Saflager S-23

Fermentation and Conditioning

Use 20 grams of properly rehydrated dry yeast, 4 liquid yeast packages, or make an appropriate starter. Ferment at 50° F (10° C). Allow the beer to lager approximately 4 weeks before bottling or serving. When finished, carbonate the beer from 2.5 to 3 volumes.

All-Grain Option

Replace the light extract with 11.6 lbs. (5.26kg) American two-row or six-row malt. Replace the rice syrup with 1 lb. (0.45kg) flaked rice. Mash at 149° F (65° C). With the low mash temperature and the need to convert the flaked rice, most brewers will need to lengthen the rest time to a minimum of 90 minutes to get full conversion. Also increase the pre-boil volume as needed to allow a 90-minute boil, which helps reduce DMS in the beer.

MUNICH HELLES

A clean, malt-focused German lager with a gentle, bready malt character. This is a smooth, easy-drinking beer often consumed by the liter. This is an advanced style that can be brewed by extract-with-grain or all-grain methods. Ferments at 50° F (10° C).

OG	FG	IBU	Color	Alcohol
1.045–1.051	1.008–1.012	16–22	3–5 SRM	4.7–5.4% ABV
(11.2–12.6 °P)	(2.1–3.1 °P)		6–10 EBC	3.7–4.3% ABW

Keys to Brewing Munich Helles:

Munich helles is a clean, pale gold German lager, with a bready malt character that starts in the aroma and lasts all the way through the finish. While there might be a slightly sweet, grainy character present, this is not a sweet beer. This beer should be well attenuated, and any sweetness should be balanced by just enough hop bitterness to keep it in check.

A common mistake when brewing a beer described as "malt focused" like Munich helles is to assume that maltiness and sweetness are the same thing. A beer with a lot of sweetness from malt is not necessarily "malty," it is sweet. It may or may not also have a lot of malt character. It is quite possible to have a dry beer that has lots of malt flavor and aroma or malt character. When most beer judges use the term "malty," they are referring to the rich grainy, bready, toasty flavors and aromas that come from the malt, not the residual malt sweetness.

There are two key things to keep in mind when brewing any German lager: the right ingredients and a good, clean fermentation with the proper level of attenuation. It is very important to use continental Pilsener malt, German noble hops, and German lager yeast. These ingredients provide certain flavors and aromas critical to brewing this beer style. Without them, the overall character of the beer just won't be brewed to style. Do not add any caramel-type malts to this beer, since those flavors are not part of the style.

Always pitch enough clean, healthy yeast and oxygenate your wort to help get a proper level of attenuation and a clean fermentation profile.

RECIPE: MÜNCHEN GROßES BIER

OG: 1.048 (12.0 °P)
FG: 1.011 (2.8 °P)
ADF: 77%
IBU: 18
Color: 4 SRM (9 EBC)
Alcohol: 5.0% ABV (3.9% ABW)
Boil: 60 minutes
Pre-Boil Volume: 7 gallons (26.5L)
Pre-Boil Gravity: 1.041 (10.3 °P)

Extract	Weight	Percent
Pilsener LME (2.3 °L)	7.6 lbs. (3.44kg)	91.0
Munich LME (9 °L)	0.5 lb. (227g)	6.0

Steeping Grains		
Melanoidin Malt (28 °L)	0.25 lb. (113g)	3.0

Hops		IBU
Hallertau 4.0% AA for 60 min.	1.1 oz. (31g)	18.1

Yeast

White Labs WLP838 Southern German Lager, Wyeast 2308 Munich Lager, or Fermentis Saflager S-23

Fermentation and Conditioning

Use 20 grams of properly rehydrated dry yeast, 4 liquid yeast packages, or make an appropriate starter. Ferment at 50° F (10° C). Allow the beer to lager at least 4 weeks before bottling or serving. When finished, carbonate the beer from 2 to 2.5 volumes.

All-Grain Option

Replace Pilsener extract with 10 lbs. (4.53kg) continental Pilsener malt. Replace Munich extract with 0.75 lb. (340g) Munich malt. Mash at 150° F (66° C). Increase the pre-boil volume as needed to allow a 90-minute boil, which helps reduce DMS in the beer.

DORTMUNDER EXPORT

A perfectly balanced beer with the malt profile of a helles, the hop character of a Pilsener, and slightly stronger than both. This is an advanced style that can be brewed by extract-with-grain or all-grain methods. Ferments at 50° F (10° C).

OG	FG	IBU	Color	Alcohol
1.048–1.056	1.010–1.015	23–30	4–6 SRM	4.8–6.0% ABV
(7.6–10 °P)	(2.6–3.8 °P)		8–12 EBC	3.8–4.7% ABW

Keys to Brewing Dortmunder Export:

Dortmunder export is all about balance, but it isn't a dull, boring beer. This is a beer with a firm, malty body and the proper hop bitterness to balance it. It has moderate-strength bready and toasted malt flavors, balanced by the fine spicy and floral flavor and aroma of German noble hops.

The key to brewing a great Dortmunder export is making sure that neither the hops nor the malt is dominant over the other. Keep a close eye on your pre-boil gravity and volume. If you have a refractometer, check the concentration of the wort at the beginning, middle, and end of the boil. If you are short at the beginning of the boil, that is the time to either extend the first part of the boil (before adding the hops) or to add some malt extract to make up for the shortage. If the wort is a bit too concentrated, add some dechlorinated water to the kettle to get it into the right range. If you are using high alpha-acid hops, use an accurate gram scale to weigh them. Balance is very important in this style, and an important part of achieving that balance is hitting your numbers while brewing.

Almost any water is fine for brewing a great Dortmunder export, but if your water is particularly soft, it can be beneficial to add a small amount of gypsum and chalk, (perhaps 0.25 oz. [7g] of each) to enhance the sharpness of the hop bitterness and the mineral background of the beer. However, you shouldn't do this unless you are sure your brewing water needs it. It is better to go without the salts than to have too much and end up with a harsh, mineral-sharp beer.

RECIPE: EXPAT EXPORT

OG: 1.055 (13.6 °P)
FG: 1.013 (3.2 °P)
ADF: 76%
IBU: 29
Color: 6 SRM (12 EBC)
Alcohol: 5.6% ABV (4.4% ABW)
Boil: 60 minutes
Pre-Boil Volume: 7 gallons (26.5L)
Pre-Boil Gravity: 1.047 (11.7 °P)

Extract	Weight	Percent
Pilsener LME (2.3 °L)	6.4 lbs. (2.9kg)	67.2
Munich LME (9 °L)	3.0 lbs. (1.36kg)	31.5

Steeping Grains		
Melanoidin Malt (28 °L)	2.0 oz. (57g)	1.3

Hops		IBU
Hallertau 4.0% AA for 60 min.	1.7 oz. (48g)	27.2
Hallertau 4.0% AA for 5 min.	0.5 oz. (14g)	1.6
Hallertau 4.0% AA for 0 min.	0.5 oz. (14g)	0

Yeast
White Labs WLP830 German Lager, Wyeast 2124 Bohemian Lager, or Fermentis Saflager S-23

Fermentation and Conditioning
Use 21 grams of properly rehydrated dry yeast, 4 liquid yeast packages, or make an appropriate starter. Ferment at 50° F (10° C). Allow the beer to lager at least 4 weeks before bottling or serving. When finished, carbonate the beer from 2 to 2.5 volumes.

All-Grain Option
Replace Pilsener extract with 8.5 lbs. (3.85kg) continental Pilsener malt. Replace Munich extract with 4 lbs. (1.81kg) Munich malt. Mash at 152° F (67° C). Increase the pre-boil volume as needed to allow a 90-minute boil, which helps reduce DMS in the beer.

6 | PILSENER

This category includes the classic Pilsener-style beers, although these are Pilseners that the average beer drinker in America might not recognize as a Pilsener. These are all pale lagers, but that is the only similarity they have with the mass-market, low-flavor lagers produced around the world. These beers all have a greater hop presence, both bittering and flavor, which makes them a much bolder, more flavorful, and aromatic beer-drinking experience than the light lager category.

GERMAN PILSENER (PILS)

A crisp, clean, refreshing lager that prominently features noble German hop bitterness. This is an advanced style that can be brewed by extract-with-grain or all-grain methods. Ferments at 50° F (10° C).

OG	FG	IBU	Color	Alcohol
1.044–1.050	1.008–1.013	25–45	2–5 SRM	4.4–5.2% ABV
(11–12.4 °P)	(2.1–3.3 °P)		4–10 EBC	3.5–4.1% ABW

Keys to Brewing German Pilsener:
The key to making a great German-style Pilsener is ensuring that the beer attenuates enough to make a crisp, dry beer. If there is too much residual malt sweetness, it is going to be too sweet and heavy for a good representation of the style. It is important to avoid crystal malts or any other specialty grain that adds non-fermentable sugars to the beer, which will work against the desired crisp, dry result. If the brand of malt extract you use does not attenuate enough, experiment with replacing a portion of the malt extract with dextrose (corn sugar). Try replacing 0.65 lb.

(295g) of the base malt extract with 0.5 lb. (227g) of dextrose. If that isn't enough, double the amount replaced the next time, or look into switching malt extracts for one that will finish drier. Don't exceed 1 lb. (0.45kg) of dextrose in this recipe, as it will begin to have a negative flavor impact.

Most water is fine for brewing a great German-style Pilsener, but if your water is particularly soft, it can be beneficial to add a small amount of gypsum (perhaps 0.25 oz. [7g]) to enhance the sharpness of the hop bittering. However, you shouldn't do this unless you are sure your brewing water needs it. It is better to go without the salts than to have too much and end up with a harsh, mineral-sharp beer.

RECIPE: MYBURGER

A friend of mine is a big fan of Bitburger, one of the classic examples of this style, and it was one of the first beers I tried to clone. The beer was great from the very first batch, but it was never quite dry enough until I got my process down and I could get it to attenuate enough. As each new batch was ready, my friend would come over and we would sample Bitburger side by side with my beer. As we compared and contrasted the two beers, we started calling the taste test Bitburger versus Myburger, and the name has stuck since.

OG: 1.048 (11.9 °P)
FG: 1.009 (2.3 °P)
ADF: 81%
IBU: 36
Color: 3 SRM (6 EBC)
Alcohol: 5.1% ABV (4.0% ABW)
Boil: 60 minutes
Pre-Boil Volume: 7 gallons (26.5L)
Pre-Boil Gravity: 1.041 (10.2 °P)

Extract	Weight	Percent
Pilsener LME (2.3 °L)	8.2 lbs. (3.72kg)	100

Hops		IBU
Perle 8.0% AA for 60 min.	1.0 oz. (27g)	32.8
Hallertau 4.0% AA for 15 min.	0.5 oz. (14g)	2.2
Hallertau 4.0% AA for 1 min.	0.5 oz. (14g)	1.4

Yeast

White Labs WLP830 German Lager, Wyeast 2124 Bohemian Lager, or Fermentis Saflager S-23

Fermentation and Conditioning

Use 20 grams of properly rehydrated dry yeast, 4 liquid yeast packages, or make an appropriate starter. Ferment at 50° F (10° C). Allow the beer to lager for at least 4 weeks before bottling or serving. When finished, carbonate the beer from 2 to 2.5 volumes.

All-Grain Option

Replace the Pilsener extract with 10.8 lbs. (4.9kg) continental Pilsener malt. Mash at 147° F (64° C). With the low mash temperature, most brewers will need to lengthen the rest time to a minimum of 90 minutes to get full conversion. Also increase the pre-boil volume as needed to allow a 90-minute boil, which will help reduce DMS in the beer.

BOHEMIAN PILSENER

A complex, well-rounded yet refreshing and crisp lager beer with plenty of malt and hop character. This is an advanced style that can be brewed by extract-with-grain or all-grain methods. Ferments at 50° F (10° C).

OG	FG	IBU	Color	Alcohol
1.044–1.056	1.013–1.017	35–45	3.5–6 SRM	4.2–5.4% ABV
(11–13.8 °P)	(3.3–4.3 °P)		4.2–5.4 EBC	3.3–4.3% ABW

Keys to Brewing Bohemian Pilsener:

Czech or Bohemian-style Pilsener is one of those styles that many new brewers want to learn to brew perfectly. While still crisp and clean like other Pilsener-style beers, Bohemian-style Pilsener has a nice, rich, complex malt and spicy hop character. Bohemian-style Pilsener usually has a bit more malt sweetness than German-style Pilsener, which helps counter the substantial hop bitterness, making a more balanced, well-rounded beer.

Bohemian-style Pilsener is typically brewed with water that is low in minerals, and it is one of the few beer styles that benefits from water adjustments. A fine example of the style can be made with most water, but low-carbonate water helps soften it. It is this softness, along with the malt and hop character, that defines this beer. If your water has moderate alkalinity, try mixing your filtered tap water 50/50 with reverse osmosis or deionized water. If you have highly alkaline water, use a 25/75 mix of tap to reverse osmosis or deionized water. It is important not to use all reverse osmosis or deionized water, as it lacks the buffering capacity and necessary minerals for all-grain brewing and for ideal fermentation.

RECIPE: TO GEORGE!

The brewing community, both amateur and professional, is filled with many bright, knowledgeable, and generous people, yet one person will always stand out in my memory, George Fix. This recipe was one of the first beers where I really felt like I had applied all that I had learned from George's work. George wrote books and articles, spoke at events, and judged competitions. Of course, it wasn't all of the things George did but the way he did them that I think most folks remember. I will always remember his enthusiasm, intelligence, kindness, and his welcoming smile when a fan like me would rush up to ask questions. George made me a better brewer not just through his knowledge but also through his spirit. Since his passing, every time I drink this beer, I say a little toast out loud or just to myself, "To George!"

OG: 1.056 (13.9 °P)
FG: 1.016 (4.2 °P)
ADF: 70%
IBU: 40
Color: 4 SRM (7 EBC)
Alcohol: 5.3% ABV (4.1% ABW)
Boil: 60 minutes
Pre-Boil Volume: 7 gallons (26.5L)
Pre-Boil Gravity: 1.048 (11.9 °P)

Extract	Weight	Percent
Pilsener LME (2.3 °L)	9.0 lbs. (4.08kg)	90

Steeping Grains		
CaraPils/Dextrine Malt (1 °L)	1.0 lb. (0.45kg)	10

Hops		IBU
Czech Saaz 3.5% AA, 60 min.	1.65 oz. (47g)	23
Czech Saaz 3.5% AA, 30 min.	2.0 oz. (57g)	14.2
Czech Saaz 3.5% AA, 10 min.	1.0 oz. (28g)	2.8
Czech Saaz 3.5% AA, 0 min.	1.0 oz. (28g)	0

Yeast
White Labs WLP800 Pilsner Lager, Wyeast 2001 Urquell, or Fermentis Saflager S-23

Fermentation and Conditioning
Use 21 grams of properly rehydrated dry yeast, 4 liquid yeast packages, or make an appropriate starter. Ferment at 50° F (10° C). Allow the beer to lager for at least 4 weeks before bottling or serving. When finished, carbonate the beer from 2 to 2.5 volumes.

All-Grain Option

Replace the Pilsener extract with 12 lbs. (5.44kg) continental Pilsener malt. Reduce the CaraPils to 0.75 lb. (340g). Mash at 154° F (67° C). Increase the pre-boil volume as needed to allow a 90-minute boil, which helps reduce DMS in the beer.

CLASSIC AMERICAN PILSENER

A clean, moderately hoppy lager, often with a substantial corn-like character. This is an advanced style that can be brewed by extract or all-grain methods. Ferments at 50° F (10° C).

OG	FG	IBU	Color	Alcohol
1.044–1.060	1.010–1.015	25–40	3–6 SRM	4.5–6% ABV
(11–14.7 °P)	(2.6–3.8 °P)		6–12 EBC	3.6–4.7% ABW

Keys to Brewing Classic American Pilsener:

Classic American Pilsener is a much richer beer, in terms of flavor and aroma, than today's American Pilseners. This isn't the light-flavored, mass-market Pilsener common around the world today. This isn't even your daddy's Pilsener. This is your grandpappy's Pilsener. This is a substantial beer with a fair level of maltiness and hoppiness, higher even than today's European-style Pilsener beers. This beer uses a substantial amount of corn or rice as an adjunct, adding either a slight corn-like sweetness or a crisp character from the rice.

The key in making the recipe below is in obtaining the freshest ingredients you can get, especially the corn adjunct. Corn can quickly take on a mealy, stale taste once processed into flakes. Grits and polenta are a little more stable but require boiling to make the starches available and conversion in the mash to turn the starches into sugar.

The flavor contribution of corn is subtle but unmistakable. The option of using brewer's (high-maltose) corn syrup for extract brewers is acceptable but not the same as getting a touch of that subtle corn sweetness from either flaked or ground corn. That is why the extract version uses Pilsener malt extract and the all-grain version uses American two-row or six-row malt. If you are an extract brewer and are serious about making a great classic American Pilsener, you will need to do a partial mash with flaked corn, per the instructions in the Appendix.

This recipe has a fairly high hop-bittering level, so if you have highly alkaline water that has a big mineral taste, you might want to cut it with reverse osmosis or deionized water to avoid a harsh mineral/hop bitterness. Try a mix of half filtered tap water and half reverse osmosis or deionized water, but only if you have highly alkaline water.

I have heard it said that Cluster hops are the hop of choice for brewing classic American Pilsener, because it is the oldest hop variety grown in the United States. For a period of time, Cluster made up the bulk of American hop production, so there might be some merit to using Cluster from an historical perspective. Some brewers enjoy Cluster. Some feel it is a bit harsh and rustic. If you want a "rustic" character without the catty aroma of Cluster, give Northern Brewer hops a try. Personally, I prefer Czech Saaz or a German noble hop in this beer, because of their more refined flavor and aroma, but feel free to substitute Cluster if you prefer.

RECIPE: SNATCH THE PEBBLE PILSENER

One of the best beer judges I know is Dave Sapsis. He has the most amazing sensory abilities and sense memory. He can tell subtle differences between two beers having tasted them a year apart. He also brews one of the best classic American Pilseners I have ever tasted. I dumped many batches of beer while trying to mimic his classic American Pilsener. My attempts were good, but they were never exactly the same and were missing a certain house character. I finally decided to make my own mark on the style and tweaked my recipe to suit my preferences.

OK, I admit it: There are too many hop additions in this recipe. However, this beer can really handle a lot more hops than you find many brewers using. The more I pushed it, the more I liked it, and the better it does in front of many judges. Perhaps it is a bit big and bold for post-Prohibition, but I like to think that there were at least a couple of pre-Prohibition brewers who enjoyed a hoppy beer. If you want to make something a bit more "classic," then either eliminate the 10- and 0-minute additions or cut all of the 20-minute and later additions in half.

OG: 1.058 (14.2 °P)
FG: 1.012 (3.1 °P)
ADF: 78%
IBU: 35
Color: 3 SRM (6 EBC)
Alcohol: 6.0% ABV (4.7% ABW)
Boil: 60 minutes

Pre-Boil Volume: 7 gallons (26.5L)
Pre-Boil Gravity: 1.049 (12.1 °P)

Grains	Weight	Percent
Pilsener LME (2.3 °L)	6.9 lbs. (3.13kg)	72.6
Brewer's Corn Syrup (0 °L)	2.6 lbs. (1.18kg)	27.4

Hops		IBU
Czech Saaz 3.5% AA, 60 min.	1.82 oz. (52g)	25.2
Czech Saaz 3.5% AA, 20 min.	1.0 oz. (28g)	4.7
Czech Saaz 3.5% AA, 10 min.	1.0 oz. (28g)	2.8
Czech Saaz 3.5% AA, 5 min.	1.0 oz. (28g)	2.3
Czech Saaz 3.5% AA, 0 min.	1.0 oz. (28g)	0

Yeast
White Labs WLP800 Pilsner Lager, Wyeast 2001 Urquell, or Fermentis Saflager S-23

Fermentation and Conditioning
Use 22 grams of properly rehydrated dry yeast, 4 liquid yeast packages, or make an appropriate starter. Ferment at 50° F (10° C). Allow the beer to lager for at least 4 weeks before bottling or serving. When finished, carbonate the beer from 2 to 2.5 volumes.

All-Grain Option
Replace the Pilsener extract with 9.5 lbs. (4.31kg) American two-row or six-row malt. Replace the brewer's corn syrup with 3.8 lbs. (1.72kg) flaked corn. Mash at 148° F (64° C). With the low mash temperature and the need to convert the flaked corn, most brewers will need to lengthen the rest time to a minimum of 90 minutes to get full conversion. Also increase the pre-boil volume as needed to allow a 90-minute boil, which will help reduce DMS in the beer.

7 | EUROPEAN AMBER LAGER

For many beer lovers, the names Oktoberfest and Vienna conjure up visions of giant pretzels, sausages, and oompah bands. These are two of the most food-friendly beer styles, and they go well with almost any food. I must admit that I get a hankering for some good bratwurst and sauerkraut if I happen to be drinking an Oktoberfest-style beer while hungry. These two European amber lagers have many similarities: Both are malt-focused beers, with Oktoberfest being slightly bigger and having more maltiness and malt sweetness than Vienna lager. Both styles have low hop character, and both are clean, easy-drinking lagers. These are good beers to brew in the dead of winter, when it is easy to keep fermentation temperatures under control. Letting these beers lager until the fall can produce some spectacular results.

It is interesting to note that the beer served at the famous Oktoberfest today is more like a strong Munich helles than it is like a traditional Oktoberfest beer of old.

VIENNA LAGER

A clean, malty lager with low hop flavors and bitterness. This is an advanced style that can be brewed by extract-with-grain or all-grain methods. Ferments at 50° F (10° C).

OG	FG	IBU	Color	Alcohol
1.046–1.052	1.010–1.014	18–30	10–16 SRM	4.5–5.5% ABV
(11.4–12.0 °P)	(2.6–3.6 °P)		20–31 EBC	3.6–4.3% ABW

Keys to Brewing Vienna Lager:

Vienna lager has a soft, moderately rich malt flavor and aroma. This clean lager beer is similar to Oktoberfest but not as intense, with less malty sweetness present and a drier finish.

There is a lot of confusion over this style, especially when trying to produce a beer that perfectly matches the style in the minds of judges. The problem stems from looking at the differences between beers like Negra Modelo and beers closer to Oktoberfest-type beers. The key to making Vienna lager is not overdoing it on the darker and/or sweet malt character. Too much roast or caramel character is inappropriate. You want to focus on a moderately toasty and bready malt character, which comes from malts like Vienna, Munich, and Pilsener.

Vienna lager should finish drier than Oktoberfest. While it is possible to add a bit of caramel-type malts to this beer, every ounce added will make for a slightly sweeter finish. It is best to brew this beer without caramel malts and make a beer more distinct from its Oktoberfest cousin.

RECIPE: NORTH OF THE BORDER VIENNA

OG: 1.050 (12.4 °P)
FG: 1.012 (3.1 °P)
ADF: 75%
IBU: 26
Color: 11 SRM (21 EBC)
Alcohol: 5.0% ABV (3.9% ABW)
Boil: 60 minutes
Pre-Boil Volume: 7 gallons (26.5L)
Pre-Boil Gravity: 1.043 (10.6 °P)

Extract	Weight	Percent
Pilsener LME (2.3 °L)	4.0 lbs. (1.81kg)	46.4
Munich LME (9 °L)	4.5 lbs. (2.04kg)	52.2

Steeping Grains		
Carafa Special II (430 °L)	2.0 oz. (57g)	1.4

Hops			IBU
Hallertau 4.0% AA for 60 min.	1.5 oz. (43g)		24.6
Hallertau 4.0% AA for 10 min.	0.5 oz. (14g)		1.6

Yeast

White Labs WLP838 Southern German Lager, Wyeast 2308 Munich Lager, or Fermentis Saflager S-23

Fermentation and Conditioning

Use 19 grams of properly rehydrated dry yeast, 4 liquid yeast packages, or make an appropriate starter. Ferment at 50° F (10° C). Allow the beer to lager at least 4 weeks before bottling or serving. When finished, carbonate the beer from 2 to 2.5 volumes.

All-Grain Option

Replace the Pilsener extract and the Munich extract with 3.4 lbs. (1.54kg) continental Pilsener malt, 3 lbs. (1.36kg) Munich malt, and 5 lbs. (2.26kg) Vienna malt. Mash at 152° F (67° C). Increase the pre-boil volume as needed to allow a 90-minute boil, which helps reduce DMS in the beer.

OKTOBERFEST/MÄRZEN

A clean, malty-rich lager with lots of smooth, complex malt character, minimal hop flavor, and minimal hop aroma. This is an advanced style that can be brewed by extract-with-grain or all-grain methods. Ferments at 50° F (10° C).

OG	FG	IBU	Color	Alcohol
1.050–1.057	1.012–1.016	20–28	7–14 SRM	4.8–5.7% ABV
(12.4–14 °P)	(3.1–4.1 °P)		14–28 EBC	3.8–4.5% ABW

Keys to Brewing Oktoberfest/Märzen:

Oktoberfest is the richest of the European amber lagers, but it is not as malty or malty-sweet as a traditional bock. This is a smooth, rich beer that starts with some malty sweetness but finishes dry enough and light enough to drink in quantity. It is often served by the liter, and it should never be cloying or too full. While balanced to the malt side, the hop bitterness helps keep the finish from being overly sweet.

The most common fault in brewing this style is making it too big: too sweet, too alcoholic, or too hoppy. I've tasted many attempts at the style that were higher in alcohol and sweeter in the finish than most commercial German doppelbocks, and many that were overly hoppy. Keep in mind this is a balanced beer, with an emphasis on malt flavor and aroma.

Oktoberfest gets its substantial bready, toasty malt character from a large percentage of Munich malt. A portion of caramel malt adds some backing sweetness, but adding too much can be an issue. Oktoberfest should not have a pronounced caramel character. Adding lots of caramel malt will also result in too high a finishing gravity, which makes it too filling and impacts the easy-drinking nature of this beer.

To get a dry-enough finish, you need the proper level of attenuation. While you want a fair amount of body and a slightly creamy feel, this beer needs to be fully fermented. Oxygenate the wort thoroughly, and make sure to use enough clean, healthy yeast.

RECIPE: MUNICH MADNESS

OG: 1.055 (13.6 °P)
FG: 1.015 (3.7 °P)
ADF: 73%
IBU: 27
Color: 11 SRM (21 EBC)
Alcohol: 5.4% ABV (4.2% ABW)
Boil: 60 minutes
Pre-Boil Volume: 7 gallons (26.5L)
Pre-Boil Gravity: 1.047 (11.7 °P)

Extract	Weight	Percent
Pilsener LME (2.3 °L)	4.4 lbs. (2kg)	44.9
Munich LME (9 °L)	4.4 lbs. (2kg)	44.9

Steeping Grains		
CaraMunich (60 °L)	1.0 lb. (0.45kg)	10.2

Hops		IBU
Hallertau 4.0% AA for 60 min.	1.5 oz. (43g)	24
Hallertau 4.0% AA for 20 min.	0.5 oz. (14g)	2.7

Yeast
White Labs WLP820 Oktoberfest/Märzen, Wyeast 2206 Bavarian Lager, or Fermentis Saflager S-23

Fermentation and Conditioning
Use 21 grams of properly rehydrated dry yeast, 4 liquid yeast packages, or make an appropriate starter. Ferment at 50° F (10° C). Allow the beer to lager at least 4 weeks before bottling or serving. When finished, carbonate the beer from 2 to 2.5 volumes.

All-Grain Option
Replace the Pilsener extract and the Munich extract with 5 lbs. (2.26kg) continental Pilsener malt, 4 lbs. (1.81kg) Munich malt, and 3 lbs. (1.36kg) Vienna malt. Mash at 151° F (66° C). Increase the pre-boil volume as needed to allow a 90-minute boil, which helps reduce DMS in the beer.

8 | DARK LAGER

Dark lager is a category often misunderstood by many beer drinkers. People assume every dark beer has a flavor and aroma similar to a stout, with lots of roasted grain character. Yet the beers in the dark lager category lack the substantial coffee, chocolate, and other roasted flavors of porters and stouts. Dark lagers are also completely devoid of any acrid or burnt flavors. American dark lager and Munich dunkel have almost no roasted flavor, and schwarzbier, the darkest of the three, has a very restrained roasted-grain character.

While dark, none of the dark lager styles are truly black like many stouts. They all use some form of dark malt that has no roasted character to it, like huskless Weyermann Carafa Special, Weyermann Sinamar (a coloring extract made from Carafa Special malt), or another debittered black malt. All of these provide color with less of the acrid, burnt, or roasted flavors that traditional dark grains add to a beer.

AMERICAN DARK LAGER

A clean, very slightly sweet, dark-colored lager with low malt and hop flavors. This is an advanced style that can be brewed by extract, extract-with-grain, or all-grain methods. Ferments at 50° F (10° C).

OG	FG	IBU	Color	Alcohol
1.044–1.056	1.008–1.012	8–20	14–22 SRM	4.2–6.0% ABV
(11–13.8 °P)	(2.1–3.1 °P)		28–43 EBC	3.3–4.7% ABW

Keys to Brewing American Dark Lager:
American dark lager, like most mass-market American lager beers, is the

least flavorful of the dark lager styles. It is a clean lager with minimal hop, malt, or roast character. While most examples are relatively light and similar to a standard or premium American lager with a dark coloring, there are some craft-brewed versions that have more body and flavor than the mass-market dark lagers.

Besides requiring a clean lager fermentation, the key to brewing American dark lager is to minimize the malt and hop character and to keep the coloring malts from having more than a minor impact on the flavor. Using a domestic light extract or domestic two-row malt is the first step in keeping the malt character at a minimum. A continental Pilsener malt or malt extract will add a sweet, grainy malt character, which can be too much in this beer style. The second step in reducing the malt character is to use a non-malt adjunct, such as rice, which leaves very little flavor in the finished beer.

While the only hop addition is one for bittering, it is important to use a clean German noble hop or something similar, as a bit of hop flavor often comes through from bittering, and you don't want it to be the wrong type of hop flavor.

It is critical that the dark coloring for this beer comes from an ingredient with very little roast character, or the resulting beer won't be an American dark lager. Make sure you use Weyermann Carafa Special, Weyermann Sinamar, or another debittered black malt.

RECIPE: PIZZA BOY DARK

I made my way through college working a number of odd jobs, and one was delivering pizza. While the pay wasn't great, the owners often gave us free pizza and beer after the store closed. The beer selection was limited to three mass-market beers, one light, one standard, and one dark. The American dark lager was the most flavorful option, so that is what we drank after a hard day of delivering pizza. More than twenty years later, eating pizza still triggers my thirst for beer.

OG: 1.052 (12.9 °P)
FG: 1.010 (2.6 °P)
ADF: 80%
IBU: 12

Color: 18 SRM (36 EBC)
Alcohol: 5.5% ABV (4.3% ABW)
Boil: 60 minutes
Pre-Boil Volume: 7 gallons (26.5L)
Pre-Boil Gravity: 1.044 (11.0 °P)

Extract	Weight	Percent
Light LME (2.2 °L)	7.5 lbs. (3.40kg)	83.3
Rice Syrup (0 °L)	1.0 lb. (0.45kg)	11.1

Steeping Grains		
Carafa Special II (430 °L)	0.5 lb. (227g)	5.6

Hops		IBU
Tettnang 4.0% AA for 60 min.	0.75 oz. (21g)	12.2

Yeast
White Labs WLP840 American Lager, Wyeast 2007 Pilsen Lager, or Fermentis Saflager S-23

Fermentation and Conditioning
Use 20 grams of properly rehydrated dry yeast, 4 liquid yeast packages, or make an appropriate starter. Ferment at 50° F (10° C). Allow the beer to lager for at least 4 weeks before bottling or serving. When finished, carbonate the beer from 2.5 to 3 volumes.

All-Extract Option
Replace the Carafa Special with 3 ounces (85g) Sinamar extract.

All-Grain Option
Replace the light extract with 10.3 lbs. (4.67kg) American two-row or six-row malt. Replace the rice syrup with 1.5 lbs. (0.68kg) flaked rice or flaked corn. Mash at 150° F (66° C). With the need to convert the flaked rice or corn, most brewers will need to lengthen the rest time to a minimum of 90 minutes to get full conversion. Also increase the pre-boil volume as needed to allow a 90-minute boil, which helps reduce DMS in the beer.

MUNICH DUNKEL

A clean, brown lager with great Munich malt depth and complexity. This is an advanced style that can be brewed by extract, extract-with-grain, or all-grain methods. Ferments at 50° F (10° C).

OG	FG	IBU	Color	Alcohol
1.048–1.056	1.010–1.016	18–28	14–28 SRM	4.5–5.6% ABV
(11.9–13.8 °P)	(2.6–4.1 °P)		28–55 EBC	3.6–4.4% ABW

Keys to Brewing Munich Dunkel:

Munich dunkel is the maltiest style in the dark lager category. Its signature flavor and aroma is a substantial toasted-bread character from the heavy use of Munich malt. It has a slightly sweet malt balance, which hides the hop bitterness, but it is never cloyingly sweet, heavy, or as intensely malty as the bock-style beers. Munich dunkel should never be roasty.

The key to brewing Munich dunkel is using a very high percentage of Munich malt. Some excellent commercial examples are made entirely from Munich malt and a dash of Weyermann Carafa Special for coloring. The question many all-grain brewers have is, what color Munich malt? I have heard some brewers report good results using dark Munich malt, around 20 °L. However, I am not sure if that is the best choice, as the flavors can be too intense when that is the bulk of the grist. It is not good to use a Munich malt that is too light, either. I prefer Munich malt in the 8 to 12 °L range, which gives plenty of melanoidin-rich character but not so much that it becomes overwhelming. When buying Munich malt, be aware that the color listed on the bag is sometimes in degrees EBC, which is roughly twice the Lovibond scale.

I have seen some recipes using half Munich malt, half Pilsener malt, and a touch of CaraMunich. This makes a completely different beer, with the CaraMunich adding a caramel sweetness that some people enjoy, but I find it out of place in this style. If you choose this alternate route for some reason, show restraint, or the flavor contribution of the CaraMunich will be too prominent and sweet, making the beer seem more like a bock than a Munich dunkel. Always use German noble hops for German lager beers.

RECIPE: OLD DARK BEAR

I have always been terrible at languages, and my attempts to translate brewing literature and beer names from German to English are quite entertaining. Still, that doesn't stop me from making up odd translations for my favorite German beers. Old Dark Bear is my nonsense translation for the name of one of my favorites, a Munich dunkel brewed just south of Munich. While the translation is lacking, this recipe closely mimics that great beer.

OG: 1.054 (13.3 °P)
FG: 1.014 (3.5 °P)
ADF: 74%
IBU: 22
Color: 19 SRM (37 EBC)
Alcohol: 5.3% ABV (4.1% ABW)
Boil: 60 minutes
Pre-Boil Volume: 7 gallons (26.5L)
Pre-Boil Gravity: 1.046 (11.4 °P)

Extract	Weight	Percent
Munich LME (9 °L)	8.5 lbs. (3.85kg)	95.8

Steeping Grains		
Carafa Special II (430 °L)	6.0 oz. (170g)	4.2

Hops		IBU
Hallertau 4.0% AA for 60 min.	1.2 oz. (34g)	19.5
Hallertau 4.0% AA for 20 min.	0.5 oz. (14g)	2.7

Yeast
White Labs WLP833 German Bock Lager, Wyeast 2308 Munich Lager, or Fermentis Saflager S-23

Fermentation and Conditioning
Use 21 grams of properly rehydrated dry yeast, 4 liquid yeast packages, or make an appropriate starter. Ferment at 50° F (10° C). Allow the beer to lager for at least 4 weeks before bottling or serving. When finished, carbonate the beer from 2 to 2.5 volumes.

All-Extract Option
Replace the Carafa Special with 3 ounces (85g) Sinamar extract.

All-Grain Option
Replace the Munich extract with 12.2 lbs. (5.53kg) Munich malt. Mash at 154° F (68° C).

SCHWARZBIER

A clean, slightly roasty, dark lager with a moderately bready malt character, balanced with hop bitterness and restrained hop character. This is an advanced style that can be brewed by extract, extract-with-grain, or all-grain methods. Ferments at 50° F (10° C).

OG	FG	IBU	Color	Alcohol
1.046–1.052	1.010–1.016	22–32	17–30 SRM	4.4–5.4% ABV
(11.4–12.9 °P)	(2.6–4.1 °P)		33–59 EBC	3.5–4.3% ABW

Keys to Brewing Schwarzbier:

Schwarzbier is another clean German-style lager with moderate malt character, somewhere between the malt character of an American dark lager and a Munich dunkel. It is the darkest and often the most roasty of the dark lager styles. While the roast flavor is more apparent in this dark lager than the others, it is still not the intense roast, burnt, or acrid flavor that you find in stouts and some porters. Most commercial examples brewed outside of the United States have less roasted-malt character than those brewed in the United States. In the United States the style tends to be a bit more roasty, slightly sweeter, and slightly bigger in malt character and alcohol than those brewed abroad.

The key to brewing schwarzbier is striking a balance between the malt, the roast, and the hops, so that no single aspect really overpowers the others. You should be able to taste and smell all of these flavors and aromas, but they should still be fairly subtle. Like other dark lagers, these two schwarzbier recipes use Weyermann Carafa Special or Weyermann Sinamar extract to increase the color without too much roasted flavor and aroma.

In this style, a subtle hop flavor and aroma is also appropriate, and it should come from noble German hops. Hop bitterness is more substantial in this style than in the other dark lagers, but it remains fairly close to balanced with the malt.

RECIPE: DOING IT IN THE DARK

I didn't have much experience with schwarzbier when I came up with this recipe. It was really a shot in the dark, based on limited samples, the BJCP style guidelines, and some detective work. This recipe makes a beer that is on the edge of the style with almost too much roasted malt character. However, from the very first batch it was a big success and has been brewed by many brewers, both professional and amateur. It has won more than twenty medals, including Best of Show, and medals at the American Homebrewers Association National Homebrew Competition. It has won at least one gold medal at the Great American Beer Festival for a commercial brewer. Over the years, I have tried to sample every schwarzbier available in the United States and abroad. I have experimented with changing this recipe in order for it to be a better example of the style, but I keep coming back to this great, a little too roasty, recipe.

OG: 1.051 (12.6 °P)
FG: 1.013 (3.3 °P)
ADF: 74%
IBU: 30
Color: 28 SRM (54 EBC)
Alcohol: 5.0% ABV (3.9% ABW)
Boil: 60 minutes
Pre-Boil Volume: 7 gallons (26.5L)
Pre-Boil Gravity: 1.043 (10.8 °P)

Extract	Weight	Percent
Munich LME (9 °L)	4.2 lbs. (1.9kg)	46.7
Pilsener LME (2.3 °L)	3.6 lbs. (1.63kg)	40

Steeping Grains		
Crystal (40 °L)	6.0 oz. (170g)	4.2
Chocolate Malt (420 °L)	6.0 oz. (170g)	4.2
Black Roasted Barley (500 °L)	3.5 oz. (99g)	2.4
Carafa Special II (430 °L)	3.5 oz. (99g)	2.4

Hops		IBU
Hallertau 4.0% AA for 60 min.	1.65 oz. (47g)	27
Hallertau 4.0% AA for 20 min.	0.5 oz. (14g)	2.8
Hallertau 4.0% AA for 0 min.	0.5 oz. (14g)	0

Yeast

White Labs WLP830 German Lager, Wyeast 2124 Bohemian Lager, or Fermentis Saflager S-23

Fermentation and Conditioning

Use 20 grams of properly rehydrated dry yeast, 4 liquid yeast packages, or make an appropriate starter. Ferment at 50° F (10° C). Allow the beer to lager for at least 4 weeks before bottling or serving. When finished, carbonate the beer from 2 to 2.5 volumes.

All-Grain Option

Replace the Pilsener extract with 4.6 lbs. (2.08kg) continental Pilsener malt. Replace the Munich extract with 6.1 lbs. (2.76kg) Munich malt. Mash at 154° F (68° C) for 60 minutes. Increase the pre-boil volume as needed to allow a 90-minute boil, which helps reduce DMS in the beer.

RECIPE: GERMAN SCHWARZBIER

For those who enjoy a schwarzbier that is very Pilsener-like, with as little roast malt character as possible, this recipe hits the mark. This recipe makes a schwarzbier very similar to Köstritzer.

OG: 1.047 (11.6 °P)
FG: 1.010 (2.6 °P)
ADF: 78%
IBU: 30
Color: 23 SRM (45 EBC)
Alcohol: 4.8% ABV (3.8% ABW)
Boil: 60 minutes
Pre-Boil Volume: 7 gallons (26.5L)
Pre-Boil Gravity: 1.040 (9.9 °P)

Extract	Weight	Percent
Pilsener LME (2.3 °L)	6.6 lbs. (2.99kg)	79.6
Munich LME (9 °L)	1.0 lb. (0.45kg)	12.1

Steeping Grains

Carafa Special II (430 °L)   11.0 oz. (312g)   8.3

Hops   IBU

Hallertau 4.0% AA for 60 min.   1.65 oz. (47g)   27.1
Hallertau 4.0% AA for 20 min.   0.5 oz. (14g)   2.8
Hallertau 4.0% AA for 0 min.   0.5 oz. (14g)   0

Yeast

White Labs WLP830 German Lager, Wyeast 2124 Bohemian Lager, or Fermentis Saflager S-23

Fermentation and Conditioning

Use 18 grams of properly rehydrated dry yeast, 4 liquid yeast packages, or make an appropriate starter. Ferment at 50° F (10° C). Allow the beer to lager for at least 4 weeks before bottling or serving. When finished, carbonate the beer from 2 to 2.5 volumes.

All-Extract Option

Replace the Carafa Special with 3.5 ounces (99g) Sinamar extract.

All-Grain Option

Replace the Pilsener extract with 9 lbs. (4.08kg) continental Pilsener malt. Replace the Munich extract with 1 lb. (0.45kg) Munich malt. Mash at 151° F (66° C). Increase the pre-boil volume as needed to allow a 90-minute boil, which helps reduce DMS in the beer.

9 | BOCK

This is one of my favorite style categories. I love the rich maltiness that these beers have in common, from the clean malt character of the maibock to the huge malty flavors and intense melanoidins of the eisbock. All of these beers are rich lagers that do better when given enough lagering time to condition fully and mature.

MAIBOCK/HELLES BOCK

A clean, higher-alcohol pale lager with rich, doughy, or grainy malt character. This is an advanced style that can be brewed by extract or all-grain methods. Ferments at 50° F (10° C).

OG	FG	IBU	Color	Alcohol
1.064–1.072	1.011–1.018	23–35	6–11 SRM	6.3–7.4% ABV
(15.7–17.5 °P)	(2.8–4.6 °P)		12–22 EBC	5–5.8% ABW

Keys to Brewing Maibock/Helles Bock:
Helles bock has a rich, full malt profile from Pilsener and Munich malts that often comes across as grainy, doughy, or very slightly toasted. Unlike the other bock beers, this style is best brewed without caramel malt. Caramel malt adds the wrong flavor for this style. You want some residual sweetness, but more of a base malt sweetness than any sort of caramelized sweetness. To get the proper effect, go with a higher starting gravity instead of using caramel malt. This fills out the beer with a touch more body and residual sweetness, but it won't be nearly as cloying as adding caramel malt.

While this style is a bit higher in alcohol than most lagers, the beer should never be hot or solvently with alcohol. A gentle warming when you drink it is OK, but anything more is considered a flaw. It is important to control the fermentation temperature and to pitch plenty of clean, healthy yeast. Hops can be a bit more apparent in this bock substyle than in the others but are still fairly restrained, with the hop flavor and aroma acting as subnotes. If you do want more late hop character, use 0.5 to 1 oz. (14 to 28g) of Hallertau during the last 10 minutes of the boil. Hop bitterness is also slightly higher in this substyle, but again, it requires restraint—just enough to cover the substantial malt sweetness and keep the beer balanced.

RECIPE: ANGEL WINGS

It is common to find maibock recipes with some sort of play on the word helles: "To Helles and Bock" and names like that. One day while enjoying a liter of this fine beer, I thought that a name like that for such a beautiful, golden, uplifting beer seemed entirely inappropriate. This beer is more like heaven than hell, and a liter of this will make you feel like you're floating on wings.

OG: 1.070 (17.1 °P)
FG: 1.017 (4.3 °P)
ADF: 75%
IBU: 27
Color: 7 SRM (14 EBC)
Alcohol: 7.1% ABV (5.5% ABW)
Boil: 60 minutes
Pre-Boil Volume: 7 gallons (26.5L)
Pre-Boil Gravity: 1.059 (14.6 °P)

Extract	Weight	Percent
Pilsener LME (2.3 °L)	8.0 lbs. (3.63kg)	66.7
Munich LME (9 °L)	4.0 lbs. (1.81kg)	33.3

Hops		IBU
Magnum 13.0% AA, 60 min.	0.56 oz. (16g)	27

Yeast
White Labs WLP833 German Bock Lager, Wyeast 2206 Bavarian Lager, or Fermentis Saflager S-23

Fermentation and Conditioning
Use 27 grams of properly rehydrated dry yeast, 5 liquid yeast packages, or make an appropriate starter. Ferment at 50° F (10° C). Allow the beer to lager for at least 4 weeks before bottling or serving. When finished, carbonate the beer to approximately 2.5 volumes.

All-Grain Option
Replace the Pilsener extract with 10.5 lbs. (4.76kg) continental Pilsener malt. Replace the Munich extract with 5.5 lbs. (2.49kg) Munich malt. Mash at 156° F (69° C). Increase the pre-boil volume as needed to allow a 90-minute boil, which helps reduce DMS in the beer.

TRADITIONAL BOCK

A slightly sweet, strong, copper lager with substantially bready malt character and no hop flavor or aroma. This is an advanced style that can be brewed by extract-with-grain or all-grain methods. Ferments at 50° F (10° C).

OG	FG	IBU	Color	Alcohol
1.064–1.072	1.013–1.019	20–27	14–22 SRM	6.3–7.2% ABV
(15.7–17.5 °P)	(3.3–4.8 °P)		28–43 EBC	5–5.7% ABW

Keys to Brewing Traditional Bock:

Traditional bock is a rich, smooth, complex, malty, strong lager beer with substantial melanoidin-derived flavors and aromas. The malt character is full of bread and toast notes, with a bit of caramel, too. The substantial malt character of this beer comes from a large percentage of Munich malt and is supported by a collection of other melanoidin-rich specialty malts.

Besides a recipe rich in malt character, the key to brewing a great traditional bock is ensuring that it is clean, not too alcoholic, and attenuates enough to avoid a cloying finish. Cool, clean fermentation using the proper amount of yeast goes a long way toward these goals.

RECIPE: LITTLE BARNABAS

The Meussdoerffer Rost malt in this recipe is a dark caramel-type malt, which has a character very much like overdone raisin cookies. If you are unable to find this malt, substitute the darkest crystal malt you can get, often 150 °L. It won't be exactly the same, but it will still turn out a really great bock.

OG: 1.070 (17.1 °P)
FG: 1.018 (4.5 °P)
ADF: 74%
IBU: 24
Color: 18 SRM (35 EBC)
Alcohol: 7.0% ABV (5.5% ABW)
Boil: 60 minutes
Pre-Boil Volume: 7 gallons (26.5L)
Pre-Boil Gravity: 1.059 (14.6 °P)

Extract	Weight	Percent
Pilsener LME (2.3 °L)	3.5 lbs. (1.58kg)	28
Munich LME (9 °L)	7.5 lbs. (3.40kg)	60

Steeping Grains		
CaraMunich (60 °L)	0.5 lb. (227kg)	4
Crystal (120 °L)	0.5 lb. (227kg)	4
Meussdoerffer Rost (200 °L)	4.0 oz. (113g)	2
Melanoidin (28 °L)	4.0 oz. (113g)	2

Hops		IBU
Magnum 13.0% AA, 60 min.	0.5 oz. (14g)	24.3

Yeast

White Labs WLP833 German Bock Lager, Wyeast 2206 Bavarian Lager, or Fermentis Saflager S-23

Fermentation and Conditioning

Use 27 grams of properly rehydrated dry yeast, 5 liquid yeast packages, or make an appropriate starter. Ferment at 50° F (10° C). Allow the beer to lager for at least 4 weeks before bottling or serving. When finished, carbonate the beer to approximately 2.5 volumes.

All-Grain Option

Replace the Pilsener extract with 4.5 lbs. (2.04kg) continental Pilsener malt. Replace the Munich extract with 10.25 lbs. (4.65kg) Munich malt. Mash at 155° F (68° C). Increase the pre-boil volume as needed to allow a 90-minute boil, which helps reduce DMS in the beer.

DOPPELBOCK

A very malty, strong lager with big, bready malt character. This is an advanced style that can be brewed by extract-with-grain or all-grain methods. Ferments at 50° F (10° C).

OG	FG	IBU	Color	Alcohol
1.072–1.112	1.016–1.024	16–26	6–25 SRM	7–10.0% ABV
(17.5–26.3 °P)	(4.1–6.1 °P)		12–49 EBC	5.5–7.9% ABW

Keys to Brewing Doppelbock:

Similar to traditional and helles bock, doppelbock is a strong, rich, very malty German-style lager, with an appreciable increase in the body, alcohol, sweetness, and malt-driven flavors and aromas. Some darker versions have very slight chocolate notes, but it is still rich, smooth, and complex.

The key to brewing a great doppelbock is similar to brewing a traditional bock, ensuring that it is clean, not too alcoholic, and attenuates enough to avoid a cloying finish. It is important to note that the sweetness present in the beer is more from low hop bitterness and not from incomplete fermentation. It is very common to find homebrew versions with fermentation problems. Often the beers did not attenuate completely and are worty sweet, or they fermented too warm and are estery and have a hot alcohol character. For the best results, pitch plenty of clean, healthy yeast and ferment under controlled conditions.

Another common flaw is making the beer overly big and alcoholic. While many brewers like to push the envelope, and there are bigger commercial examples out there, avoid the temptation to go too big on the alcohol and keep this an easier-drinking beer. All German beers are beers that are easy-drinking, and doppelbock should be no exception.

The last flaw is making the beer too melanoidin-rich. While we want to get a lot of those rich melanoidin flavors, too much can make it taste meaty or brothy. The cause is often excessive boiling, excessive decoction, or overuse of specialty grains. If you find your beer too melanoidin-rich, consider adjusting your process or recipe.

RECIPE: MR. MALTINATOR

OG: 1.086 (20.6 °P)
FG: 1.020 (5.2 °P)
ADF: 75%
IBU: 24
Color: 18 SRM (35 EBC)
Alcohol: 8.7% ABV (6.7% ABW)
Boil: 60 minutes
Pre-Boil Volume: 7 gallons (26.5L)
Pre-Boil Gravity: 1.073 (17.7 °P)

Extract	Weight	Percent
Munich LME (9 °L)	10.4 lbs. (4.71kg)	67.5
Pilsener LME (2.3 °L)	3.0 lbs. (1.36kg)	19.5

Steeping Grains		
CaraMunich (60 °L)	2.0 lbs. (0.90kg)	13.0

Hops		IBU
Hallertau 4.0% AA for 60 min.	1.50 oz. (43g)	20.9
Hallertau 4.0% AA for 30 min.	0.50 oz. (14g)	3.5

Yeast
White Labs WLP833 German Bock Lager, Wyeast 2206 Bavarian Lager, or Fermentis Saflager S-23

Fermentation and Conditioning
Use 32 grams of properly rehydrated dry yeast, 6 liquid yeast packages, or make an appropriate starter. Ferment at 50° F (10° C). Allow the beer to lager for at least 4 weeks before bottling or serving. When finished, carbonate the beer to approximately 2.5 volumes.

All-Grain Option
Replace the Pilsener extract with 4 lbs. (1.81kg) continental Pilsener malt. Replace the Munich extract with 14 lbs. (6.35kg) Munich malt. Mash at 155° F (68° C). Increase the pre-boil volume as needed to allow a 90-minute boil, which helps reduce DMS in the beer.

EISBOCK

An extremely strong, full, and malty dark lager. This is an advanced style that can be brewed by extract-with-grain or all-grain methods. Ferments at 50° F (10° C) and then requires temperatures below freezing to concentrate the beer.

OG	FG	IBU	Color	Alcohol
1.078–1.120	1.020–1.035	25–35	18–30 SRM	9–14% ABV
(18.9–28.1 °P)	(5.1–8.8 °P)		35–59 EBC	7.1–11.1% ABW

Keys to Brewing Eisbock:

Eisbock is a doppelbock that has been concentrated through freezing. This transforms the already rich, full-bodied, intensely malty doppelbock into the biggest of the bock family. In addition to concentrating the bread, toast, and caramel malt flavors and aromas, this beer also picks up some dark fruit notes from the process, like figs and plums.

The mistake many brewers make when attempting this style is that they start with a beer that has too much alcohol and caramel flavor. They end up with a beer that is overly sweet and candy-like or one that is very hot with solvent-like alcohol. It is important to brew a very clean, doppelbock-type beer, with a good level of attenuation. Once it is concentrated by freezing, any fermentation flaws become concentrated and more intense. If you don't start with a very clean lager beer with a dry-enough finish, or you don't allow enough lagering time for the beer flavors to mellow, you won't end up with a very good eisbock.

The key is to use less caramel and Munich malt than in a typical doppelbock. Remember, all of the flavors are going to get concentrated, presenting a much more intense profile. If you don't back down on certain ingredients, the beer will become cloying and over-the-top after freezing. You can run into the same problem by removing too much water. It is best not to freeze-concentrate it by more than 25 percent.

When making eisbock the same tips as for fermenting a doppelbock apply. In addition it is important to choose a clean lager yeast that will attenuate a bit more than a yeast you might use for a doppelbock. This keeps the flavors from being over-the-top and the finished beer from being too sweet.

RECIPE: STEVE'S FIFTY

One day at my friend Steve's house, we were sampling beers and talking about how some judges would never give a perfect score of 50 points to any beer. While the discussion progressed, Steve brought out an eisbock he had brewed nearly five years earlier. It turned out to be not only the best eisbock I had ever tasted, but also one of the best beers I had ever tasted. I exclaimed, "Now, this is a 50-point beer!" It was a perfect, flawless eisbock. I encouraged Steve to enter the beer in an upcoming competition, and it took second place. Later he came over to my place and showed me how to brew it. It has placed first and was a Best of Show runner-up, but the highest score it ever got was a 49. No 50.

OG: 1.090 (21.5 °P)
FG: 1.021 (5.3 °P)
ADF: 75%
IBU: 27
Color: 13 SRM (25 EBC)
Alcohol: 9.2% ABV (7.1% ABW)
Boil: 60 minutes
Pre-Boil Volume: 7 gallons (26.5L)
Pre-Boil Gravity: 1.076 (18.5 °P)

Extract	Weight	Percent
Pilsener LME (2.3 °L)	8.75 lbs. (3.97kg)	55.6
Munich LME (9 °L)	6.0 lbs. (2.72kg)	38.1

Steeping Grains		
CaraMunich (60 °L)	1.0 lb. (0.45kg)	6.3

Hops		IBU
Magnum 13.0% AA, 60 min.	0.53 oz. (15g)	23.6
Hallertau 4.0% AA, 30 min.	0.50 oz. (14g)	3.5

Yeast
White Labs WLP830 German Lager, Wyeast 2124 Bohemian Lager, or Fermentis Saflager S-23

Fermentation and Conditioning

Use 34 grams of properly rehydrated dry yeast, 7 liquid yeast packages, or make an appropriate starter. Ferment at 50° F (10° C).

Once the beer has finished fermentation, let it lager for 1 month at near freezing temperatures. Transfer it to a Cornelius keg or similar container that can be flushed with CO_2 and can withstand the freezing process without cracking. Put it in the freezer, checking every 30 minutes by shaking the container. Once ice crystals form you will hear them sloshing against the side of the keg. Initially, the sound of the ice crystals will be faint, but as more ice forms, the sound will increase. You want to pull it out of the freezer when approximately 20 percent of the beer has turned to ice. (You will need to guess the first few times you do this.) Transfer the still-liquid portion to another container, leaving behind the ice portion. If you wish, you can let the ice portion thaw and measure the volume to use in calculating the beer's strength post-concentration. If you remove 20 percent of the water, it will be equivalent to:

OG 1.109 (25.8 °P)
FG 1.030 (7.6 °P)
10.6 ABV (8.2 ABW)

And the color will be a bit darker as well.

Allow the beer to lager at least another 4 weeks before bottling or serving, but it will continue to improve for much longer. When finished, carbonate the beer to approximately 2.5 volumes.

All-Grain Option

Replace the Pilsener extract with 11.6 lbs. (5.26kg) continental Pilsener malt. Replace the Munich extract with 8 lbs. (3.63kg) Munich malt. Mash at 155° F (68° C). Increase the pre-boil volume as needed to allow a 90-minute boil, which helps reduce DMS in the beer.

10 | LIGHT HYBRID BEER

The light hybrid beer category is really more of a collection of lighter ales, some of which use special yeast at lower temperatures or extended periods of cold conditioning. All are fairly clean, light-colored beers with no overwhelming malt or hop character. These beers tend to be easy introductions for drinkers new to the rich flavors of the craft beer world.

CREAM ALE

This is a clean, crisp, refreshing ale, similar to an American light lager, with low malt and hop flavors but brewed as an ale. This is an intermediate style that can be brewed by extract or all-grain methods. Ferments at 65° F (18 ° C).

OG	FG	IBU	Color	Alcohol
1.042–1.055	1.006–1.012	15–20	2.5–5 SRM	4.2–5.6% ABV
(10.5–13.6 °P)	(1.5–3.1 °P)		5–10 EBC	3.3–4.4% ABW

Keys to Brewing Cream Ale:

Cream ale is a crisp, clean, dry beer, like an American standard lager with a little too much malt presence. A common mistake is associating cream ale with cream soda. The two have nothing to do with each other. Trying to make a sweet cream ale or adding vanilla to this beer is incorrect. A cream ale is similar to a mass-market, American-style lager, but it is made with ale yeast at cool temperatures. That being the case, the recipe is very similar to an American light lager and uses a fair amount of adjunct. Some brewers prefer to use a corn-based adjunct for this style, although almost any non-malt adjunct will do. In this case I like rice, as it has a very clean flavor. If you have trouble finding flaked rice or rice syrup, you can use any simple sugar (corn sugar, table sugar) in its place, and it will still make a fine example of the style. In fact, some brewers consider the use of simple sugar critical to getting that crisp, dry finish to the beer. If your cream ale doesn't ferment dry enough, consider replacing 10 percent of the malt with simple sugar the next time you brew this recipe.

This recipe uses some Pilsener malt for the base to give it a slightly grainy, sweet aroma, even though the beer itself will be dry and not sweet. If you want an even cleaner, drier, less malty beer, replace the Pilsener malt with light extract or American two-row.

While White Labs WLP001 California Ale and Wyeast 1056 American Ale both produce a nice cream ale, an interesting alternative is to use Kölsch yeast. Most Kölsch yeast seems a little more lager-like, and some can add a slight fruity note to the beer.

RECIPE: WEED, FEED, AND MOW

OG: 1.050 (12.4 °P)
FG: 1.009 (2.2 °P)
ADF: 75%
IBU: 18
Color: 3 SRM (6 EBC)
Alcohol: 5.4% ABV (4.3% ABW)
Boil: 60 minutes
Pre-Boil Volume: 7 gallons (26.5L)
Pre-Boil Gravity: 1.042 (10.6 °P)

Extract	Weight	Percent
Pilsener LME (2.3 °L)	3.3 lbs. (1.49kg)	39.8
Light LME (2.2 °L)	3.3 lbs. (1.49kg)	39.8
Rice Syrup (0 °L)	1.7 lbs. (0.77kg)	20.5

Hops		IBU
Liberty 4% AA for 60 min.	1.0 oz. (28g)	16.4
Liberty 4% AA for 1 min.	0.5 oz. (14g)	1.4

Yeast

White Labs WLP001 California Ale, Wyeast 1056 American Ale, or Fermentis Safale US-05

Fermentation and Conditioning

Use 10 grams of properly rehydrated dry yeast, 2 liquid yeast packages, or make a starter. Ferment at 65° F (18° C). When finished, carbonate the beer to approximately 2.5 volumes.

All-Grain Option

Replace the Pilsener extract with 4.75 lbs. (2.15kg) continental Pilsener malt. Replace the light extract with 4.75 lbs. (2.15kg) American two-row malt. Replace the rice syrup with 1 lb. (0.45kg) flaked rice or flaked corn and 0.75 lb. (340g) cane or corn sugar. Mash at 149° F (65° C). With the low mash temperature and the need to convert the flaked rice, most brewers will need to lengthen the rest time to a minimum of 90 minutes to get full conversion. Also increase the pre-boil volume as needed to allow a 90-minute boil, which helps reduce DMS in the beer.

BLONDE ALE

A fairly clean, easy-drinking, and slightly malty ale. This is a beginner style that can be brewed by extract-with-grain or all-grain methods. Ferments at 67° F (19° C).

OG	FG	IBU	Color	Alcohol
1.038–1.054	1.008–1.013	15–28	3–6 SRM	3.8–5.5% ABV
(9.5–13.3 °P)	(2.1–3.3 °P)		6–12 EBC	3–4.3% ABW

Keys to Brewing Blonde Ale:

Blonde ale is a smooth, easy-to-drink beer, with low fruity esters and just a touch of malt character. Often it is one of the lower-alcohol beers in an American pub's offerings and has just enough hop bitterness to keep things balanced. It is a very approachable beer for people new to craft beer.

This is also a relatively easy style of beer to brew, with the key being a balanced recipe and a clean fermentation. You might find recipes out there with all sorts of additional grains and sugars, but a simple recipe is best for this style. Choose quality malt or malt extract, and let the fine flavors of the base malt shine through with a clean fermentation. Most brewpubs make this as an ale, but it can also be done as a lager at slightly warmer than normal lager fermentation temperatures. If you want to add some late hop additions, keep them restrained, and use only one hop variety to keep things simple.

RECIPE: CALL ME!

OG: 1.050 (12.5 °P)
FG: 1.011 (2.8 °P)
ADF: 78%
IBU: 20
Color: 4 SRM (8 EBC)
Alcohol: 5.2% ABV (4.1% ABW)
Boil: 60 minutes
Pre-Boil Volume: 7 gallons (26.5L)
Pre-Boil Gravity: 1.043 (10.7 °P)

Extract	Weight	Percent
Light LME (2.2 °L)	8.3 lbs. (3.76kg)	94.3

Steeping Grains	Weight	Percent
Crystal (15 °L)	0.5 lb. (227g)	5.7

Hops		IBU
Willamette 5.0% AA, 60 min.	0.98 oz. (28g)	20.1

Yeast
White Labs WLP001 California Ale, Wyeast 1056 American Ale, or Fermentis Safale US-05

Fermentation and Conditioning
Use 10 grams of properly rehydrated dry yeast, 2 liquid yeast packages, or make a starter. Ferment at 67° F (19° C). When finished, carbonate the beer to approximately 2.5 volumes.

All-Grain Option
Replace the light extract with 11.5 lbs. (5.21kg) American two-row malt. Mash at 152° F (67° C).

KÖLSCH

A clean, crisp, delicate beer with soft malt and hop character. This is an intermediate style that can be brewed by extract or all-grain methods. Ferments at 60° F (16° C).

OG	FG	IBU	Color	Alcohol
1.044–1.050	1.007–1.011	20–30	3.5–5 SRM	4.4–5.2% ABV
(11–12.4 °P)	(1.8–2.8 °P)		7–10 EBC	3.5–4.1% ABW

Keys to Brewing Kölsch:

Kölsch is a subtle beer, with a light grainy Pilsener malt aroma and flavor. It is subtle and soft with some grainy malt sweetness up front but with a crisp enough finish that the beer never really seems sweet. The other flavors often attributed to this beer, such as sulfur, hop flavor, hop aroma, and fruitiness, are usually very subtle in the examples that have them or not present at all.

A mistake some brewers make is to take any mention of fruitiness in the style guide and use that as carte blanche to brew really fruity beers. While you might find a touch of fruitiness in some examples, I am of the opinion that any fruit note in a Kölsch should be very subtle and more in the imagination than on the palate. Sometimes small amounts of sulfur from certain yeasts during cold fermentation can give a slight peach note to the beer, but again, this is something that should be very light or not present at all. Make sure your fermentation procedures minimize the production of fruity esters.

If you want to brew a great Kölsch, it is very important to use the right yeast for this beer. It is impossible to get the right flavor and aroma without the right yeast at the right temperature. The dry yeast below will produce a clean beer, but it really won't be a Kölsch. Both liquid yeasts listed below do an excellent job, although you will find that they do not flocculate easily and it will take quite a bit of time, finings, or filtering to clear the beer. I prefer a nice long lager period to clear my Kölsch.

RECIPE: JZ FRÜH

After a particularly wonderful trip to Cologne, Germany, I was determined to make a Kölsch identical to the beers I tasted there. I brewed batch after batch and finally made a beer that compared well in side-by-side tests with samples I carried back from Cologne. However, something was still missing in my beers when I compared them to my memory of those I had in Cologne.

Glassware, I know, can have a significant impact on the perception of a beer, so I obtained the traditional Kölsch glass called a stange, but that wasn't the answer. I figured it must be the way it was being served, so I suggested to my wife that she should dress as a traditional German barmaid and serve me. Completely ignoring this fine idea, my wife reminded me how important "the moment" is to the enjoyment of a beer. She reminded me of how perception and enjoyment of a beer are affected by much more than the ingredients or the glassware.

A beer may taste extra special because of the feel of the table where you're sitting. It may be better because of the beauty of the historic old building and the friendly locals. Perhaps the warm weather, the comfortable clothes you're wearing, and the extra Euros you discovered in your pocket help it taste really good, too! Everything that affects you affects your perception and ultimately your enjoyment of any beer. Perhaps, in the end, there isn't anywhere else in the world that a Kölsch will taste as good as it did that special day in Cologne, but one never knows what unique joy the next beer moment may bring. So, make the most of each moment and enjoy each beer as if it were completely unique, because in reality it is unique to you and the moment you are enjoying.

OG: 1.048 (11.9 °P)
FG: 1.009 (2.3 °P)
ADF: 81%
IBU: 25
Color: 4 SRM (7 EBC)
Alcohol: 5.1% ABV (4.0% ABW)
Boil: 60 minutes
Pre-Boil Volume: 7 gallons (26.5L)
Pre-Boil Gravity: 1.041 (10.2 °P)

Extract	Weight	Percent
Pilsener LME (2.3 °L)	8.0 lbs. (3.63kg)	97.0
Munich LME (9 °L)	0.25 lb. (113g)	3.0

Hops		IBU
Hallertau 4% AA for 60 min.	1.5 oz. (43g)	24.6

Yeast

White Labs WLP029 German Ale/Kölsch, Wyeast 2565 Kölsch, or Fermentis Safale US-05

Fermentation and Conditioning

Use 12 grams of properly rehydrated dry yeast, 2.5 liquid yeast packages, or make a starter. Ferment at 60° F (16° C). Allow the beer to lager for at least 4 weeks before bottling or serving. When finished, carbonate the beer to approximately 2.5 volumes.

All-Grain Option

Replace the Pilsener extract with 10.3 lbs. (4.67kg) continental Pilsener malt. Replace the Munich malt extract with 0.5 lb. (227g) Vienna malt. Mash at 149° F (65° C). With the low mash temperature, you might need to lengthen the rest time to 90 minutes to get full conversion. Also increase the pre-boil volume as needed to allow a 90-minute boil, which helps reduce DMS in the beer.

AMERICAN WHEAT OR RYE BEER

Refreshing wheat or rye beers can display more hop character and less yeast character than their German cousins. This is a beginner-level style that can be brewed by extract or all-grain methods. Ferments at 65° F (18° C).

OG	FG	IBU	Color	Alcohol
1.040–1.055	1.008–1.013	15–30	3–6 SRM	4–5.5% ABV
(10–13.6 °P)	(2.1–3.3 °P)		6–12 EBC	3.2–4.3% ABW

Keys to Brewing American Wheat or Rye Beer:

This easy-drinking beer style usually has a subtly grainy wheat character, slightly reminiscent of crackers. The hop flavor and aroma are more variable, with some versions having no hop character, while others have a fairly noticeable citrus or floral flair. Even when the hops are more prominent, they should not be overwhelming, and the hop bitterness should be balanced. The rye version of this style has a slight spicy, peppery note from the addition of rye in place of some or all of the wheat.

The key mistake many brewers make is in assuming that American wheat beer should be similar to German hefeweizen. However, this style should not have the clove and banana character of a hefeweizen. This beer should not be as malty (bready) as a German hefeweizen, either, so all-grain brewers will want to use a less malty American two-row malt.

To get the right fermentation profile, it is important to use a fairly neutral yeast strain, one that doesn't produce a lot of esters like the German wheat yeasts do. While you can substitute yeast like White Labs WLP001 California Ale, Wyeast 1056 American Ale, or Fermentis Safale US-05, a better choice is one that provides some crispness, such as an altbier or Kölsch yeast, and fermentation at a cool temperature.

RECIPE: KENT'S HOLLOW LEG

It was the dead of winter and I was in Amarillo, Texas, on a business trip with Kent, my co-worker. That evening at dinner I watched as Kent drank a liter of soda, several glasses of water, and three or four liters of American wheat beer. I had a glass of water and one liter of beer, and I went to the bathroom twice. Kent never left the table. When I asked Kent about his superhuman bladder capacity, he thought it was due to years of working as a programmer glued to his computer and to the wonderful, easy-drinking wheat beer. This recipe is named in honor of Kent's amazing bladder capacity.

This recipe has a touch more hop character than many bottled, commercial examples on the market, but a lot less than some examples you might find. If you want less hop character, feel free to drop the late hop additions. If you really love hops and want to make a beer with lots of hop flavor and aroma, increase the late hop amounts as you see fit. However, going past the amounts listed below might knock it out of consideration in many competitions for being "too hoppy for style," no matter how well it is brewed.

OG: 1.052 (12.8 °P)
FG: 1.012 (3.0 °P)
ADF: 77%
IBU: 20
Color: 5 SRM (10 EBC)
Alcohol: 5.3% ABV (4.1% ABW)
Boil: 60 minutes
Pre-Boil Volume: 7 gallons (26.5L)
Pre-Boil Gravity: 1.044 (11.0 °P)

Extract	Weight	Percent
Wheat LME (4 °L)	8.9 lbs. (4.03kg)	100

Hops		IBU
Willamette 5.0% AA, 60 min.	1.0 oz. (28g)	20.3
Willamette 5.0% AA, 0 min.	0.3 oz. (9g)	0
Centennial 9.0% AA, 0 min.	0.3 oz. (9g)	0

Yeast
White Labs WLP320 American Hefeweizen, Wyeast 1010 American Wheat, or Fermentis Safale US-05

Fermentation and Conditioning

Use 10 grams of properly rehydrated dry yeast, 2 liquid yeast packages, or make a starter. Ferment at 65° F (18° C). When finished, carbonate the beer to approximately 2.5 volumes.

All-Grain Option

Replace the wheat extract with 6 lbs. (2.72kg) American two-row malt and 6 lbs. (2.72kg) wheat malt. Mash at 152° F (67° C).

Rye Option

This beer can also be made with a portion of malted rye. The rye gives the beer a slightly spicy note and adds a certain creamy mouthfeel. Replace the wheat extract with 6 lbs. (2.72kg) American two-row malt, 3.75 lbs. (1.70kg) rye malt, and 3 lbs. (1.36kg) wheat malt. Mash at 152° F (67° C).

11 | AMBER HYBRID BEER

This category is a mix of unique, amber-colored beers. This includes two traditional German styles that are rarely seen outside of Germany and one of the few styles that can be considered uniquely American. All three are really enjoyable, unique beers and should be high on anybody's list of beers to brew.

NORTHERN GERMAN ALTBIER

A very clean, slightly bitter beer with a smooth malt character. This is an intermediate style that can be brewed by extract-with-grain or all-grain methods. Ferments at 60° F (16° C).

OG	FG	IBU	Color	Alcohol
1.046–1.054	1.010–1.015	25–40	13–19 SRM	4.5–5.2% ABV
(11.4–13.3 °P)	(2.6–3.8 °P)		26–37 EBC	3.6–4.1% ABW

Keys to Brewing Northern German Altbier:

Northern German altbier is a very clean beer with a smooth malt character, often with touches of toast, biscuit, and caramel. This style of alt doesn't have much in the way of hop aroma or flavor. If it does, it should always be from German noble hops.

Like most alts, Northern German altbier has a fair amount of hop bittering. However, this is not the blow-your-head-off, hop-bitter monster that some folks seem to think all altbiers should be. Northern German altbier usually has a little less bitterness and a little more malt sweetness than many Düsseldorf altbiers, which results in a more balanced beer. This style should have a firm hop backbone, but don't overdo it. If you want a more bitter version, look at the next category, Düsseldorf altbier.

The key to brewing a good Northern German altbier is using restraint in hopping, a malt bill that will leave a moderate level of bready and caramel notes, and clean fermentation. While this style is sometimes made with lager yeast, I like it a lot better when it is made with a good alt yeast. The alt yeast gives a nice, clean fermentation character, but makes it seem more like an alt than just a brown lager.

RECIPE: ALT.BEER.RECIPE

OG: 1.050 (12.3 °P)
FG: 1.014 (3.5 °P)
ADF: 72%
IBU: 32
Color: 16 SRM (31 EBC)
Alcohol: 4.7% ABV (3.7% ABW)
Boil: 60 minutes
Pre-Boil Volume: 7 gallons (26.5L)
Pre-Boil Gravity: 1.042 (10.5 °P)

Extract	Weight	Percent
Pilsener LME (2.3 °L)	7.4 lbs. (3.35kg)	84.2
Munich LME (9 °L)	0.7 lb. (318g)	8.0

Steeping Grains		
Carafa Special II (430 °L)	0.25 lb. (113g)	2.8
CaraMunich (60 °L)	0.25 lb. (113g)	2.8
Pale Chocolate Malt (200 °L)	3.0 oz. (85g)	2.1

Hops		IBU
Magnum 13.0% AA for 60 min.	0.6 oz. (17g)	32

Yeast

White Labs WLP036 Düsseldorf Alt, Wyeast 1007 German Ale, or Fermentis Saflager S-23

Fermentation and Conditioning

Use 13 grams dry yeast, 2.5 liquid yeast packages, or make an appropriate starter. Ferment at 60° F (16° C). Allow the beer to lager for at least 4 weeks before bottling or serving. When finished, carbonate the beer from 2 to 2.5 volumes.

All-Grain Option

Replace the Pilsener extract with 9.8 lbs. (4.44kg) continental Pilsener malt. Replace the Munich extract with 1 lb. (0.45kg) Munich malt. Mash at 152° F (67° C). Increase the pre-boil volume as needed to allow a 90-minute boil, which helps reduce DMS in the beer.

CALIFORNIA COMMON BEER

A lightly fruity beer with firm, grainy maltiness, interesting toasty and caramel flavors, and showcasing the signature Northern Brewer varietal hop character. This is an intermediate style that can be brewed by extract-with-grain or all-grain methods. Ferments at 62° F (17° C).

OG	FG	IBU	Color	Alcohol
1.048–1.054	1.011–1.014	30–45	10–14 SRM	4.5–5.5% ABV
(11.9–13.3 °P)	(2.8–3.6 °P)		20–28 EBC	3.6–4.3% ABW

Keys to Brewing California Common Beer:

California common is a fairly malty but dry beer. It has noticeable toasted, grainy, and caramel notes in both the flavor and aroma. The hop bittering is quite firm, balancing the beer toward bitter but not overwhelmingly so. Northern Brewer hops provide a moderate- to high level of woody (some people say rustic or minty) flavors and aromas, which are a big part of this beer. The hops help it to finish dry and firm.

The key to making a great California common is using the proper yeast at the proper temperature. This will give it just the right profile, with a light, fruity note. There is no substitute for the proper San Francisco-style lager yeast.

While there are some examples out there that use all sorts of different hops, if you want to make a beer like Anchor Steam, you will need to use Northern Brewer hops. To me any other hops just don't seem right. Whichever hop variety you choose, don't pick one with lots of citrus or fruity notes. They tend to cover up the light, fruity ester of the yeast.

RECIPE: UNCOMMONLY LUCKY

I am very lucky to live close enough to Anchor Brewing Company to have visited there several times. While they make many great beers, there is one that is both unique and wonderful, Anchor Steam Beer. When served in the bottle, far from the brewery, it is still a great beer, traveling as well as any other commercial beer out there, but it just seems to lose a bit of that special something that makes it truly world-class when on draft. If you are ever in the San Francisco area, try Anchor Steam on draft. Until then, here is a recipe that makes a beer similar in flavor to Anchor Steam but a bit bigger in mouthfeel, hops, and malt flavors. It is going to finish on the high end for the style, but it is delicious. If you want a beer that's a bit drier and more like Anchor Steam, eliminate the Munich, Victory, and pale chocolate malts, and it will be closer.

OG: 1.054 (13.3 °P)
FG: 1.016 (4.1 °P)
ADF: 69%
IBU: 41
Color: 11 SRM (21 EBC)
Alcohol: 5.0% ABV (3.9% ABW)
Boil: 60 minutes
Pre-Boil Volume: 7 gallons (26.5L)
Pre-Boil Gravity: 1.046 (11.4 °P)

Extract	Weight	Percent
Light LME (2.2 °L)	7.0 lbs. (3.17kg)	72.0
Munich LME (9 °L)	1.1 lbs. (0.49kg)	11.3

Steeping Grains		
Crystal (40 °L)	1.0 lb. (0.45kg)	10.3
Victory (28 °L)	0.5 lb. (227g)	5.1
Pale Chocolate (200 °L)	2.0 oz. (57g)	1.3

Hops		IBU
Northern Brewer 6.5% AA for 60 min.	0.9 oz. (26g)	23.5
Northern Brewer 6.5% AA for 15 min.	1.5 oz. (43g)	10.5
Northern Brewer 6.5% AA for 1 min.	1.5 oz. (43g)	6.5

Yeast
White Labs WLP810 San Francisco Lager, Wyeast 2112 California Lager

Fermentation and Conditioning
Use 3 liquid yeast packages or make an appropriate starter. Ferment at 62° F (17° C). When finished, carbonate the beer from 2.5 to 3 volumes.

All-Grain Option
Replace the light extract with 10 lbs. (4.53kg) American two-row malt. Replace the Munich extract with 1.25 lbs. (0.56kg) Munich malt. Mash at 150° F (66° C).

DÜSSELDORF ALTBIER

A well-balanced, bitter yet malty, clean, smooth, well-attenuated, copper-colored German ale. This is an intermediate style that can be brewed by extract-with-grain or all-grain methods. Ferments at 60° F (16° C).

OG	FG	IBU	Color	Alcohol
1.046–1.054	1.010–1.015	35–50	11–17 SRM	4.5–5.2% ABV
(11.4–13.3 °P)	(2.6–3.8 °P)		22–33 EBC	3.6–4.1% ABW

Keys to Brewing Düsseldorf Altbier:

Düsseldorf altbier is another clean, German beer with a full, rich, and complex malt character. The flavor and aroma are both full of dark bread, and often spicy or floral hop notes, too. Hop bitterness ranges from moderate to quite high, leaving it balanced nearly evenly in some examples and very firmly bittered in others. In all cases, the malt character is apparent, the fermentation is clean, and the overall beer finishes fairly dry.

The key to brewing a Düsseldorf altbier is using the proper yeast and fermenting cool, but still getting enough attenuation to avoid too much residual sweetness. There is a little balancing act going on in this beer. You don't want it to finish too sweet, but it seems that many people appreciate it much more with a dash of CaraMunich, which will enhance the residual sweetness. Just keep that dash to no more than 5 percent. The same goes for the later hop additions. Most pubs in Düsseldorf are not adding late hops, so the late addition can be dropped, if you prefer.

When I first started brewing altbier, I was told you really couldn't make one without German grown Spalt hops, so I went to great lengths to obtain them for my beer. Unfortunately, Spalt has a uniquely bold and spicy flavor that most people find a bit unusual in beer. No beer with noticeable Spalt character that I have entered in competition has ever done well, so I have switched to other, more subtle German hops for brewing altbier.

RECIPE: COWBOY ALT

One of the greatest beer experiences I have had was while wandering the Altstadt of Düsseldorf, Germany. This is the old section of Düsseldorf, with pubs that have been brewing the same beer for eight hundred years. Just the sense of history and the quality of the beer makes this an amazing destination for a beer geek. They still serve their beer from wooden kegs, rolling them out with their feet from the cellar through the pub to the bar. All of these pubs brew and serve just one kind of beer, and it is served in one size of glass. It is served by gravity, and the keg is tapped with a simple faucet. You only need to go in and ask for ein bier bitte. They keep a tally of how many beers you drink by making a mark on your coaster. When you are done, they count up the checkmarks.

Some travelers like to take pictures of buildings and statues. I like to take photos of the beers I drink. When I stopped at *Brauerei Zum Schlüssel* for a second time (because the beer was so incredibly good the first time), I took a picture of the beer, and a very large fellow at the end of the bar, speaking German, said in a very gruff voice, "Hey, Cowboy, are you taking a picture of me?" I quickly explained that I was taking a picture of the beer, because I felt it was the best one in all of Düsseldorf. Several locals also chimed in that I just loved the beer and that it was OK. The big guy laughed. He, of course, was just kidding around. They were all pleased that I thought the beer at their favorite pub was the best in town.

Every time I brew the recipe below, I think of the wonderful people of Düsseldorf and the great beer moment I had at *Brauerei Zum Schlüssel*.

OG: 1.050 (12.4 °P)
FG: 1.013 (3.2 °P)
ADF: 74%
IBU: 45
Color: 14 SRM (27 EBC)
Alcohol: 4.9% ABV (3.9% ABW)
Boil: 60 minutes
Pre-Boil Volume: 7 gallons (26.5L)
Pre-Boil Gravity: 1.042 (10.6 °P)

Extract	Weight	Percent
Pilsener LME (2.3 °L)	6.1 lbs. (2.76kg)	67.1
Munich LME (9 °L)	1.3 lbs. (0.59kg)	14.3

Steeping Grains		
Aromatic Malt (20 °L)	1.0 lb. (0.45kg)	11.0
CaraMunich (60 °L)	0.5 lb. (227g)	5.5
Carafa Special II (430 °L)	3.0 oz. (85g)	2.1

Hops		IBU
Magnum 13.0% AA, 60 min.	0.8 oz. (23g)	42.7
Tettnang 4.0% AA, 15 min.	0.5 oz. (14g)	2.2

Yeast

White Labs WLP036 Düsseldorf Alt, Wyeast 1007 German Ale, or Fermentis Safale US-05

Fermentation and Conditioning

Use 13 grams dry yeast, 2.5 liquid yeast packages, or make an appropriate starter. Ferment at 60° F (16° C). Allow the beer to lager for at least 4 weeks before bottling or serving. When finished, carbonate the beer from 1.5 to 2.5 volumes.

All-Grain Option

Replace the Pilsener extract with 8 lbs. (3.63kg) continental Pilsener malt. Replace the Munich extract with 2 lbs. (0.9kg) Munich malt. Mash at 149° F (65° C). With the low mash temperature, you might need to lengthen the rest time to 90 minutes to get full conversion. Also increase the pre-boil volume as needed to allow a 90-minute boil, which helps reduce DMS in the beer.

12 | ENGLISH PALE ALE

This category of beers is also often called "bitter," yet they tend to be much less bitter than many of the modern American pale ales. The style names—ordinary, special, and strong or extra special—generally differentiate the commercial examples by starting gravity. However, you will find that these styles also vary considerably in other ways, such as hop flavor and aroma, malt characteristics, caramel or roasted notes, or the fermentation characteristics of each beer's particular yeast. A beer lover with a chance to sample the diverse world of English bitter is in for a treat, especially when enjoyed on cask as real ale. While English pale ales were the forerunners of today's American pale ales, they really don't have a lot in common in terms of flavor or aroma anymore, as American pale ales tend to have far less yeast character and a much narrower malt character range.

STANDARD/ORDINARY BITTER

Low gravity, low alcohol levels, and low carbonation make this an easy-drinking beer with plenty of English yeast character. This is a beginner-level style that can be brewed by extract-with-grain or all-grain methods. Ferments at 68° F (20° C).

OG	FG	IBU	Color	Alcohol
1.032–1.040	1.007–1.011	25–35	4–14 SRM	3.2–3.8% ABV
(8.1–10 °P)	(1.8–2.8 °P)		8–28 EBC	2.5–3% ABW

Keys to Brewing Standard/Ordinary Bitter:
This style is one of my favorites. It is a beer I try to always have available,

and it is one I turn to when I am craving a lot of flavor but not a lot of alcohol. It has balanced but firm hop bitterness, low hop character, and a nice touch of fermentation character from the yeast. Ordinary bitter should have some malt character in the aroma, often biscuit-like with a touch of caramel. This malt character carries through to the flavor and finish, helping balance the bitterness. Some examples have more toasted malt flavors and some will have less, as there is a fair range among the different examples.

The yeast for an ordinary bitter should be one that does not highly attenuate the beer. Using yeast that attenuates around 70 percent is a good choice. The yeast used also needs to contribute a fair amount of esters and other compounds that add interest. Subtle fruit-like flavors and aromas ranging from pale fruits like apple and pear to dark fruits like fig and plum are common from many of these yeasts. Some odd strains will even produce flavors that are slightly earthy.

It is very important to use English pale ale malt extract or grain. This is what adds a slight, English biscuit-like malt note to the beer.

A common error in brewing this style is overhopping the beer, especially the hop aroma and flavor. It should be fairly subtle even in the hoppiest examples. Keeping the hops subtle and balanced with the other flavors is an important part of brewing a great bitter.

RECIPE: NO SHORT MEASURE

I vividly remember one of my first times in a proper British pub. I stepped up to the bar and ordered a pint of bitter. The bartender pulled the pint and set it on the counter. Being the get-it-quick American that I am, I immediately reached over and picked it up. I then heard a loud voice behind me, "Eh, don't let her screw you like that!" The two chaps standing behind me then began to lambaste the poor lady, "You can't get away with that. How dare you try to cheat him!"

They were upset because they saw that the pint I was holding was about 97 percent beer and 3 percent foam. I could barely keep it from spilling on my shoes as I held it, but they felt the glass was not full. This is a great issue in most British pubs. Many feel that when you pay for a pint of beer, it should be a full pint, with liquid beer all the way to the top of the glass. Getting any foam is considered thievery by the pub. There is even a campaign to fight these "short measures."

Well, it turns out the fault was all mine. The bartender explained to the two men that she had placed the pint on the bar as she was waiting for the head to settle. I just reached over and grabbed it before she was done. Now, so you won't think me a completely uncouth ape, in this case the difference in position between the pint belonging to the bartender and the pint belonging to the patron is a little more than a hand's breadth. The two guys admitted that what she said was probably the case and let it drop. However, throughout the evening as we chatted and bought each other pints, I could see they still kept a watchful eye for any short measures.

OG: 1.038 (9.6 °P)
FG: 1.011 (2.8 °P)
ADF: 71%
IBU: 32
Color: 10 SRM (19 EBC)
Alcohol: 3.6% ABV (2.8% ABW)
Boil: 60 minutes
Pre-Boil Volume: 7 gallons (26.5L)
Pre-Boil Gravity: 1.033 (8.2 °P)

Extract	Weight	Percent
English Pale Ale LME (3.5 °L)	6.1 lbs. (2.76kg)	89.1

Steeping Grains		
Crystal (120 °L)	0.5 lb. (227g)	7.3
Special Roast (50 °L)	0.25 lb. (113g)	3.6

Hops		IBU
Kent Goldings 5% AA, 60 min.	1.2 oz. (34g)	24.6
Kent Goldings 5% AA, 30 min.	0.5 oz. (14g)	5.2
Kent Goldings 5% AA, 1 min.	0.5 oz. (14g)	1.7

Yeast
White Labs WLP002 English Ale, Wyeast 1968 London ESB, or Fermentis Safale S-04

Fermentation and Conditioning

Use 5 grams of properly rehydrated dry yeast, 1 liquid yeast package, or make an appropriate starter. Ferment at 68° F (20° C). When finished, carbonate the beer to approximately 1 to 1.5 volumes and serve at 52 to 55° F (11 to 13° C). Since this beer has a fairly light body, excessive carbon dioxide can make it seem extra thin, harsh, and hard to drink. With the right level of CO_2, the body of the beer will be just right, and it won't seem watery or harsh.

All-Grain Option

Replace the English pale ale extract with 8 lbs. (3.63kg) British pale ale malt. Mash at 152° F (67° C).

SPECIAL/BEST/PREMIUM BITTER

A flavorful yet refreshing session beer. Some examples can be more malt balanced, but this should not override the overall bitter impression. Drinkability is a critical component of the style. This is a beginner-level style that can be brewed by extract-with-grain or all-grain methods. Ferments at 68° F (20° C).

OG	FG	IBU	Color	Alcohol
1.040–1.048	1.008–1.012	25–40	5–16 SRM	3.8–4.6% ABV
(10–11.9 °P)	(2.1–3.1 °P)		10–31 EBC	3–3.6% ABW

Keys to Brewing Special/Best/Premium Bitter:

Special bitter is slightly bigger than the previous style but otherwise very similar. It has been said that traditionally this was the breweries' best or special beer, using their best ingredients and made to a higher standard than their ordinary effort. This is certainly a very enjoyable beer and one of my favorites. It has balanced but firm hop bitterness, low hop character, and a touch of fermentation character from the yeast. While it is bigger than ordinary bitter, it is still an easy-drinking style that is   simple to brew. The higher gravity of this style results in a few noticeable differences between the styles. Special bitter tends to have a fuller malt backbone and the appropriate bitterness to balance the additional malt. The additional malt creates a little more alcohol, a bit more body, and a touch more flavor.

The keys for brewing this style are the same as for ordinary bitter. Use an appropriate English yeast with plenty of character and lower attenuation, high-quality English base malt, and don't overhop the beer.

RECIPE: I'M NOT BITTER, I'M THIRSTY

OG: 1.047 (11.7 °P)
FG: 1.012 (3.2 °P)
ADF: 73%
IBU: 30
Color: 11 SRM (21 EBC)
Alcohol: 4.6% ABV (3.6% ABW)
Boil: 60 minutes
Pre-Boil Volume: 7 gallons (26.5L)
Pre-Boil Gravity: 1.040 (10.0 °P)

Extract	Weight	Percent
English Pale Ale LME (3.5 °L)	6.8 lbs. (3.08kg)	84.5

Steeping Grains	Weight	Percent
Aromatic (20 °L)	0.5 lb. (227g)	6.2
Crystal (120 °L)	0.5 lb. (227g)	6.2
Special Roast (50 °L)	0.25 lb. (113g)	3.1

Hops		IBU
Kent Goldings 5% AA, 60 min.	1.2 oz. (34g)	24.6
Kent Goldings 5% AA, 20 min.	0.5 oz. (14g)	3.5
Kent Goldings 5% AA, 1 min.	0.5 oz. (14g)	1.7

Yeast
White Labs WLP002 English Ale, Wyeast 1968 London ESB, or Fermentis Safale S-04

Fermentation and Conditioning
Use 9 grams of properly rehydrated dry yeast, 2 liquid yeast packages, or make an appropriate starter. Ferment at 68° F (20° C). When finished, carbonate the beer to approximately 1.5 to 2 volumes. Since this beer has a fairly light body, excessive carbon dioxide can make it seem extra thin, harsh, and hard to drink. With the right level of CO_2, the body will be just right, and it won't seem watery or harsh.

All-Grain Option
Replace the English pale ale extract with 9.5 lbs. (4.31kg) British pale ale malt. Mash at 151° F (66° C).

EXTRA SPECIAL/STRONG BITTER

An average-strength to moderately strong English ale. The balance may be fairly even between malt and hops to somewhat bitter. Drinkability is a critical component of the style. This is a beginner-level style that can be brewed by extract-with-grain or all-grain methods. Ferments at 68° F (20° C).

OG	FG	IBU	Color	Alcohol
1.048–1.060	1.010–1.016	30–50	6–18 SRM	4.6–6.2% ABV
(11.9–14.7 °P)	(2.6–4.1 °P)		12–35 EBC	3.6–4.9% ABW

Keys to Brewing Extra Special/Strong Bitter:
Similar to the other bitters, strong bitter has balanced but firm hop bitterness, moderate hop character, and a touch of fermentation character from the yeast. While still in the same family as the special and ordinary bitter, this style very often has significant caramel malt sweetness and a complex biscuity, toasty, nutty malt character in the background. Of course, this additional malt sweetness and character gets balanced with more hop bitterness and flavor.

The keys for brewing this style are similar to the other bitters. Use an appropriate English yeast with plenty of character, high-quality English base malt, and don't overhop. While this bitter has the most hop flavor and aroma of the beers in this category, it should not have a big late-hop character as is common in many American pale ales.

RECIPE: PROGRAMMER'S ELBOW

One of the great things about many English beers is their creative names, such as Bishop's Finger, Old Speckled Hen, and Fiddler's Elbow. During my years as a software programmer, I used to get a terrible pain in my elbow toward the end of some particularly brutal projects. Lifting a few pints of this beer to work the kinks out of my elbow was one of the small joys in life. It kept me sane enough to code for sixteen hours at a stretch.

OG: 1.056 (13.8 °P)
FG: 1.015 (3.8 °P)
ADF: 73%
IBU: 40

Color: 8 SRM (16 EBC)
Alcohol: 5.4% ABV (4.2% ABW)
Boil: 60 minutes
Pre-Boil Volume: 7 gallons (26.5L)
Pre-Boil Gravity: 1.048 (11.8 °P)

Extract	Weight	Percent
English Pale Ale LME (3.5 °L)	8.6 lbs. (3.9kg)	92.0

Steeping Grains		
Crystal (15 °L)	0.5 lb. (227g)	5.3
Crystal (120 °L)	0.25 lb. (113g)	2.7

Hops		IBU
Kent Goldings 5% AA for 60 min.	2.0 oz. (57g)	39.8
Kent Goldings 5% AA for 0 min.	1.0 oz. (28g)	0

Yeast

White Labs WLP002 English Ale, Wyeast 1968 London ESB, or Fermentis Safale S-04

Fermentation and Conditioning

Use 11 grams of properly rehydrated dry yeast, 2 liquid yeast packages, or make an appropriate starter. Ferment at 68° F (20° C). When finished, carbonate the beer to approximately 1.5 to 2 volumes.

All-Grain Option

Replace the English pale ale extract with 12 lbs. (5.44kg) British pale ale malt. Mash at 152° F (67° C).

13 | SCOTTISH AND IRISH ALE

Scottish ales and strong Scotch ale are delightfully malty beers that are differentiated mainly by their alcohol content. They are much cleaner (lower esters and other fermentation elements) and are balanced far more toward malt sweetness than English pale ales. They range from low-alcohol session beers (Scottish ales) to the big, warming, strong Scotch ale.

Irish red ale is similar to Scottish ale. It is somewhere between a too clean, not bitter enough English bitter and a little too hoppy, too dry Scottish ale.

SCOTTISH LIGHT 60/-, SCOTTISH HEAVY 70/- AND SCOTTISH EXPORT 80/-

All of the Scottish ales are clean, malty, and slightly sweet with little or no hop flavor. They range in alcohol from very low to moderate. This is a beginner style that can be brewed by extract-with-grain or all-grain methods. Ferments at 65° F (18° C).

	OG	FG	IBU	Color	Alcohol
60/-	1.030–1.035 (7.6–8.9 °P)	1.010–1.013 (2.6–3.3 °P)	10–20	9–17 SRM 18–33 EBC	2.5–3.2% ABV 2–2.5% ABW
70/-	1.035–1.040 (8.8–10 °P)	1.010–1.015 (2.6–3.8 °P)	10–25	9–17 SRM 19–33 EBC	3.2–3.9% ABV 2.5–3.1% ABW
80/-	1.040–1.054 (10–13.3 °P)	1.010–1.016 (2.6–4.1 °P)	15–30	9–17 SRM 18–33 EBC	3.9–5.0% ABV 3.1–4% ABW

Keys to Brewing Scottish Ales:

Scottish ales are another beer style favorite of mine. I like to keep the lower-shilling versions on hand when I am craving something malty but without a lot of alcohol. Since they have a low level of bittering, Scottish ales are also nice beers to use when cooking. Most range in color from very light amber to a deep copper color. They have a malt-focused aroma, with bread and toasted malt notes, caramel, and some malty sweetness.

Some people will detect peat smoke notes in this beer style, even when there is no peat malt used. It might be the combination of roasted malt and malt sweetness, or it might be that minor oxidation is what they perceive as a very slight smoky, earthy, or peat-like note. I have heard some people say it is the water or the yeast that provides this peat character, but then, the water and California ale yeast I use don't produce any peat character in any of my other beers. Regardless, the use of peat-smoked malt is not correct, and it is not found in good examples of this style. Much confusion was caused early on when some written descriptions mentioned peat or smoked character in these beers. Brewers took this description to heart and started adding peat-smoked malt to Scottish beers, and judges started hunting for any suggestion of it. While judging continues to improve, every now and then I still hear of judges asking brewers to add peat-smoked malt, which is completely wrong. Don't do it. Do not add peat malt to any of the beers in this category.

If you went to Scotland and wanted to order Scottish ale, you would ask for a "seventy" or an "eighty." Many years ago the price of a cask of Scottish ale, including the tax, was given in shillings. This was written as the number of shillings, a slash, and then the number of pence (shillings/pence). When there are no pence, they would write a dash instead (shillings/-). When you see 70/-, read it as "seventy shilling" or "seventy shillings."

Today the shilling number is still a relative indication of one beer's strength in relation to another. And because they are so similar in character, the 60/-, 70/-, and 80/- beers all share the same basic recipe. The only difference is in the amount of base malt, hop bitterness, and the amount of yeast needed for each substyle.

My first attempts at perfecting this recipe were based on an idea by Ray Daniels that the rich malty and caramel notes of this style could be created through specialty malts instead of an extended boil. Sure enough, with a bit of tweaking and experimentation, this basic recipe resulted in numerous medals, including four medals in the final round of the American Homebrewers Association National Homebrew Competition. Many other brewers have had great success with this recipe, too.

Keep in mind that the hop bitterness in this style is quite subdued, just enough to keep the beer from being overly sweet or cloying. Hop flavor and aroma should be very low to none at all. These beers need a clean, cool fermentation, using neutral ale yeast. The result is a beer with low esters and lots of clean malt flavors. Do not add any type of smoked malt to Scottish ale.

RECIPE: SCOTTISH HEAVY 70/-

The recipe below can be easily adjusted to make varying strengths of the same beer. The specialty grains remain the same; it is only the base malt and hop bittering that changes. Many new brewers mistakenly think it is necessary to increase the level of specialty malts when making a higher-alcohol beer. That is incorrect, and doing so will make an over-the-top version of the beer. The increased base malt will add the additional body, alcohol, and some malty flavors and aromas, so there is no need to change the specialty grain amounts, unless you are making a larger or smaller volume of beer.

OG: 1.038 (9.6 °P)
FG: 1.014 (3.5 °P)
ADF: 63%
IBU: 15
Color: 13 SRM (26 EBC)
Alcohol: 3.2% ABV (2.5% ABW)
Boil: 60 minutes
Pre-Boil Volume: 7 gallons (26.5L)
Pre-Boil Gravity: 1.032 (8.2 °P)

Extract	Weight	Percent
English Pale Ale LME (3.5 °L)	4.75 lbs. (2.15kg)	68.5
Munich LME (9 °L)	0.25 lb. (113g)	3.6

Steeping Grains

Crystal (40 °L)	1.0 lb. (0.45kg)	14.4
Honey Malt (18 °L)	0.5 lb. (227g)	7.2
Crystal (120 °L)	0.25 lb. (113g)	3.6
Pale Chocolate (200 °L)	3.0 oz. (85g)	2.7

Hops

		IBU
Kent Goldings 5% AA, 60 min.	0.75 oz. (21g)	15.4

Yeast

White Labs California Ale WLP001, Wyeast American Ale 1056, or Fermentis Safale US-05

Fermentation and Conditioning

Use 7 grams of properly rehydrated dry yeast, 1.5 liquid yeast packages, or make an appropriate starter. Ferment at 65° F (18° C). When finished, carbonate the beer to approximately 1.5 to 2 volumes and serve at 48 to 52° F (9 to 11° C). Allowing the beer to cold condition around 40° F (4° C) for several months will improve the beer.

All-Grain Option

Replace the English pale ale extract with 6.5 lbs. (2.95kg) British pale ale malt. Replace the Munich extract with 0.5 lb. (227g) Munich malt. Mash at 158° F (70° C).

Scottish Light 60/- Option:

To make a 60/- ale, decrease the English malt extract to 4 lbs. (1.81kg) and the hops to 0.67 oz. (19g). For an all-grain beer use 5.5 lbs. (2.49kg) British pale ale malt, 0.5 lb. (227g) Munich malt, and mash at 158° F (70° C). Use 5 grams of properly rehydrated dry yeast or use 1 liquid yeast package.

Scottish Export 80/- Option:

To make an 80/- ale, increase the English malt extract to 7 lbs. (3.17kg) and the hops to 1 oz. (28g). For an all-grain beer use 9.5 lbs. (4.31kg) British pale ale malt, 0.5 lb. (227g) Munich malt, and mash at 158° F (70° C). Increase the amount of yeast to handle the increased gravity. Use

10 grams of properly rehydrated dry yeast, 2 liquid yeast packages, or make an appropriate starter.

RECIPE: SCOTTISH HEAVY 70/-, CARAMELIZED

This recipe is for a Scottish ale made with a more traditional recipe, which relies on some kettle caramelization and an extended boil to increase the level of melanoidins. When making this beer, you will need to boil 1 gallon of the wort, reducing it down until the sugars begin to caramelize, and then add that to the main wort. If you're an all-grain brewer, you can boil the first gallon of runnings from the mash. You may need to add back some water to end up at the correct starting gravity and volume.

There is one thing to note before going this route, which is that heavy kettle caramelization can lend a toffee note, which some people may describe as buttery and a flaw in the beer.

As with the previous recipe, this recipe can be easily adjusted to make varying strengths of the same beer. The specialty grains remain the same; it is only the base malt and hop bittering that changes.

OG: 1.038 (9.4 °P)
FG: 1.013 (3.3 °P)
ADF: 65%
IBU: 15
Color: 12 SRM (23 EBC)
Alcohol: 3.2% ABV (2.5% ABW)
Boil: 120 minutes
Pre-Boil Volume: 8.6 gallons (32.6L)
Pre-Boil Gravity: 1.026 (6.6 °P)

Extract	Weight	Percent
English Pale Ale LME (3.5 °L)	6.0 lbs. (2.72kg)	97.0

Steeping Grains		
Black Roasted Barley (500 °L)	3.0 oz. (85g)	3.0

Hops		IBU
Kent Goldings 5% AA, 60 min.	0.75 oz. (21g)	15.4

Yeast
White Labs WLP028 Edinburgh Ale, Wyeast 1728 Scottish Ale, or Fermentis Safale US-05

Fermentation and Conditioning
Use 7 grams of properly rehydrated dry yeast, 1.5 liquid yeast packages, or make an appropriate starter. Ferment at 65° F (18° C). When finished, carbonate the beer to approximately 1.5 to 2 volumes and serve at 48 to 52° F (9 to 11° C). Allowing the beer to cold condition around 40° F (4° C) for a few months will improve the beer.

All-Grain Option
Replace the English pale ale extract with 8.5 lbs. (3.85kg) British pale ale malt. Mash at 154° F (68° C).

Scottish Light 60/- Option:
To make a 60/- ale, decrease the English malt extract to 5.4 lbs. (2.45kg) and the hops to 0.67 oz. (19g). For an all-grain beer use 7.5 lbs. (3.4kg) British pale ale malt, and mash at 154° F (68° C). Use 5 grams of properly rehydrated dry yeast or use 1 liquid yeast package.

Scottish Export 80/- Option:
To make an 80/- ale, increase the English malt extract to 8.3 lbs. (3.76kg) and the hops to 1 oz. (28g). For an all-grain beer use 11.5 lbs. (5.21kg) British pale ale malt, and mash at 154° F (68° C). Increase the amount of yeast to handle the increased gravity. Use 10 grams of properly rehydrated dry yeast, 2 liquid yeast packages, or make an appropriate starter.

IRISH RED ALE

A malt-focused beer with an initial sweetness and a roasted dryness in the finish. This is a beginner style that can be brewed by extract-with-grain or all-grain methods. Ferments at 66° F (19° C).

OG	FG	IBU	Color	Alcohol
1.044–1.060	1.010–1.014	17–28	9–18 SRM	4.0–6.0% ABV
(11–14.7 °P)	(2.6–3.6 °P)		18–35 EBC	3.2–4.7% ABW

Keys to Brewing Irish Red Ale:

Irish red ale is a balanced beer with moderate malt character that often comes across as toasted and subtle caramel notes. The deep-reddish-copper color comes from a small dose of highly kilned malt that also adds to the dry finish. Sometimes the roast can add a very slight touch of roasted flavor, too. Hop bitterness is evenly balanced, but the beer can seem a little more bitter from the dark malt addition. Hop character is low, although it is still higher than in Scottish ales. This beer can be brewed as either a lager or ale, but my preference is to use ale yeast that ferments clean at low temperatures.

It is important to use restraint with dark malts, caramel malts, and hops in this style. If any one of the elements is out of balance or too prominent, it is going to cover up the toasted notes that are key to the overall background of the beer. Temperature control during fermentation is also very important. You want it to attenuate enough so that it doesn't have a sweet finish, and you want to ferment it cold enough that any esters are restrained and it has a fairly clean character. While some commercial examples have a touch of diacetyl, keep any buttery flavors and aromas to a minimum for the best results in competition.

RECIPE: RUABEOIR

OG: 1.054 (13.4 °P)
FG: 1.014 (3.6 °P)
ADF: 73%
IBU: 25
Color: 17 SRM (33 EBC)
Alcohol: 5.2% ABV (4.0% ABW)

Boil: 60 minutes
Pre-Boil Volume: 7 gallons (26.5L)
Pre-Boil Gravity: 1.046 (11.4 °P)

Extract	Weight	Percent
English Pale Ale LME (3.5 °L)	8.1 lbs. (3.67kg)	87.8

Steeping Grains		
Crystal (40 °L)	6.0 oz. (170g)	4.1
Crystal (120 °L)	6.0 oz. (170g)	4.1
Roasted Barley (300 °L)	6.0 oz. (170g)	4.1

Hops		IBU
Kent Goldings 5% AA, 60 min.	1.25 oz. (35g)	25.1

Yeast
White Labs WLP004 Irish Ale, Wyeast 1084 Irish Ale, or Fermentis Safale US-05

Fermentation and Conditioning
Use 10 grams of properly rehydrated dry yeast, 2 liquid yeast packages, or make an appropriate starter. Ferment at 66° F (19° C). When finished, carbonate the beer from 2 to 2.5 volumes.

All-Grain Option
Replace the English pale ale extract with 11.25 lbs. (5.1kg) British pale ale malt. Mash at 153° F (67° C).

STRONG SCOTCH ALE

Rich, malty, and usually sweet, which can be suggestive of a dessert. Complex secondary malt flavors prevent a one-dimensional impression. This is an intermediate style that can be brewed by extract-with-grain or all-grain methods. Ferments at 65° F (18° C).

OG	FG	IBU	Color	Alcohol
1.070–1.130	1.018–1.030	17–35	14–25 SRM	6.5–10% ABV
(17.1–30.2 °P)	(4.6–7.6 °P)		28–49 EBC	5.1–7.9% ABW

Keys to Brewing Strong Scotch Ale:

Strong Scotch ale, also known as wee heavy, is related to the lower-alcohol Scottish ales, but the higher starting gravity brings changes that make it substantially different. This beer has a rich, deep malt character plus a fair amount of residual malt sweetness. Enhancing that perception of sweetness is a low level of hop bitterness and often considerable melanoidin development from long boil times. Along with the higher starting gravity comes higher alcohol, although the alcohol should always be just warming and never harsh. The higher-gravity fermentation creates more esters, so this beer is not as clean as the Scottish ales. It isn't highly fruity, either, but it does tend to have some dark fruit notes, like plums, raisins, and figs.

The key to a good wee heavy is in controlling the recipe and process to make a beer that is slightly sweet but not cloying, and making it alcoholic but not hot or harsh. Cool, steady fermentation and pitching the right amount of yeast are important. Fermenting too warm or not pitching the right amount of clean, healthy yeast will often result in a solvency taste and aroma.

As with Scottish ales, do not add peat-smoked malt.

RECIPE: MCZAINASHEFF'S WEE

OK, I'll admit it; the name for this beer came to me while taking a "break" from enjoying a pint.

OG: 1.099 (23.4 °P)
FG: 1.026 (6.6 °P)
ADF: 72%

IBU: 28
Color: 16 SRM (31 EBC)
Alcohol: 9.7% ABV (7.5% ABW)
Boil: 90 minutes
Pre-Boil Volume: 7.7 gallons (29.3L)
Pre-Boil Gravity: 1.076 (18.5 °P)

Extract	Weight	Percent
English Pale Ale LME (3.5 °L)	14.5 lbs. (6.57kg)	86.6
Munich LME (9 °L)	0.25 lb. (113g)	1.5

Steeping Grains		
Crystal (40 °L)	1.0 lb. (0.45kg)	6.0
Honey Malt (18 °L)	0.5 lb. (227g)	3.0
Crystal (120 °L)	0.25 lb. (113g)	1.5
Pale Chocolate (200 °L)	0.25 lb. (113g)	1.5

Hops		IBU
Kent Goldings 5% AA, 60 min.	1.6 oz. (45g)	26.4
Kent Goldings 5% AA, 10 min.	0.5 oz. (14g)	1.7

Yeast
White Labs WLP028 Edinburgh Ale, Wyeast 1728 Scottish Ale, or Fermentis Safale US-05

Fermentation and Conditioning
Use 18 grams of properly rehydrated dry yeast, 4 liquid yeast packages, or make an appropriate starter. Ferment at 65° F (18° C). When finished, carbonate the beer from 2 to 2.5 volumes. A period of cold conditioning for several months will improve it.

All-Grain Option
Replace the English pale ale extract with 20 lbs. (9.07kg) British pale ale malt. Replace the Munich extract with 0.5 lb. (227g) Munich malt. Mash at 154° F (68° C).

14 | AMERICAN ALE

The American ale category started as "Americanized" versions of English beers, with American pale ale featuring more hops and less caramel than English pale ale. American brown ale also has significantly more hops and is roastier and bigger than Northern English brown ale. Yet these styles are not just hoppier versions of English beers anymore; they have really become unique styles of their own, and American amber ale is altogether original. In general the American ales tend to be clean, moderately bigger beers, with a wonderful range of American hop character that goes from restrained to way over the top.

What is really cool, at least to me, is that this is a uniquely American category. As a beer traveler, I realize that the most wonderful English ales are made in England. The great Belgian beers are still found in Belgium. The finest German-style ales and lagers are brewed in Germany. Not so long ago, in the United States, low-flavor lagers were pretty much the only game in town. Now, through the efforts of amateur and professional brewers in the United States, there are very distinct beer styles where the best examples are found right here. This is very cool, indeed.

AMERICAN PALE ALE

A clean, fresh, hoppy beer with enough malt backbone to carry moderate hop character and bitterness. This is beginner style that can be brewed by extract-with-grain or all-grain methods. Ferments at 67° F (19° C).

OG	FG	IBU	Color	Alcohol
1.045–1.060	1.010–1.015	30–45	5–14 SRM	4.5–6.2% ABV
(11.2–14.7 °P)	(2.6–3.8 °P)		10–18 EBC	3.6–4.9% ABW

Keys to Brewing American Pale Ale:

Every year or so I come across yet another great American pale ale, either homebrewed or commercial. What makes a great pale ale is balance between the hop bitterness and malt sweetness, between the bready, toasty and the citrus, floral. Avoiding a harsh hop bitterness is also important. The hop bittering can be strong, but it shouldn't be harsh. When all of these characteristics are in harmony, it makes for a great beer with a high level of drinkability. The level of carbonation and the amount of alcohol also affect drinkability. A really big or highly carbonated pale ale is often a less drinkable pale ale.

The keys to brewing American pale ale are fresh ingredients, a balanced recipe, a fair amount of late hops, and a clean fermentation featuring neutral ale yeast.

RECIPE: AMERICAN PALE ALE

There are so many different American pale ales out there. Some have a definite caramel note, of varying intensity, up to the point where you stop calling it a pale ale and start calling it an American amber. Other interpretations of the style focus on a slightly drier beer with a gentle bready, toasty, biscuity malt background and very little or no crystal malt flavor. This recipe makes the latter version, which I really prefer as I brew it more. If you want a version with some caramel, try the next recipe. If you want to increase the biscuity malt background, substitute English pale ale extract for the light extract.

OG: 1.056 (13.8 °P)
FG: 1.013 (3.2 °P)

ADF: 77%
IBU: 40
Color: 6 SRM (12 EBC)
Alcohol: 5.7% ABV (4.5% ABW)
Boil: 60 minutes
Pre-Boil Volume: 7 gallons (26.5L)
Pre-Boil Gravity: 1.048 (11.8 °P)

Extract	Weight	Percent
Light LME (2.2 °L)	8.1 lbs. (3.67kg)	82.2
Munich LME (9 °L)	0.5 lb. (227g)	5.1
Wheat LME (4 °L)	0.5 lb. (227g)	5.1

Steeping Grains		
Victory (28 °L)	0.75 lb. (340g)	7.6

Hops		IBU
Horizon 13% AA, 60 min.	0.66 oz. (19g)	34.2
Cascade 6% AA, 10 min.	0.25 oz. (7g)	2.4
Centennial 9% AA, 10 min.	0.25 oz. (7g)	3.6
Cascade 6% AA, 0 min.	0.5 oz. (14g)	0
Centennial 9% AA, 0 min.	0.5 oz. (14g)	0

Yeast
White Labs California Ale WLP001, Wyeast American Ale 1056, or Fermentis Safale US-05

Fermentation and Conditioning
Use 11 grams of properly rehydrated dry yeast, 2 liquid yeast packages, or make an appropriate starter. Ferment at 67° F (19° C). When finished, carbonate the beer from 2 to 2.5 volumes.

All-Grain Option
Replace the light extract with 11.3 lbs. (5.1kg) American two-row malt. Replace the Munich extract with 0.75 lb. (340g) Munich malt. Replace the wheat extract with 0.5 lb. (227g) wheat malt. Mash at 152° F (67° C).

RECIPE: AMERICAN PALE ALE WITH CARAMEL

OG: 1.052 (12.9 °P)
FG: 1.013 (3.3 °P)
ADF: 74%
IBU: 40
Color: 7 SRM (13 EBC)
Alcohol: 5.1% ABV (4.0% ABW)
Boil: 60 minutes
Pre-Boil Volume: 7 gallons (26.5L)
Pre-Boil Gravity: 1.044 (11.0 °P)

Extract	Weight	Percent
Light American LME (2.2 °L)	7.9 lbs. (3.58kg)	86.3
Munich LME (9 °L)	0.5 lb. (227g)	5.5

Steeping Grains		
Crystal (40 °L)	0.75 lb. (340g)	8.2

Hops		IBU
Horizon 13% AA, 60 min.	0.66 oz. (19g)	34.9
Columbus 14% AA, 10 min.	0.25 oz. (7g)	2.8
Centennial 9% AA, 10 min.	0.25 oz. (7g)	1.8
Columbus 14% AA, 0 min.	0.5 oz. (14g)	0
Centennial 9% AA, 0 min.	0.5 oz. (14g)	0

Yeast

White Labs California Ale WLP001, Wyeast American Ale 1056, or Fermentis Safale US-05

Fermentation and Conditioning

Use 10 grams of properly rehydrated dry yeast, 2 liquid yeast packages, or make an appropriate starter. Ferment at 67° F (19° C). When finished, carbonate the beer from 2 to 2.5 volumes.

All-Grain Option

Replace the light extract with 10.9 lbs. (4.94kg) American two-row malt. Replace the Munich extract with 0.75 lb. (340g) Munich malt. Mash at 154° F (68° C).

AMERICAN AMBER ALE

Similar to an American pale ale but with more body, more caramel richness, and a balance more towards malt than hops (although hop rates can be significant). This is a beginner style that can be brewed by extract-with-grain or all-grain methods. Ferments at 67 °F (19 °C).

OG	FG	IBU	Color	Alcohol
1.045–1.060	1.010–1.015	25–40	10–17 SRM	4.5–6.2% ABV
(11.2–14.7 °P)	(2.6–3.8 °P)		20–33 EBC	3.6–4.9% ABW

Keys to Brewing American Amber Ale:

American amber is another of one of my favorite beer styles. Well-made American amber ale is a very drinkable beer, with lots of hop flavor and aroma. These beers have significant caramel flavors and a little more residual malt sweetness than American pale ales. This can help to better balance the hop bitterness. Of course, like many styles, this one has a wide range. Some examples are going to be quite big and hoppy, especially on the West Coast of the United States, while others will be much more restrained. Some examples are toasty, while others show a touch of roast. Either way, this is a great, easy-drinking style.

The key to my favorite American amber ales is the right percentage of caramel-type malts and a high level of late hopping. Moving hops to later in the boil increases the hop flavor and aroma while keeping the bitterness restrained. If you are making a bigger version of the style, make sure you increase the amount of yeast pitched, and ferment it on the cool side to keep the higher alcohols in check.

RECIPE: AMERICAN AMBER

OG: 1.052 (12.8 °P)
FG: 1.013 (3.3 °P)
ADF: 74%
IBU: 35
Color: 13 SRM (25 EBC)
Alcohol: 5.1% ABV (4.0% ABW)
Boil: 60 minutes
Pre-Boil Volume: 7 gallons (26.5L)

Pre-Boil Gravity: 1.044 (10.9 °P)

Extract	Weight	Percent
English Pale Ale LME (3.5 °L)	6.6 lbs. (3kg)	72.9
Munich LME (9 °L)	0.7 lb. (318g)	7.7

Steeping Grains		
Crystal (40 °L)	0.75 lb. (340g)	8.3
Crystal (120 °L)	0.5 lb. (227g)	5.5
Victory (28 °L)	0.5 lb. (227g)	5.5

Hops		IBU
Horizon 13% AA, 60 min.	0.6 oz. (17g)	31.7
Cascade 6% AA, 10 min.	0.25 oz. (7g)	1.2
Centennial 9% AA, 10 min.	0.25 oz. (7g)	1.8
Cascade 6% AA, 0 min.	0.25 oz. (7g)	0
Centennial 9% AA, 0 min.	0.25 oz. (7g)	0

Yeast

White Labs California Ale WLP001, Wyeast American Ale 1056, or Fermentis Safale US-05

Fermentation and Conditioning

Use 10 grams of properly rehydrated dry yeast, 2 liquid yeast packages, or make an appropriate starter. Ferment at 67° F (19° C). When finished, carbonate the beer from 2 to 2.5 volumes.

All-Grain Option

Replace the English pale ale extract with 9.25 lbs. (4.19kg) British pale ale malt. Replace the Munich extract with 1 lb. (0.45kg) Munich malt. Mash at 154° F (68° C).

RECIPE: WEST COAST BLASTER

This is how red ales are done on the West Coast. Just about every brewery out here needs a beer on their menu that has a lot of hop flavor, and many of them turn to this style of beer. They are big, bold statements balancing lots of citrusy hops and specialty malt. While this beer is a bit bigger than the current style guidelines suggest, it is an example of the direction red ales are going out in California.

OG: 1.067 (16.3 °P)
FG: 1.015 (3.9 °P)
ADF: 76%
IBU: 66
Color: 16 SRM (31 EBC)
Alcohol: 6.8% ABV (5.3% ABW)
Boil: 60 minutes
Pre-Boil Volume: 7 gallons (26.5L)
Pre-Boil Gravity: 1.057 (14 °P)

Extract	Weight	Percent
English Pale Ale LME (3.5 °L)	8.75 lbs. (3.97kg)	75.2
Munich LME (9 °L)	0.7 lb. (318g)	6.0

Steeping Grains		
Crystal (40 °L)	1.0 lb. (0.45kg)	8.6
Crystal (120 °L)	0.5 lb. (227g)	4.3
Victory (28 °L)	0.5 lb. (227g)	4.3
Pale Chocolate Malt (200 °L)	3.0 oz. (85g)	1.6

Hops		IBU
Horizon 13% AA, 60 min.	1.1 oz. (31g)	54.2
Cascade 6% AA, 10 min.	1.0 oz. (28g)	4.5
Centennial 9% AA, 10 min.	1.0 oz. (28g)	6.8
Cascade 6% AA, 0 min.	1.0 oz. (28g)	0
Centennial 9% AA, 0 min.	1.0 oz. (28g)	0

Yeast
White Labs California Ale WLP001, Wyeast American Ale 1056, or Fermentis Safale US-05

Fermentation and Conditioning

Use 13 grams of properly rehydrated dry yeast, 2.5 liquid yeast packages, or make an appropriate starter. Ferment at 67° F (19° C). When finished, carbonate the beer from 2 to 2.5 volumes.

All-Grain Option

Replace the English pale ale extract with 12.25 lbs. (5.55kg) British pale ale malt. Replace the Munich extract with 1 lb. (0.45kg) Munich malt. Mash at 152° F (67° C).

AMERICAN BROWN ALE

A bold, hoppy brown ale with lots of chocolate and some caramel flavors. This is a beginner style that can be brewed by extract-with-grain or all-grain methods. Ferments at 67° F (19° C).

OG	FG	IBU	Color	Alcohol
1.045–1.060	1.010–1.016	20–40	18–35 SRM	4.3–6.2% ABV
(11.2–14.7 °P)	(2.6–4.1 °P)		35–69 EBC	3.4–4.9% ABW

Keys to Brewing American Brown Ale:

American brown ales vary from being very hoppy, very bitter beers to beers with a more restrained hop bitterness and character. Some examples have a lot of sweetness and a rich background malt flavor that balances the hops, while others are drier, letting the hops come straight through to poke you in the tastebuds.

All American brown ales need some chocolate, toasty, and caramel flavors and aromas. How bold those flavors are, and the amount of residual malt sweetness as compared to the hopping, make up the wide range of interpretations of this style.

Besides the right grain bill, the key areas to focus on for brewing a great American brown ale are hop type and fermentation. It is important to use good citrusy/fruity American hops. Yes, you could make this beer without characteristic American-type hops, but it really isn't the same. The same can be said for fermentation. It should be quite clean and neutral. If you are not using a typical American ale yeast, you will want to use a nice, cool fermentation temperature to keep the esters as low as possible.

RECIPE: DIRTY WATER BROWN

Don't ask ... some things are better left unexplained. This recipe makes an American brown on the lighter side of the style, hoppy but lower in alcohol and bitterness, for those times when you want to have a couple of pints.

OG: 1.048 (11.8 °P)
FG: 1.011 (2.7 °P)

ADF: 77%
IBU: 34
Color: 20 SRM (40 EBC)
Alcohol: 4.9% ABV (3.8% ABW)
Boil: 60 minutes
Pre-Boil Volume: 7 gallons (26.5L)
Pre-Boil Gravity: 1.041 (10.1 °P)

Extract	Weight	Percent
Light LME (2.2 °L)	7.2 lbs. (3.26kg)	82.8

Steeping Grains		
Crystal (40 °L)	0.5 lb. (227g)	5.7
Chocolate Malt (420 °L)	0.5 lb. (227g)	5.7
Crystal (60 °L)	0.25 lb. (113g)	2.9
Victory (28 °L)	0.25 lb. (113g)	2.9

Hops		IBU
Horizon 13% AA, 60 min.	0.45 oz. (13g)	24.0
Amarillo 9% AA, 15 min.	1.0 oz. (28g)	9.8
Amarillo 9% AA, 0 min.	1.75 oz. (50g)	0

Yeast
White Labs California Ale WLP001, Wyeast American Ale 1056, or Fermentis Safale US-05

Fermentation and Conditioning
Use 9 grams of properly rehydrated dry yeast, 2 liquid yeast packages, or make an appropriate starter. Ferment at 67° F (19° C). When finished, carbonate the beer from 2 to 2.5 volumes.

All-Grain Option
Replace the light extract with 10 lbs. (4.53kg) American two-row malt. Mash at 152° F (67° C).

RECIPE: JANET'S BROWN ALE

This is a recipe from my good friend Mike McDole. He is one of the best brewers I know, and I would drink anything he brews without question. It is a little bit outside the style guidelines, but not so much so that you would call it out of style. Mike has won many awards with this beer, and in 2004 it was the National Homebrew Competition gold medal winner for its category. However, Mike tells me the most important critique he ever received was from his late wife, Janet. She really loved this brown ale. It was her favorite. Brew this beer and every time you have a pint, make a toast to the memory of a fine lady with great taste. Mike always does.

OG: 1.066 (16.2 °P)
FG: 1.016 (4.2 °P)
ADF: 74%
IBU: 63
Color: 21 SRM (41 EBC)
Alcohol: 6.6% ABV (5.1% ABW)
Boil: 60 minutes
Pre-Boil Volume: 7 gallons (26.5L)
Pre-Boil Gravity: 1.056 (13.9 °P)

Extract	Weight	Percent
Light LME (2.2 °L)	8.4 lbs. (3.81kg)	67.7
Wheat LME (4 °L)	1.0 lb. (0.45kg)	8.1

Steeping Grains		
CaraPils Dextrin Malt (1 °L)	1.25 lbs. (0.56kg)	10.1
Crystal (40 °L)	1.25 lbs. (0.56kg)	10.1
Chocolate Malt (420 °L)	0.5 lb. (227g)	4.0

Hops		IBU
Northern Brewer 6.5% AA, 60 min.	2.0 oz. (57g)	49.3
Northern Brewer 6.5% AA, 15 min.	1.0 oz. (28g)	7.1
Cascade 6% AA, 10 min.	1.5 oz. (43g)	6.8

Cascade 6% AA, 0 min.	1.5 oz. (43g)	0
Centennial 9% AA, dry	2.0 oz. (57g)	0

Yeast

White Labs California Ale WLP001, Wyeast American Ale 1056, or Fermentis Safale US-05

Fermentation and Conditioning

Use 13 grams of properly rehydrated dry yeast, 2.5 liquid yeast packages, or make an appropriate starter. Ferment at 67° F (19° C). When finished, carbonate the beer from 2 to 2.5 volumes.

All-Grain Option

Replace the light extract with 12 lbs. (5.44kg) American two-row malt. Replace the wheat extract with 1 lb. (0.45kg) wheat malt. Reduce the 60-minute Northern Brewer hop addition by 0.75 oz. (21g) and instead add a 1 oz. (28g) mash hop addition of Northern Brewer. Mash at 154° F (68° C).

15 | ENGLISH BROWN ALE

English brown ales are similar to many other English beers, with a toasty/biscuit malt background and a fair amount of yeast-derived character. This category also tends to have a sweeter overall character and far more roasted, nutty, and toffee notes than you would find in the English pale ales category.

MILD

A lower-alcohol, easy-drinking beer with plenty of malt character and very low hop presence. This is a beginner style that can be brewed by extract-with-grain or all-grain methods. Ferments at 68° F (20° C).

OG	FG	IBU	Color	Alcohol
1.030–1.038	1.008–1.013	10–25	12–25 SRM	2.8–4.5% ABV
(7.6–9.5 °P)	(2.1–3.3 °P)		24–49 EBC	2.2–3.6% ABW

Keys to Brewing Mild:

Mild is a style on the brink of extinction in England, but its popularity is slowly growing with a subset of amateur brewers who desire a beer with lots of rich flavors and a low level of alcohol.

The majority of the flavor and aroma in mild comes from the yeast and the malts. Mild has very little in the way of hop flavor or aroma, and hop bitterness should be just enough to balance the bulk of the malt sweetness. It is most often dark in color, from copper to very dark brown, but there are pale versions, too. The pale version focuses on the biscuity, toasty malt notes, while darker milds may have caramel, chocolate, coffee, licorice, raisin, and other flavors. I have even come across a mild in England with a firm tobacco note, which was actually a pleasant part of the overall beer. There is such a huge range of flavors in mild that it allows for a great deal of creativity.

Being a low-gravity, low-alcohol beer, brewing a great example requires enough dextrins and other residual sugars to keep it from seeming thin. Using a relatively high percentage of specialty malts and a good base of English pale ale malt helps create a nice, broad malt backbone and plenty of malt character. Keep the hops simple, with just a bittering addition. Ferment with an English yeast that provides character but attenuates lower to help keep the beer from seeming thin. Also, serve it warmer and with restrained carbonation. The warmer serving temperature allows the character to come out, and the restrained carbonation prevents that harsh biting feel when a low-gravity beer has too much carbon dioxide.

RECIPE: THROUGH A MILD DARKLY

It was family vacation time and we were in London, visiting the incredibly beautiful and interesting sites of that great city. At least once each day I would drag the family to one pub or another, hunting down this or that favorite English ale. One day I took the family into a pub serving Harvey's Sussex Mild. I went on and on for such a long time, telling them what a rare treat it was to find mild, that my wife took pictures of me ordering and drinking the beer. I always wonder what impression I must be leaving behind in my travels. I like to think that people appreciate seeing someone so passionate about beer, but they probably just think I'm nuts.

OG: 1.036 (9.0 °P)
FG: 1.011 (2.8 °P)
ADF: 69%
IBU: 17
Color: 17 SRM (33 EBC)
Alcohol: 3.2% ABV (2.5% ABW)
Boil: 60 minutes
Pre-Boil Volume: 7 gallons (26.5L)
Pre-Boil Gravity: 1.030 (7.7 °P)

Extract	Weight	Percent
English Pale Ale LME (3.5 °L)	5.0 lbs. (2.26kg)	80.0

Steeping Grains		
Crystal (60 °L)	0.5 lb. (227g)	8.0
Crystal (120 °L)	6.0 oz. (170g)	6.0
Pale Chocolate Malt (200 °L)	0.25 lb. (113g)	4.0
Black Patent (525 °L)	2.0 oz. (57g)	2.0

Hops		IBU
Kent Goldings 5% AA, 60 min.	0.85 oz. (24g)	17.4

Yeast

White Labs WLP002 English Ale, Wyeast 1968 London ESB Ale, or Fermentis Safale S-04

Fermentation and Conditioning

Use 5 grams of properly rehydrated dry yeast, 1 liquid yeast package, or make an appropriate starter. Ferment at 68° F (20° C). When finished, carbonate the beer to approximately 1 to 1.5 volumes and serve at 52 to 55° F (11 to 13° C).

All-Grain Option

Replace the English pale ale extract with 7 lbs. (3.17kg) British pale ale malt. Mash at 154° F (68° C).

SOUTHERN ENGLISH BROWN

A luscious, malt-oriented brown ale with a caramel and dark fruit complexity of malt flavors. It may seem somewhat like a smaller version of a sweet stout or a sweet version of a dark mild. This is a beginner style that can be brewed by extract-with-grain or all-grain methods. Ferments at 68° F (20° C).

OG	FG	IBU	Color	Alcohol
1.035–1.042	1.011–1.014	12–20	19–35 SRM	2.8–4.2% ABV
(8.8–10.5 °P)	(2.8–3.6 °P)		37–69 EBC	2.2–3.3% ABW

Keys to Brewing Southern English Brown:

Another rare beer style, Southern English brown is a dark, rich, smooth, malty-sweet beer with plenty of caramel and dark fruit. This beer has little in the way of hop character and just enough hop bitterness to keep the malt sweetness from being cloying. It is similar in many ways to mild, but it is bigger and sweeter.

Just like brewing a great mild, you want to brew this beer leaving enough dextrins and other residual sugars to give it plenty of mouthfeel. Using lots of specialty malts and a good base of English pale ale malt creates a nice broad malt backbone and plenty of malt character. Keep the hops simple, with just a bittering addition, and ferment with English yeast that has a low level of attenuation. Also, serving it warmer and with restrained carbonation allows the character to come out and helps it seem richer and sweeter.

RECIPE: NUTTY MAN BROWN ALE

OG: 1.041 (10.3 °P)
FG: 1.013 (3.2 °P)
ADF: 69%
IBU: 17
Color: 26 SRM (51 EBC)
Alcohol: 3.8% ABV (3.0% ABW)
Boil: 60 minutes
Pre-Boil Volume: 7 gallons (26.5L)
Pre-Boil Gravity: 1.035 (8.8 °P)

Extract	Weight	Percent
English Pale Ale LME (3.5 °L)	5.0 lbs. (2.26kg)	64.5

Steeping Grains		
Crystal (80 °L)	1.0 lb. (0.45kg)	12.9
Crystal (120 °L)	10.0 oz. (284g)	8.1
Special Roast (50 °L)	0.5 lb. (227g)	6.5
Pale Chocolate (200 °L)	6.0 oz. (170g)	4.8
Carafa Special II (430 °L)	0.25 lb. (113g)	3.2

Hops		IBU
Kent Goldings 5% AA, 60 min.	0.85 oz. (24g)	17.4

Yeast
White Labs WLP002 English Ale, Wyeast 1968 London ESB Ale, or Fermentis Safale S-04

Fermentation and Conditioning
Use 8 grams of properly rehydrated dry yeast, 1.5 liquid yeast packages, or make an appropriate starter. Ferment at 68° F (20° C). When finished, carbonate the beer to approximately 1 to 1.5 volumes and serve at 52 to 55° F (11 to 13° C).

All-Grain Option
Replace the English pale ale extract with 6.9 lbs. (3.13kg) British pale ale malt. Mash at 153° F (67° C).

NORTHERN ENGLISH BROWN ALE

A nutty, biscuity, easy-drinking English ale. It has less sweetness and caramel character than Southern English brown. This is a beginner style that can be brewed by extract-with-grain or all-grain methods. Ferments at 68° F (20° C).

OG	FG	IBU	Color	Alcohol
1.040–1.052	1.008–1.013	20–30	12–22 SRM	4.2–5.4% ABV
(10–12.9 °P)	(2.1–3.3 °P)		24–43 EBC	3.3–4.3% ABW

Keys to Brewing Northern English Brown Ale:

Many beer lovers have tried Newcastle Brown Ale or Samuel Smith's Nut Brown Ale. Both of these dark amber to light brown beers are considered examples of Northern English brown ale. Both are relatively balanced, with neither the malt sweetness nor the hop bitterness overwhelming the other. Malt character tends toward the biscuity and nutty flavors and aromas, and hop character is usually low to none. This is a drier, slightly more hop-bittered beer than its Southern cousin. The Southern will have more caramel character, too, and is usually darker in color than the Northern.

The biggest key to brewing a proper Northern English brown ale is having the right malt base. English pale ale malt is essential, as it provides a touch of biscuit malt background that is common in English beers. You want it to have more of a nutty character than a caramel character. The Victory and pale chocolate malts help create that nutty note. Use restraint on the caramel malts and the hop bitterness to balance it, so that it doesn't become too big and full. The beer needs to remain quite drinkable, and too much malt and hops fighting each other can leave the drinker with a cloying, heavy palate.

RECIPE: NUTCASTLE

OG: 1.051 (12.6 °P)
FG: 1.013 (3.2 °P)
ADF: 75%
IBU: 26
Color: 13 SRM (26 EBC)
Alcohol: 5.1% ABV (4.0% ABW)
Boil: 60 minutes
Pre-Boil Volume: 7 gallons (26.5L)
Pre-Boil Gravity: 1.043 (10.8 °P)

Extract	Weight	Percent
English Pale Ale LME (3.5 °L)	7.0 lbs. (3.17kg)	77.8

Steeping Grains		
Special Roast (50 °L)	0.75 lb. (340g)	8.3
Victory (28 °L)	0.5 lb. (227g)	5.6
Crystal (40 °L)	0.5 lb. (227g)	5.6
Pale Chocolate (200 °L)	0.25 lb. (113g)	2.8

Hops		IBU
Kent Goldings 5% AA, 60 min.	1.2 oz. (34g)	24.5
Kent Goldings 5% AA, 5 min.	0.5 oz. (14g)	1.7

Yeast
White Labs WLP013 London Ale, Wyeast 1028 London Ale, or Danstar Nottingham

Fermentation and Conditioning
Use 10 grams of properly rehydrated dry yeast, 2 liquid yeast packages, or make an appropriate starter. Ferment at 68° F (20° C). When finished, carbonate the beer to approximately 1 to 1.5 volumes and serve at 52 to 55° F (11 to 13° C).

All-Grain Option
Replace the English pale ale extract with 9.75 lbs. (4.42kg) British pale ale malt. Mash at 152° F (67° C).

16 | PORTER

Porter is reputed to have been a favorite of the working class in England. In the early eighteenth century, the industrialization of breweries allowed porter to become the first real industrial, mass-produced beer of its time. As technologies advanced, breweries built larger and larger aging vats. By the late eighteenth century, vats as large as 20,000 barrels (nearly one million U.S. gallons) were being built to age porter. In 1894 one vat was reported to have burst open, knocking down buildings, flooding streets, and killing eight people. During the early nineteenth century, there was a brewery producing as much as 300,000 barrels of porter annually. Indeed, porter was a very popular beer.

All three porters—brown, robust, and Baltic—are similar in that they have some level of roasty character—less than a stout but usually more than brown ale. Baltic porter is said to have its roots in English porters or Russian imperial stout, and its big flavor and richness leads me to believe the Russian imperial stout angle.

BROWN PORTER

A fairly substantial English dark ale with restrained roasty characteristics. It typically has a higher gravity and more roast flavor and aroma than English brown ales. This is a beginner style that can be brewed by extract-with-grain or all-grain methods. Ferments at 67° F (19° C).

OG	FG	IBU	Color	Alcohol
1.040–1.052	1.008–1.014	18–35	20–30 SRM	4.0–5.4% ABV
(10–12.9 °P)	(2.1–3.6 °P)		39–59 EBC	3.2–4.3% ABW

Keys to Brewing Brown Porter:

Brown porter claims the ground between English brown ale, mild, and robust porter. It is a dark ale that often has the light caramel and toasty malt character and low hop character of a Southern English brown ale, but it is bigger and roastier than that. It is not as big and roasty as a robust porter, but it shares a lot of the same chocolate malt notes. However, brown porter doesn't have any of the more burnt and acrid notes of robust porter. Brown and robust porter are fairly close style types, and the differences are minor in some commercial examples.

As with mild and Southern English brown, you want a lot of malt character from the use of specialty malts and a good base of English pale ale malt. This will create a nice, broad malt backbone. Keep the hops simple, with just a bittering addition, and ferment with an English yeast that has plenty of character and a moderate level of attenuation. While this beer requires a bit more roasted malt than English brown ale, it is easy to add too much, so don't overdo it. This beer is less roasty than a robust porter, so it is best to show some restraint.

The secret ingredient for creating a great brown porter is brown malt. Brown malt provides the nutty, slightly roasty, gentle chocolate background note that is apparent in some commercial examples. Without it, most recipes lean too heavily upon darker roasted malts and end up with too much roast character. The same thing can be said for residual sweetness. A little residual sweetness is OK, but it is important to use a more attenuative English yeast to keep the beer from being too sweet. If you're using a less attenuative strain than listed below, you will need to add some simple sugar to help dry it out a little. It also needs to ferment fairly clean, so cool fermentation temperatures are better than warmer ones. I used to make a version of this beer using the very neutral California/American ale yeast, but it wasn't exactly right. It attenuated enough but was far too clean for the style. It needs a touch of English yeast character to be considered a great brown porter.

RECIPE: WHO'S YOUR TADDY PORTER

There are some nice similarities between this beer and a very popular commercial example. I had been trying for some time to figure how to make this recipe more like the commercial example. When I finally discovered that it was brown malt, I have to admit to yelling at the commercial bottle, "Who's your Taddy!" Gosh, that is embarrassing to admit.

OG: 1.052 (12.8 °P)
FG: 1.013 (3.3 °P)
ADF: 74%
IBU: 27
Color: 24 SRM (48 EBC)
Alcohol: 5.1% ABV (4.0% ABW)
Boil: 60 minutes
Pre-Boil Volume: 7 gallons (26.5L)
Pre-Boil Gravity: 1.044 (11.0 °P)

Extract	Weight	Percent
English Pale Ale LME (3.5 °L)	6.8 lbs. (3.08kg)	72.1

Steeping Grains		
Brown Malt (70 °L)	1.0 lb. (0.45kg)	10.6
Crystal (40 °L)	1.0 lb. (0.45kg)	10.6
Chocolate Malt (350 °L)	10.0 oz. (284g)	6.6

Hops		IBU
Fuggles 5% AA, 60 min.	1.25 oz. (35g)	25.4
Fuggles 5% AA, 10 min.	0.5 oz. (14g)	2.0

Yeast
White Labs WLP013 London Ale, Wyeast 1028 London Ale, or Danstar Nottingham

Fermentation and Conditioning
Use 10 grams of properly rehydrated dry yeast, 2 liquid yeast packages, or make an appropriate starter. Ferment at 67° F (19° C). When finished, carbonate the beer to approximately 1.5 to 2.0 volumes and serve at 52 to 55° F (11 to 13° C).

All-Grain Option
Replace the English extract with 9.5 lbs. (4.31kg) British pale ale malt. Mash at 152° F (67° C) for 60 minutes.

ROBUST PORTER

A substantial, malty dark ale with a complex and flavorful roasty character. This is a beginner style that can be brewed by extract-with-grain or all-grain methods. Ferments at 67° F (19° C).

OG	FG	IBU	Color	Alcohol
1.048–1.065	1.012–1.016	25–50	22–35 SRM	4.8–6.5% ABV
(11.9–15.9 °P)	(3.1–4.1 °P)		43–69 EBC	3.8–5.1% ABW

Keys to Brewing Robust Porter:

Robust porter is a roasty, complex, rich ale. This beer ranges from very dark brown to black, with most of the color coming from dark roasted malts, such as black patent. Examples of the style range quite a bit, from bigger, bolder American interpretations to less bold English interpretations. This style should always have a fair amount of roasted character, full of coffee and chocolate. It also needs some bread and caramel flavors and aromas to help carry the roast. Hop bitterness is fairly firm, but the balance varies from slightly sweet to firmly bitter.

The common mistake many brewers make on this style is either too much or too little roasted character. A portion of malt sweetness and a touch of caramel help soften the roastiness. Not including any caramel malt makes it much more like a dry stout. If brewing an American-style robust porter, use clean, neutral ale yeast and a higher starting gravity. The hop bitterness, flavor, and aroma are also higher in an American version. If brewing an English version, use a lower starting gravity, less hops and typical English yeast.

RECIPE: BLACK WIDOW PORTER

If you think the name of this recipe has something to do with its deep, dark color, you are wrong. I like to brew outside, and my brewing system and hoses stay outside three hundred and sixty-five days a year. Every so often, there might be a bug or two that finds its way into a piece of equipment, so I have gotten used to checking for unwanted brewing assistants before I brew. However, over the many times I have brewed this recipe, a very large black widow has escaped detection three times. Usually it pops out a hose and into the boil kettle during sparging. I have to admit, fishing a very upset black widow from hot wort is not my favorite brew-day task. I never seem to have the proper tool at hand, and when the spider is finally fished out, it tends to be missing a few parts. As I later pour myself a pint, I assume the boil killed anything nasty and denatured any toxins, yet I can't help but taste a bit of spidery goodness in every sip. (Caution: Do not add spiders to your beer.)

OG: 1.064 (15.7 °P)
FG: 1.015 (3.8 °P)
ADF: 76%
IBU: 37
Color: 35 SRM (69 EBC)
Alcohol: 6.5% ABV (5.1% ABW)
Boil: 60 minutes
Pre-Boil Volume: 7 gallons (26.5L)
Pre-Boil Gravity: 1.055 (13.5 °P)

Extract	Weight	Percent
Light LME (2.2 °L)	8.6 lbs. (3.90kg)	72.6
Munich LME (9 °L)	1.0 lb. (0.45kg)	8.4

Steeping Grains		
Crystal (40 °L)	1.0 lb. (0.45kg)	8.4
Chocolate Malt (350 °L)	0.75 lb. (340g)	6.3
Black Patent Malt (525 °L)	0.5 lb. (227g)	4.2

Hops		IBU
Kent Goldings 5% AA, 60 min.	1.75 oz. (50g)	33.5
Fuggles 5% AA, 15 min.	0.75 oz. (21g)	3.8
Kent Goldings 5% AA, 0 min.	0.75 oz. (21g)	0

Yeast
White Labs WLP001 California Ale, Wyeast 1056 American Ale, or Fermentis Safale US-05

Fermentation and Conditioning

Use 12 grams of properly rehydrated dry yeast, 2.5 liquid yeast packages, or make an appropriate starter. Ferment at 67° F (19° C). When finished, carbonate the beer to approximately 2 to 2.5 volumes.

All-Grain Option

Replace the light extract with 11.75 lbs. (5.33kg) American two-row malt. Replace Munich extract with 1.5 lbs. (0.68kg) Munich malt. Mash at 153° F (67° C).

BALTIC PORTER

A big, complex, and flavorful malty dark lager or ale with a restrained roasty character. This is an advanced style that can be brewed by extract-with-grain or all-grain methods. Ferments at 53° F (12° C).

OG	FG	IBU	Color	Alcohol
1.060–1.090	1.016–1.024	20–40	17–30 SRM	5.5–9.5% ABV
(14.7–21.6 °P)	(4.1–6.1 °P)		33–59 EBC	4.3–7.5% ABW

Keys to Brewing Baltic Porter:

Baltic porter is bigger, richer, sweeter, and more alcoholic than robust porter. Robust porter is usually hoppier and roastier than Baltic porter. Baltic porter, in many examples, is a malty sweet, slightly roasty beer with a fair amount of alcohol. While lower-alcohol examples are generally clean and have little in the way of esters, the higher-alcohol examples often carry lots of dark fruit notes, like plums, prunes, raisins, cherries, and currants. Imported samples often have some sherry- or port-type notes from age and transportation stress, so don't let that fool you into thinking that is always appropriate.

Baltic porter requires a couple of brewing tricks to pull off the dark, rich flavor with no highly burnt or acrid notes. The first is to use debittered black malt for a portion of the grain bill. This will give some roasted flavors but without the bitterness commonly associated with that grain. The second is to have some residual malt sweetness, which helps ameliorate the perception of the roasted malt, just like adding sugar to coffee changes the bitter perception of coffee. Third and equally important are the yeast and fermentation. If using ale yeast, this beer needs cold fermentation. Colder fermentation often leaves a bit more residual sugar and helps restrain the fruity esters typical of many ale yeasts. Otherwise, ferment with lager yeast and count on the specialty grains and alcohol to give you the dark fruit character. If you want to brew a smaller Baltic porter, go with neutral ale yeast or lager yeast and keep the fermentation character as clean as possible.

RECIPE: ZEK'S PORTER

There are a couple of great Baltic porters made in Russia, which happens to be where my grandparents came from, before the Communists took power. My grandparents fled Russia, with one of them later being captured and imprisoned in the gulag after fighting against the Soviets. The colloquial name for a Soviet gulag inmate was *zek*. This recipe is for those who died under Communism, especially those who died in the gulag. Raise a pint and be sure to say something out loud that the Soviet Communists would have hated … which is pretty much anything.

OG: 1.089 (21.3 °P)
FG: 1.018 (4.6 °P)
ADF: 78%
IBU: 38
Color: 28 SRM (55 EBC)
Alcohol: 9.4% ABV (7.3% ABW)
Boil: 60 minutes
Pre-Boil Volume: 7 gallons (26.5L)
Pre-Boil Gravity: 1.075 (18.3 °P)

Extract	Weight	Percent
Munich LME (9 °L)	8.9 lbs. (4.03kg)	56.2
Pilsener LME (2.3 °L)	5.3 lbs. (2.4kg)	33.5

Steeping Grains		
Crystal (60 °L)	0.5 lb. (227g)	3.2
Special "B" (120 °L)	0.5 lb. (227g)	3.2
Carafa Special II (430 °L)	6.0 oz. (170g)	2.4
Chocolate Malt (350 °L)	0.25 lb. (113g)	1.6

Hops		IBU
Lublin 3.5% AA, 60 min.	2.9 oz. (82g)	34.9
Lublin 3.5% AA, 15 min.	1.0 oz. (28g)	3.2

Yeast
White Labs WLP885 Zurich Lager, White Labs WLP830 German Lager, Wyeast 2206 Bavarian Lager, or Fermentis Saflager S-23

Fermentation and Conditioning

Use 33 grams of properly rehydrated dry yeast, 6.5 liquid yeast packages, or make an appropriate starter. Ferment at 53° F (12° C). When finished, carbonate the beer to approximately 2 to 2.5 volumes.

All-Grain Option

Replace the Pilsener extract with 7 lbs. (3.17kg) continental Pilsener malt. Replace the Munich extract with 12 lbs. (5.44kg) Munich malt. Mash at 150° F (66° C). Increase the pre-boil volume as needed to allow a 90-minute boil, which helps reduce DMS in the beer.

17 | STOUT

All that can be said for certain about any stout is that it is a very dark beer and it has some level of roast character. I find it very frustrating to hear some people talk about stouts as if they were the equivalent of used motor oil with enough alcohol to launch a rocket. I can't count the number of times I have heard people say, "I don't drink really heavy beers like stout." That is just not true, and misconceptions like that keep a lot of people from trying the wonderful beers in this category. The stout category has a huge range, from low-alcohol, refreshing, easy-drinking beers to huge, roasty, thick, high-alcohol warmers perfect for an evening by the fire. Please do me one favor, make sure you're always helping people understand that a dark beer is not always high in alcohol or thick like used motor oil.

DRY STOUT

A lower-alcohol, very dark, roasty, bitter, creamy ale. This is an advanced style that can be brewed by extract-with-grain but is best brewed by partial mash or all-grain methods to convert the flaked barley properly. Ferments at 65 to 71° F (18 to 22° C).

OG	FG	IBU	Color	Alcohol
1.036–1.050	1.007–1.011	30–45	25–40 SRM	4.0–5.0% ABV
(9.1–12.4 °P)	(1.81–2.8 °P)		49–79 EBC	3.2–4% ABW

Keys to Brewing Dry Stout:
The most often-cited and most well-known dry stout is Guinness. This is a sharp, dry beer with a long coffee and bittersweet chocolate finish. It

is a low-gravity, low-alcohol, and light-bodied beer with a high level of hop bittering. It is dry and bitter but easy to drink by the pint because of its dryness, low alcohol, and low carbonation.

The dry, roasted character of this beer comes from highly kilned unmalted barley and substantial hop bitterness. A mistake many brewers make is including caramel malt in a dry stout recipe. Caramel malts add non-fermentable sugar and caramel flavor, which negatively affect the dryness. This beer must have roasted unmalted barley to get that distinctive stout taste and some flaked unmalted barley to add to the mouthfeel. Irish ale yeast provides the right low-ester profile but is not highly attenuative. You will need to pitch the proper amount of clean, healthy yeast and keep a close eye on fermentation temperatures to ensure good attenuation. As an alternative, you can use a neutral ale yeast with higher attenuation, such as White Labs WLP001 California Ale, Wyeast 1056 American Ale, or Fermentis Safale US-05.

RECIPE: CERVEZA DE MALTO SECA

This is a classic dry stout recipe. It makes a great dry stout, but you need to crush the roasted barley very fine. Run it through a coffee mill or use a rolling pin to turn it almost to dust. That is critical to getting the right flavor and color with this recipe.

OG: 1.042 (10.4 °P)
FG: 1.010 (2.6 °P)
ADF: 75%
IBU: 41
Color: 32 SRM (63 EBC)
Alcohol: 4.1% ABV (3.2% ABW)
Boil: 60 minutes
Pre-Boil Volume: 7 gallons (26.5L)
Pre-Boil Gravity: 1.035 (8.9 °P)

Extract	Weight	Percent
English Pale Ale LME (3.5 °L)	5.0 lbs. (2.26kg)	62.5

Steeping Grains		
Flaked Barley (2.2 °L)	2.0 lbs. (0.9kg)	25.0
Black Roasted Barley (500 °L)	1.0 lb. (0.45kg)	12.5

Hops		IBU
Kent Goldings 5% AA, 60 min.	2.0 oz. (57g)	41.0

Yeast

White Labs WLP004 Irish Ale, Wyeast 1084 Irish Ale, or Fermentis Safale US-05

Fermentation and Conditioning

Use 8 grams of properly rehydrated dry yeast, 1.5 liquid yeast packages, or make an appropriate starter. Ferment at 65° F (18° C). Slowly raise the temperature during the final third of fermentation by 6° F (3° C) to reduce diacetyl levels in the beer. When finished, carbonate the beer to approximately 1 to 1.5 volumes and serve at 52 to 55° F (11 to 13° C).

Partial Mash Option

Reduce the English extract to 3.6 lbs. (1.63kg) British pale ale malt. Mash the grains along with 2 lbs. (0.9kg) of American two-row malt following the partial mash instructions in Appendix C.

All-Grain Option

Replace the English extract with 7 lbs. (3.17kg) British pale ale malt. Mash at 120° F (49° C) for 15 minutes, then raise the temperature to 150° F (64° C) for 60 minutes.

SWEET STOUT

A dark, sweet, rich ale full of roasted flavors and aromas. This is a beginner-level style that can be brewed by extract-with-grain or all-grain methods. Ferments at 68° F (20° C).

OG	FG	IBU	Color	Alcohol
1.044–1.060	1.012–1.024	20–40	30–40 SRM	4.0–6.0% ABV
(10.9–14.7 °P)	(3.1–6.1 °P)		59–79 EBC	3.2–4.7% ABW

Keys to Brewing Sweet Stout:

This English-style stout is historically known as milk or cream stout. The name comes from the practice of adding lactose (milk sugar) to sweeten it. Sweet stout is dark, sweet, rich, and full of roasted flavors and aromas. It is full-bodied and has substantial coffee and chocolate notes. While some commercial examples are drier than others, you will have more success in competitions focusing on the sweet side of the style.

Brewing a sweet stout is similar to other stouts with the exception of two critical areas: sweetness and mouthfeel. Sweetness is accomplished by reducing the bitterness of the beer, adding some crystal malt and a significant dose of lactose powder for sweetness, and using restrained carbonation. Lactose is only mildly sweet, but it is also unfermentable by brewing yeasts, which helps add to the mouthfeel. This recipe also has a slightly higher starting gravity, which also adds to the mouthfeel and sweetness.

It is important not to add any hop flavor or hop aroma to the beer. Those flavors tend to detract from the overall impression of sweetened espresso.

RECIPE: TRIPLE-X

OG: 1.060 (14.8 °P)
FG: 1.023 (5.7 °P)
ADF: 61%
IBU: 29
Color: 39 SRM (78 EBC)
Alcohol: 4.9% ABV (3.8% ABW)
Boil: 60 minutes
Pre-Boil Volume: 7 gallons (26.5L)
Pre-Boil Gravity: 1.051 (12.7 °P)

Extract	Weight	Percent
English Pale Ale LME (3.5 °L)	7.2 lbs. (3.26kg)	68.9
Lactose Powder (Milk Sugar) (0 °L)	1.0 lb. (0.45kg)	9.6

Steeping Grains		
Black Patent Malt (525 °L)	1.0 lb. (0.45kg)	9.6
Crystal (80 °L)	0.75 lb. (340g)	7.2
Pale Chocolate Malt (200 °L)	0.5 lb. (227g)	4.8

Hops		IBU
Kent Goldings 5% AA, 60 min.	1.5 oz. (43g)	29.3

Yeast
White Labs WLP006 Bedford British, Wyeast 1099 Whitbread Ale, or Fermentis Safale S-04

Fermentation and Conditioning
Use 11 grams of properly rehydrated dry yeast, 2 liquid yeast packages, or make an appropriate starter. Ferment at 68° F (20° C). When finished, carbonate the beer to approximately 1.5 to 2 volumes.

All-Grain Option
Replace the English extract with 10 lbs. (4.53kg) British pale ale malt. Mash at 151° F (66° C).

OATMEAL STOUT

A dark, full-bodied, roasty ale with a slight oatmeal note in the background. This is an advanced style that can be brewed by extract-with-grain but is best brewed by partial mash or all-grain methods to convert the oatmeal properly. Ferments at 68° F (20° C).

OG	FG	IBU	Color	Alcohol
1.048–1.065	1.010–1.018	25–40	22–40 SRM	4.2–5.9% ABV
(11.9–15.9 °P)	(2.6–4.6 °P)		44–79 EBC	3.3–4.7% ABW

Keys to Brewing Oatmeal Stout:

Oatmeal stout is sweeter than dry stout but not as sweet as sweet stout. This beer uses oats instead of lactose to provide a slightly creamy mouthfeel and complexity. It has a slight roasted-grain flavor and aroma, like bitter chocolate, which helps dry the finish. A subtle background fruity/earthy character from fermentation and hop notes round out the character of this style.

While oats can add a fair amount of silkiness to a beer, they tend to add very little flavor. It isn't a distinct flavor where someone might say, "Hey, you've added oats." Oats add more of a background complexity to the beer's base malt character. The problem is, many people tend to expect that the oatmeal in this stout should have a huge impact on flavor and mouthfeel. They are looking for a significant nutty/biscuity flavor and aroma from the oats. They are also usually expecting the beer's body to be quite thick and full but not overly sweet. The trick here is to give the customer what he wants. Toasting the oats in the oven at around 300° F (149° C) until they begin to slightly color up and give off a nutty oatmeal cookie character tends to help them stand out a bit more. A little Briess Victory malt in the recipe also adds a nice nutty/biscuity character to back up the oats. Adding flaked oats and using a high mash temperature adds body and a creamy mouthfeel. Keeping the hop bittering restrained and using low-attenuating yeast adds just the right touch of sweetness.

RECIPE: MCQUAKER'S OATMEAL STOUT

OG: 1.055 (13.5 °P)
FG: 1.016 (4.1 °P)
ADF: 70%
IBU: 36
Color: 35 SRM (69 EBC)
Alcohol: 5.1% ABV (4.0% ABW)
Boil: 60 minutes
Pre-Boil Volume: 7 gallons (26.5L)
Pre-Boil Gravity: 1.047 (11.6 °P)

Extract	Weight	Percent
English Pale Ale LME (3.5 °L)	6.8 lbs. (3.08kg)	66.0

Steeping Grains		
Flaked Oats (1 °L)	1.0 lb. (0.45kg)	9.7
Chocolate Malt (350 °L)	0.75 lb. (340g)	7.3
Victory Malt (28 °L)	0.75 lb. (340g)	7.3
Crystal (80 °L)	0.5 lb. (227g)	4.9
Black Roasted Barley (500 °L)	0.5 lb. (227g)	4.9

Hops		IBU
Kent Goldings 5% AA, 60 min.	1.8 oz. (51g)	36.1

Yeast
White Labs WLP002 English Ale, Wyeast 1968 London ESB, or Fermentis Safale S-04

Fermentation and Conditioning
Use 11 grams of properly rehydrated dry yeast, 2 liquid yeast packages, or make an appropriate starter. Ferment at 68° F (20° C). When finished, carbonate the beer to approximately 2 to 2.5 volumes.

Partial Mash Option
Reduce the English extract to 5.4 lbs. (2.45kg). Mash all of the grains, including the oats, along with 2 lbs. (0.9kg) of American two-row malt following the partial mash instructions in the Appendix.

All-Grain Option

Replace the English extract with 9.4 lbs. (4.26kg) British pale ale malt. Mash at 154° F (68° C). With the need to convert the flaked oats, you may need to lengthen the rest time to 90 minutes to get full conversion.

FOREIGN EXTRA STOUT

A very dark, roasty, and moderately strong ale. This is an intermediate style that can be brewed by extract-with-grain or all-grain methods. Ferments at 67 to 70° F (19 to 21° C).

OG	FG	IBU	Color	Alcohol
1.056–1.075	1.010–1.018	30–70	30–40 SRM	5.5–8.0% ABV
(13.8–18.2 °P)	(2.6–4.6 °P)		59–79 EBC	4.3–6.3% ABW

Keys to Brewing Foreign Extra Stout:

Foreign extra stout is a style originally brewed for tropical markets. It is usually bigger than both oatmeal and sweet stouts, with a full body, a touch of sweetness, and a gentle warming from the higher level of alcohol. Good examples have a firm coffee and chocolate character in both the aroma and flavor. The presence of higher alcohols, dark malts, and some esters from fermentation lend dried fruit or dark fruit notes to these beers.

The style ranges from a drier, less fruity export version to a sweeter, fruitier tropical version. The difference in making these two versions is mostly the choice of yeast. If you want to make a drier, cleaner export version, use yeast like White Labs WLP001 California Ale, Wyeast 1056 American Ale, or Fermentis Safale US-05. This yeast will attenuate a bit more and will leave a cleaner, drier finish. It is going to seem a little roastier, too. If you want to make the tropical version, use the English yeast listed below. It will attenuate less, leaving more sweetness and some fruitiness in the finished beer. If you go with the English yeast, you will need to perform a diacetyl rest near the last third of fermentation, as this beer should not have much diacetyl.

RECIPE: EXTRA LYING STOUT

OG: 1.071 (17.2 °P)
FG: 1.017 (4.4 °P)
ADF: 75%
IBU: 45
Color: 39 SRM (77 EBC)
Alcohol: 7.1% ABV (5.5% ABW)

Boil: 60 minutes
Pre-Boil Volume: 7 gallons (26.5L)
Pre-Boil Gravity: 1.060 (14.8 °P)

Extract	Weight	Percent
English Pale Ale LME (3.5 °L)	10 lbs. (4.53kg)	80.0

Steeping Grains

Black Roasted Barley (500 °L)	0.75 lb. (340g)	6.0
Crystal (40 °L)	10.0 oz. (284g)	5.0
Crystal (80 °L)	10.0 oz. (284g)	5.0
Chocolate Malt (420 °L)	0.5 lb. (227g)	4.0

Hops		IBU
Kent Goldings 5% AA, 60 min.	2.4 oz. (68g)	44.6

Yeast
White Labs WLP013 London Ale, Wyeast 1028 London Ale, or Danstar Nottingham

Fermentation and Conditioning
Use 13 grams of properly rehydrated dry yeast, 3 liquid yeast packages, or make an appropriate starter. Ferment at 67° F (19° C), raising the temperature to 70° F (21° C) during the last third of fermentation to help reduce diacetyl and assure complete attenuation. When finished, carbonate the beer to approximately 2 to 2.5 volumes.

All-Grain Option
Replace the English extract with 13.9 lbs. (6.3kg) British pale ale malt. Mash at 152° F (67° C).

AMERICAN STOUT

A roastier, hoppier, Americanized version of foreign extra stout. This is an intermediate style that can be brewed by extract-with-grain or all-grain methods. Ferments at 67° F (19° C).

OG	FG	IBU	Color	Alcohol
1.050–1.075	1.010–1.022	35–75	30–40 SRM	5.0–7.0% ABV
(12.4–18.2 °P)	(2.6–5.6 °P)		78–105 EBC	4–5.5% ABW

Keys to Brewing American Stout:

American stout is similar in many ways to foreign extra stout, being a higher-alcohol stout that ranges between sweeter and drier versions. However, American stout generally has a more strongly roasted flavor and aroma, almost bordering on burnt coffee in some examples. The other difference is that hop character in this beer can be quite high and is often full of citrusy and fruity American hop varieties.

There is a lot of leeway in making an American-style stout, but there are two ingredients common to the best versions: bold American hops and clean, neutral ale yeast. It is important not to let the beer finish too sweet and also to include a nice, firm hop bitterness to overcome any residual sweetness.

RECIPE: REPROBATE STOUT

OG: 1.072 (17.5 °P)
FG: 1.017 (4.4 °P)
ADF: 75%
IBU: 73
Color: 45 SRM (89 EBC)
Alcohol: 7.2% ABV (5.6% ABW)
Boil: 60 minutes
Pre-Boil Volume: 7 gallons (26.5L)
Pre-Boil Gravity: 1.061 (15 °P)

Extract	Weight	Percent
Light LME (2.2 °L)	10.8 lbs. (4.90kg)	81.2

Steeping Grains		
Black Roasted Barley (500 °L)	1.0 lb. (0.45kg)	7.5
Chocolate Malt (420 °L)	0.75 lb. (340g)	5.6
Crystal (40 °L)	0.75 lb. (340g)	5.6

Hops		IBU
Horizon 13% AA, 60 min.	1.4 oz. (40g)	67.4
Centennial 9% AA, 5 min.	1.0 oz. (28g)	5.6

Yeast

White Labs WLP001 California Ale, Wyeast 1056 American Ale, or Fermentis Safale US-05

Fermentation and Conditioning

Use 14 grams of properly rehydrated dry yeast, 3 liquid yeast packages, or make an appropriate starter. Ferment at 67° F (19° C). When finished, carbonate the beer to approximately 2.5 to 3 volumes.

All-Grain Option

Replace the light extract with 15 lbs. (6.80kg) American two-row malt. Mash at 154° F (68° C).

RUSSIAN IMPERIAL STOUT

An intense and rich, dark, roasty ale with substantial alcohol warming. This is an advanced style that can be brewed by extract-with-grain or all-grain methods. Ferments at 67 to 70° F (19 to 21° C) and requires several months or more until ready to drink.

OG	FG	IBU	Color	Alcohol
1.075–1.115	1.018–1.030	50–90	30–40 SRM	8.0–12% ABV
(18.2–26.9 °P)	(4.6–7.6 °P)		78–105 EBC	6.3–9.5% ABW

Keys to Brewing Russian Imperial Stout:

Russian imperial stout is as big, rich, and bold as a stout can be. It seems that in this style, there are really no upper limits, only minimums. A good version of this beer needs to have a big roasted malt character, coming across in the flavor and aroma as coffee, dark chocolate, and even tar-like notes. There are also a lot of dark fruits, hops, and alcohol, although the alcohol shouldn't be overly hot or harsh.

There are two very important considerations when brewing a Russian imperial stout. The first is ensuring that the beer is attenuated enough to avoid being overly sweet or syrupy. Yes, this can be a sweeter dessert beer, but don't overdo it. The second is a controlled fermentation to ensure that the beer's substantial alcohol doesn't end up hot and solventy, which is a very common problem in many amateur examples. A long aging period will really help soften some of the harsh edges, so plan accordingly.

RECIPE: THE CZAR'S REVENGE

OG: 1.098 (23.4 °P)
FG: 1.030 (7.5 °P)
ADF: 68%
IBU: 77
Color: 57 SRM (113 EBC)
Alcohol: 9.2% ABV (7.0% ABW)
Boil: 60 minutes
Pre-Boil Volume: 7 gallons (26.5L)
Pre-Boil Gravity: 1.084 (20.2 °P)

Extract	Weight	Percent
English Pale Ale LME (3.5 °L)	13.7 lbs. (6.21kg)	77.4

Steeping Grains

Black Roasted Barley (500 °L)	1.5 lbs. (0.68kg)	8.5
Special "B" (120 °L)	1.0 lb. (0.45kg)	5.6
CaraMunich (60 °L)	0.5 lb. (227g)	2.8
Chocolate Malt (350 °L)	0.5 lb. (227g)	2.8
Pale Chocolate Malt (200 °L)	0.5 lb. (227g)	2.8

Hops		IBU
Horizon 13% AA, 60 min.	1.5 oz. (43g)	64.4
Kent Goldings 5% AA, 10 min.	2.0 oz. (57g)	6.6
Kent Goldings 5% AA, 1 min.	2.0 oz. (57g)	5.5

Yeast

White Labs WLP001 California Ale, Wyeast 1056 American Ale, or Fermentis Safale US-05

Fermentation and Conditioning

Use 18 grams of properly rehydrated dry yeast, 3.5 liquid yeast packages, or make an appropriate starter. Ferment at 67° F (19° C). When finished, carbonate the beer to approximately 2 to 2.5 volumes. Store the beer in a cool, dark place, and allow to age. The beer will improve over time and ideally should mature 6 or more months before consumption.

All-Grain Option

Replace the English extract with 19 lbs. (8.62kg) British pale ale malt. Mash at 154° F (68° C).

RECIPE: MIKE RIDDLE'S TRICENTENNIAL STOUT

When I was just starting out in brewing, I sought advice from the best brewers in my area. I spent a fair amount of time speaking with Mike Riddle. I asked him all sorts of questions, and he gave me a lot of good advice and encouragement. He also dispensed samples of his incredible Russian imperial stout. Mike is hailed as one of the best brewers of this style, and he considers it one of his signature beers. He has won many awards with the recipe below, including yet another Best of Show while this was being written. This is one serious winner.

I asked Mike about the keys to brewing his recipe to get optimum results. He told me that his recipe pushes the envelope in every aspect, and the results are going to be slightly different for each brewer and their equipment, so they will need to invest in some trial and error to get this right. One area of concern is the efficiency of the mash for all-grain brewers. Mike's system, like that of many brewers, has a lower efficiency when making a really big beer like this. He suggests starting with 20 to 22 lbs. (9 to 10kg) of base malt, instead of the 15.7 lbs. (7.12kg) that 70 percent efficiency would require.

Mike also said:

"The key to this beer, as for most good beers, is balance. To make the perfect Russian imperial stout, the brewer needs to consider the balance of bitterness, residual sugar, alcohol, roastiness, diacetyl, hop flavor, hop aroma, astringency, oxidation, and body. All of these characteristics are major players in the final aged beer.

"The final gravity should be around 1.037 (9.2 °P) to give the right balance of bitterness, residual sugar, alcohol, and roastiness. Anything lower and it will be too dry, roasty, and astringent. Anything higher and it will be syrupy sweet. You also want some diacetyl in this beer to help balance the roastiness and bitterness and to improve the mouthfeel and aromatic complexity. To increase the amount of diacetyl with this yeast, ferment at 70° F (21° C), as any colder will not produce enough diacetyl.

"Some oxidation aromas and flavors are important to the complexity of this beer. You want some wine/sherry notes but not any cardboard character. Bottle the beer instead of kegging it, and store it at 40° F (4° C), giving it plenty of time to age before drinking. This beer will easily improve for three years if stored properly.

"The Northern Brewer hops in the recipe add a woody note that complements the roastiness. The Kent Goldings flavor and aroma hop additions are assertive enough to be noticed but won't clash with all the other aspects. The resin from dry-hopping not only adds flavor and aroma, it adds to the complexity of the mouthfeel."

OG: 1.100 (23.8 °P)
FG: 1.037 (9.2 °P)
ADF: 61%
IBU: 100
Color: 101 SRM (198 EBC)
Alcohol: 8.5% ABV (6.5% ABW)
Boil: 60 minutes
Pre-Boil Volume: 7.7 gallons (29.3L)
Pre-Boil Gravity: 1.085 (20.5 °P)

Extract	Weight	Percent
English Pale Ale LME (3.5 °L)	10.75 lbs. (4.87kg)	57.8
Wheat LME (4 °L)	2.0 lbs. (0.9kg)	10.8

Steeping Grains		
Roasted Barley (575 °L)	2.5 lbs. (1.13kg)	13.4
Chocolate Malt (475 °L)	2.5 lbs. (1.13kg)	13.4
Crystal (120 °L)	0.85 lb. (386g)	4.6

Hops		IBU
Northern Brewer 6.5% AA, 60 min.	2.6 oz. (74g)	55.4
Northern Brewer 6.5% AA, 30 min.	2.0 oz. (57g)	21.8
Northern Brewer 6.5% AA, 15 min.	1.0 oz. (28g)	5.7
Kent Goldings 5% AA, 15 min.	2.0 oz. (57g)	8.7
Kent Goldings 5% AA, 3 min.	3.0 oz. (85g)	8.2
Kent Goldings 5% AA, dry	2.0 oz. (57g)	0

Yeast
White Labs WLP004 Irish Ale or Wyeast 1084 Irish Ale

Fermentation and Conditioning
Use 4 liquid yeast packages or make an appropriate starter. Ferment at 70° F (21° C) until kraeusen falls through, about 9 days. Transfer to secondary and add dry hops. Allow it to finish fermenting until

completely settled, about 7 additional days. Prime the beer with 6 oz. (170g) corn sugar and bottle, allowing the beer to carbonate at 70° F (21° C) for 1 month. Once carbonated, store the beer at 40° F (4° C) for 1 to 3 years before drinking.

All-Grain Option

Replace the wheat extract with 2 lbs. (0.9kg) wheat malt and the English extract with 15.7 lbs. (7.12kg) British pale ale malt for 70% efficiency. If your system loses efficiency on big beers, Mike suggests starting with 20 to 22 lbs. (9 to 10kg) of base malt. Mash at 149° F (65° C) for 90 minutes.

18 | INDIA PALE ALE

As much as I love beers with a lot of rich malt character, I find that I get cravings for highly hopped beers, too. India pale ale was first created when an enterprising brewer crafted a beer to better survive the long sea voyage from England to India in the late eighteenth century. The beer had more hop bitterness than other beers of its time, because the hops helped preserve it against spoilage.

English commercial examples of the style have since become a lot more restrained in both hops and alcohol. Currently, many beers labeled as IPA in England are much closer to bitters than the India pale ales of old. There are still a few that hold onto some of the past glory, but they are not common. Luckily, American brewers embraced and expanded on the style, brewing not only the traditional English version of yesterday, but creating an Americanized version and even an imperialized version.

This category, India pale ale, has three beers that all can be considered hoppy, but there are worlds of difference in the level of hops. On the lower end you will find English IPA, which, while hoppy, does not have quite as bold a hop character as is found in American IPA. On the high end, the imperial IPA style is so hoppy that in some cases it is like drinking hop squeezings. If you think you have tasted a hoppy beer before, a good example of the imperial IPA category will open up a whole new world of hoppiness.

ENGLISH IPA

A hoppy, moderately strong pale ale that features characteristics consistent with the use of English malt, hops, and yeast. It has less hop character and a more pronounced malt flavor than American versions. This is a beginner style that can be brewed by extract-with-grain or all-grain methods. Ferments at 68° F (20° C).

OG	FG	IBU	Color	Alcohol
1.050–1.075	1.010–1.018	40–60	8–14 SRM	5.0–7.5% ABV
(12.4–18.2 °P)	(2.6–4.6 °P)		16–28 EBC	4–5.9% ABW

Keys to Brewing English IPA:

The late hop character is more pronounced in an IPA than in any other English beer. Most other English beers, if they feature hops at all, focus more on the hop bittering or flavor. In this style, there is often a fair amount of hop bitterness and flavor as well as a substantial late hop aroma. Even so, the hop character in English IPA is usually much lower than that in the other beers in this category and often lower than in many American pale ales. The trick is to get the right level of hop aroma and flavor using traditional English hops without going completely overboard. It takes a balance of early and late hopping to create this character, and it is important to chill the entire wort rapidly after the last hop addition in order to trap the late hop character. If that is not possible, then the use of a hopjack to infuse hop character just prior to the wort reaching the chiller is a good idea.

Ensuring a traditional English toasty/biscuity background malt character is also important in brewing this beer. While a good example of the style can have some caramel malt sweetness, don't overdo it. The bulk of the malt character should come from the use of high-quality English pale ale malt or malt extract, supported with a moderate amount of crystal malt.

A common mistake with higher-gravity English ales is lack of attenuation. In this style you want a reasonably crisp finish, so choose a yeast that finishes drier rather than sweeter. While it is possible to some extent to balance malt sweetness with hop bitterness, too much of both eventually ends up being cloying and more barley wine-like. When making an English IPA with a higher starting gravity, or when using less attenuative yeast, lower the mash temperature and/or replace a portion of the base malt with corn sugar to aid in drying out the final beer.

Almost any water is fine for brewing a great English IPA, but if your water is particularly soft, it can be beneficial to add a small amount, perhaps 0.25 oz. (7g) of gypsum and 0.25 oz. (7g) of chalk to enhance the sharpness of the hop bitterness and the mineral background of the beer. However, you shouldn't do this unless you are sure your brewing water needs it. It is better to go without the salts than to end up with a harsh, mineral-sharp beer.

RECIPE: BIÈRE DE L'INDE

OG: 1.062 (15.2 °P)
FG: 1.015 (4.0 °P)
ADF: 74%
IBU: 50
Color: 11 SRM (22 EBC)
Alcohol: 6.2% ABV (4.8% ABW)
Boil: 60 minutes
Pre-Boil Volume: 7 gallons (26.5L)
Pre-Boil Gravity: 1.053 (13.0 °P)

Extract	Weight	Percent
English Pale Ale LME (3.5 °L)	8.7 lbs. (3.94kg)	82.3
Wheat LME (4 °L)	0.5 lb. (227g)	4.7

Steeping Grains		
Biscuit (25 °L)	0.5 lb. (227g)	4.7
Crystal (40 °L)	0.5 lb. (227g)	4.7
Crystal (120 °L)	6.0 oz. (170g)	3.5

Hops		IBU
Challenger 8% AA, 60 min.	1.43 oz. (41g)	44.3
Fuggles 5% AA, 10 min.	1.5 oz. (43g)	5.8
Kent Goldings 5% AA, 0 min.	1.5 oz. (43g)	0

Yeast
White Labs WLP013 London Ale, Wyeast 1028 London Ale, or Danstar Nottingham

Fermentation and Conditioning

Use 12 grams of properly rehydrated dry yeast, 2.5 liquid yeast packages, or make an appropriate starter. Ferment at 68° F (20° C). When finished, carbonate the beer to approximately 2 to 2.5 volumes and serve at 52 to 55° F (11 to 13° C).

All-Grain Option

Replace the English extract with 12.25 lbs. (5.55kg) British pale ale malt. Replace the wheat extract with 0.5 lb. (227g) wheat malt. Mash at 152° F (67° C).

AMERICAN IPA

A decidedly hoppy and bitter, moderately strong American pale ale. This is a beginner style that can be brewed by extract-with-grain or all-grain methods. Ferments at 67° F (19° C).

OG	FG	IBU	Color	Alcohol
1.056–1.075	1.010–1.018	40–70	6–15 SRM	5.5–7.5% ABV
(13.8–18.2 °P)	(2.6–4.6 °P)		12–30 EBC	4.3–5.9% ABW

Keys to Brewing American IPA:

American IPA should always have high hop bitterness with a lot of American hop character up front. American hop character is generally described as being citrusy, piney, fruity, and resiny.

The malt character of American IPA generally should be low and clean. Some crystal malt is OK, but overall, the malt flavors and aromas should be less than in the English variety of IPA. It is best to use American two-row malt or a light extract made from it. American two-row has a clean malt flavor and aroma that is very subtle. Some brewers prefer to use English pale ale malt, but that can be a bit much in a beer like this. If you do use a more malt-forward base, drop the Munich malt to avoid too high a level of malt-based flavors and aromas for this style.

A clean, neutral ale yeast is important for a great American IPA. Some brewers use more estery yeasts, such as English strains, but those yeasts often pose two problems. One is a lower attenuation level, and the other is a higher level of fruity esters. Low attenuation of a big beer can make it overly sweet, and too high a level of fruity esters can compete with the hops. Both are not really typical of a well-brewed American IPA.

If you are brewing with extract and not quite reaching the final gravity listed below, try replacing about 1.3 lbs. (0.59kg) of the light malt extract with 1 lb. (0.45kg) of corn or cane sugar. This will enhance the fermentability of the wort and result in a lower final gravity. You can push this higher if needed, but don't exceed 20 percent simple sugars.

RECIPE: HOPPINESS IS AN IPA

OG: 1.065 (15.9 °P)
FG: 1.012 (3.1 °P)
ADF: 81%
IBU: 64
Color: 7 SRM (13 EBC)
Alcohol: 7% ABV (5.5% ABW)
Boil: 60 minutes
Pre-Boil Volume: 7 gallons (26.5L)
Pre-Boil Gravity: 1.055 (13.6 °P)

Extract	Weight	Percent
Light LME (2.2 °L)	9.75 lbs. (4.42kg)	84.8
Munich LME (9 °L)	0.5 lb. (227g)	4.3

Steeping Grains		
Crystal (15 °L)	1.0 lb. (0.45kg)	8.7
Crystal (40 °L)	0.25 lb. (113g)	2.2

Hops		IBU
Horizon 13% AA, 60 min.	1.0 oz. (28g)	49.7
Centennial 9% AA, 10 min.	1.0 oz. (28g)	6.9
Simcoe 12% AA, 5 min.	1.0 oz. (28g)	7.6
Amarillo 9% AA, 0 min.	1.0 oz. (28g)	0

Yeast

White Labs WLP001 California Ale, Wyeast 1056 American Ale, or Fermentis Safale US-05

Fermentation and Conditioning

Use 12 grams of properly rehydrated dry yeast, 2.5 liquid yeast packages, or make an appropriate starter. Ferment at 67° F (19° C). When finished, carbonate the beer to approximately 2 to 2.5 volumes.

All-Grain Option

Replace the light extract with 12.75 lbs. (5.78kg) American two-row malt. Replace the Munich extract with 0.75 lb. (340g) Munich malt.

Mash at 149° F (65° C). With the low mash temperature, you may need to lengthen the rest time to 90 minutes to get full conversion.

IMPERIAL IPA

An intensely hoppy, very strong pale ale without the big maltiness and/or deeper malt flavors of an American barley wine. Strongly hopped but clean, lacking harshness. This is an advanced style that can be brewed by extract-with-grain or all-grain methods. Ferments at 67 to 70° F (19 to 21° C).

OG	FG	IBU	Color	Alcohol
1.070–1.090	1.010–1.020	60–120	8–15 SRM	7.5–10% ABV
(17–21.6 °P)	(2.6–5.1 °P)		16–30 EBC	5.9–7.9% ABW

Keys to Brewing Imperial IPA:

Besides adding lots of hops to get intense hop bitterness, flavor, and aroma, the key to brewing a great imperial IPA is to avoid having too much crystal malt flavor and too high a finishing gravity. It is important that the finishing gravity is in the 1.012 to 1.015 (3.1 to 3.8 °P) range, no matter how big the starting gravity. This is what keeps the beer drinkable.

To get a low-enough finishing gravity, all-grain brewers will need to use a low mash temperature and add simple sugars. The addition of simple sugars is critical to making a great example of this style. Put aside any fears that adding sugar will make your beer too thin or "cidery." That is only an issue when using large percentages in lighter-flavored beers, and there is more than enough flavor to go around in this one.

The intense hop character of this beer is a combination of an insane amount of hops and selecting just the right varieties. One very important thing to keep in mind is that in this beer the hop varieties and quantities are more important than their alpha acid levels. Once the bittering gets past a certain level (reportedly, 100 to 120 IBU), you are only interested in the oils, resins, and other hop compounds that add flavor, aroma, and mouthfeel. If you can't find Warrior at 15 percent, don't worry about it. Warrior at 13 percent or 17 percent is just fine. Keep all the quantities the same, regardless of the AA percentage.

The amount of hop material at the end of the boil and the hop material when dry-hopping will be massive. You might want to bump up the 5-gallon (19L) recipe below to 6 gallons (23L) to get a finished 5 gallons (19L) at the end—otherwise, expect to end up with around 4 gallons (15L) of finished beer. You might ask yourself if such a huge amount of hops and such losses in wort volume are worth the trouble. If you're a hop aficionado, the answer is, absolutely yes! One taste of this intense beer, and you will be hooked.

You will need to ferment this beer with plenty of healthy, clean yeast at a restrained temperature. This helps control any hot, solvent-like notes. As the fermentation begins to slow, gently ramp up the temperature to ensure complete attenuation. If you are a brewer who repitches yeast from one batch to another, do not reuse the yeast from this batch. The high hopping level has considerable impact on yeast viability (as does the alcohol content of this beer), so it is better not to reuse this yeast.

RECIPE: HOP HAMMER

Vinnie Cilurzo of Russian River Brewing Company brews what is arguably the best example of this style, Pliny the Elder. Vinnie very generously shared his recipe with the brewing world, and just about everyone interested in this style has seen it. The recipe below, while a little bigger than Vinnie's, is a direct descendant of his. If there is any difference, it is an unintentional consequence of translating commercial-sized batches down to homebrew size.

OG: 1.080 (19.3 °P)
FG: 1.013 (3.3 °P)
ADF: 83%
IBU: 100+ (284 calculated)
Color: 6 SRM (12 EBC)
Alcohol: 8.9% ABV (7.0% ABW)
Boil: 90 minutes
Pre-Boil Volume: 7.74 gallons (29.3L)
Pre-Boil Gravity: 1.062 (15.2 °P)

Extract	Weight	Percent
Light LME (2.2 °L)	10.9 lbs. (4.94kg)	81.3
Corn Sugar (0 °L)	1.5 lbs. (0.68kg)	11.2
Wheat LME (4 °L)	0.5 lb. (227g)	3.7

Steeping Grains

Crystal (40 °L)	0.5 lb. (227g)	3.7

Hops		**IBU**
Warrior 15% AA, 90 min.	2.0 oz. (57g)	117.8
Chinook 13% AA, 90 min.	2.0 oz. (57g)	102.1
Simcoe 12% AA, 45 min.	1.0 oz. (28g)	38.4
Columbus 14% AA, 30 min.	1.0 oz. (28g)	25.5
Centennial 9% AA, 0 min.	2.25 oz. (64g)	0
Simcoe 12% AA, 0 min.	1.0 oz. (28g)	0
Columbus 14% AA, dry	3.25 oz. (92g)	0
Centennial 9% AA, dry	1.75 oz. (50g)	0
Simcoe 12% AA, dry	1.75 oz. (50g)	0

Yeast

White Labs WLP001 California Ale, Wyeast 1056 American Ale, or Fermentis Safale US-05

Fermentation and Conditioning

Use 15 grams of properly rehydrated dry yeast, 3 liquid yeast packages, or make an appropriate starter. Ferment at 67° F (19° C), slowly raising the temperature to 70° F (21° C) as the fermentation begins to slow.

As soon as the bulk of the yeast begins to drop, transfer the beer to a second fermenter and add the dry hops. The pellets should break up and eventually settle to the bottom of the fermenter. This might take a few days, so don't panic. Let the beer sit on the hops for another 7 days, approximately 7 to 10 days total.

When finished, carbonate the beer to approximately 2 to 2.5 volumes.

All-Grain Option

Replace the light extract with 15.25 lbs. (6.91kg) American two-row malt. Replace the wheat extract with 0.5 lb. (227g) wheat malt. Mash at 150° F (66° C).

19 | GERMAN WHEAT AND RYE BEER

Most people seem to either love or hate German wheat and rye beers. These styles all include a large portion (50 percent or more) of wheat or rye malt, and they all feature a unique banana/clove yeast character. I think those who love these styles have had the chance to try great examples with the proper level of fermentation-derived esters and phenols. Those who dislike them probably have experienced some bad examples, where the yeast character was overwhelming or completely out of balance. Properly made, these are really wonderful beers.

WEIZEN/WEISSBIER

A pale, spicy, fruity, refreshing wheat-based ale. This is a beginner style that can be brewed by extract or all-grain methods. Ferments at 62° F (17° C).

OG	FG	IBU	Color	Alcohol
1.044–1.052	1.010–1.014	8–15	2–8 SRM	4.3–5.6% ABV
(11–12.9 °P)	(2.6–3.6 °P)		4–16 EBC	3.4–4.4% ABW

Keys to Brewing Weizen/Weissbier:
When I was a new brewer, I brewed a number of less than perfect German-style wheat beers. I kept playing around with the grain bill, assuming that there was some secret ingredient for that soft, bready, and slightly sweet malt flavor that the best examples showed. In the end the best recipe was the simplest—at least 50 percent wheat malt and the rest good continental Pilsener malt. Yes, a decoction mash might add a slight richness to the beer, but more important is using the best quality malt or malt extract you can find.

The other vital key I lacked in my quest for a great weizen was the proper fermentation temperature. Everyone told me that higher temperatures produce more banana esters and fewer clove phenols. Cooler temperatures produced only clove and no banana. I tried everything from 65 to 72° F (18 to 22° C), but then my dear friend Harold Gulbransen told me the best temperature for fermenting this beer was 62° F (17° C). I was skeptical that the yeast would even ferment well at that temperature, but the results were spectacular. Along with the proper amount of yeast and oxygen, this temperature creates a beautiful balance of fermentation flavors, helps keep some unpleasant flavors in check, and produces a fantastic beer.

RECIPE: HAROLD-IS-WEIZEN

OG: 1.050 (12.4 °P)
FG: 1.012 (3.1 °P)
ADF: 75%
IBU: 13
Color: 5 SRM (10 EBC)
Alcohol: 5.0% ABV (3.9% ABW)
Boil: 60 minutes
Pre-Boil Volume: 7 gallons (26.5L)
Pre-Boil Gravity: 1.043 (10.6 °P)

Extract	Weight	Percent
Wheat LME (4 °L)	8.6 lbs. (3.9kg)	100

Hops		IBU
Hallertau 4% AA, 60 min.	0.8 oz. (23g)	13.1

Yeast
White Labs WLP300 Hefeweizen Ale, Wyeast 3068 Weihenstephan Weizen

Fermentation and Conditioning
Use 2 liquid yeast packages or make an appropriate starter. Ferment at 62° F (17° C). When finished, carbonate the beer to approximately 2.5 to 3 volumes.

All-Grain Option

Replace the wheat extract with 5.6 lbs. (2.54kg) continental Pilsener malt and 5.6 lbs. (2.54kg) wheat malt. Mash at 152° F (67° C). Increase the pre-boil volume as needed to allow a 90-minute boil, which will help reduce DMS in the beer.

DUNKELWEIZEN

A moderately dark, spicy, fruity, malty, refreshing wheat-based ale. This is a beginner style that can be brewed by extract-with-grain or all-grain methods. Ferments at 62° F (17° C).

OG	FG	IBU	Color	Alcohol
1.044–1.056	1.010–1.014	10–18	14–23 SRM	4.3–5.6% ABV
(11–13.8 °P)	(2.6–3.6 °P)		28–45 EBC	3.4–4.4% ABW

Keys to Brewing Dunkelweizen:

Dunkelweizen has the same spicy/fruity character as hefeweizen, but it also has a rich Munich malt character, similar to but not as intense as a Munich dunkel. At least half of the base needs to be malted wheat, while the rest can be Munich malt. The problem with such a recipe is that many people expect a little caramel-type sweetness from this style, and you won't get much unless you add some caramel-type malts. It doesn't take a lot, and too much can be overwhelming. A decoction mash might add a slight richness to the beer, as it can when brewing hefeweizen, but more important is using the best quality malt or malt extract you can find.

The proper fermentation temperature will create a beautiful balance of fermentation flavors and helps keep some unpleasant flavors in check. It is very important to follow the recommended fermentation temperature for this beer.

RECIPE: TRIGO OSCURO

Many people expect a darker beer to be bigger and richer, even though that is not always the case. However, I believe in giving people what they want, so this recipe is on the bigger end of the style. If you prefer it not so big, just back down on the wheat extract a little.

OG: 1.056 (13.8 °P)
FG: 1.014 (3.5 °P)
ADF: 75%
IBU: 16
Color: 16 SRM (31 EBC)

Alcohol: 5.6% ABV (4.4% ABW)
Boil: 60 minutes
Pre-Boil Volume: 7 gallons (26.5L)
Pre-Boil Gravity: 1.048 (11.8 °P)

Extract	Weight	Percent
Wheat LME (4 °L)	6.8 lbs. (3.08kg)	68.4
Munich LME (9 °L)	2.2 lbs. (3.08kg)	22.1

Steeping Grains		
Special "B" (120 °L)	6.0 oz. (170g)	3.8
Crystal (40 °L)	6.0 oz. (170g)	3.8
Carafa Special II (430 °L)	2.0 oz. (57g)	1.9

Hops		IBU
Hallertau 4% AA, 60 min.	1.0 oz. (28g)	15.9

Yeast

White Labs WLP300 Hefeweizen Ale, Wyeast 3068 Weihenstephan Weizen

Fermentation and Conditioning

Use 2 liquid yeast packages or make an appropriate starter. Ferment at 62° F (17° C). When finished, carbonate the beer to approximately 2.5 to 3 volumes.

All-Grain Option

Replace the wheat extract with 2 lbs. (0.9kg) continental Pilsener malt and 6.9 lbs. (3.13kg) wheat malt. Replace the Munich extract with 3 lbs. (1.36kg) Munich malt. Mash at 152° F (67° C). Increase the pre-boil volume as needed to allow a 90-minute boil, which will help reduce DMS in the beer.

WEIZENBOCK

A strong, malty, fruity, spicy, wheat-based ale combining the best flavors of a dunkelweizen and the rich strength and body of a bock. This is an intermediate style that can be brewed by extract-with-grain or all-grain methods. Ferments at 62° F (17° C).

OG	FG	IBU	Color	Alcohol
1.064–1.090	1.015–1.022	15–30	12–25 SRM	6.5–8.0% ABV
(15.7–21.5 °P)	(3.8–5.6 °P)		24–49 EBC	5.1–6.3% ABW

Keys to Brewing Weizenbock:

Weizenbock is like dunkelweizen on steroids. This beer is rich, malty, and warming like a bock, but full of dark fruit and spicy notes like a good weizen. Like dunkelweizen, at least half of the base needs to be malted wheat, but unlike dunkelweizen not all of the remaining base can be Munich malt. While most bock beers require a fair amount of Munich malt, this style seems too heavy with lots of Munich malt and all the other rich flavors in this beer.

The proper fermentation temperature will create a beautiful balance of fermentation flavors and helps keep some unpleasant, hotter alcohol flavors in check. It is very important to follow the recommended fermentation temperature for this beer.

RECIPE: TRICK OR TREAT BOCK

Taking my kids out for Halloween has always been one of my favorite "Dad" things to do. I get a kick out of seeing their excitement, how much fun they have, and seeing all of the neighborhood kids in costume. Every year for the past ten years, I have dragged along our little red wagon. Early on it was just in case anyone got tired. More recently it has morphed into a place to store the giant loads of candy, bottles of water, coats, flashlights, and a bottle of weizenbock for Dad, which makes wagon pulling a little more enjoyable. Weizenbock is the perfect Halloween beer. The rich, malty character, the gently warming alcohol, and the spicy and fruity notes make it seem like an adult candy, perfect for the cooler weather of fall.

OG: 1.081 (19.6 °P)
FG: 1.021 (5.3 °P)
ADF: 73%
IBU: 23
Color: 16 SRM (31 EBC)
Alcohol: 8.0% ABV (6.2% ABW)
Boil: 60 minutes
Pre-Boil Volume: 7 gallons (26.5L)
Pre-Boil Gravity: 1.069 (16.9 °P)

Extract	Weight	Percent
Wheat LME (4 °L)	11.0 lbs. (4.99kg)	80
Munich LME (9 °L)	1.5 lbs. (0.68kg)	10.9

Steeping Grains		
Special "B" (120 °L)	0.5 lb. (227g)	3.6
Crystal (40 °L)	0.5 lb. (227g)	3.6
Pale Chocolate (200 °L)	0.25 lb. (113g)	1.8

Hops		IBU
Hallertau 4% AA, 60 min.	1.6 oz. (45g)	22.7

Yeast

White Labs WLP300 Hefeweizen Ale, Wyeast 3068 Weihenstephan Weizen

Fermentation and Conditioning

Use 3 liquid yeast packages or make an appropriate starter. Ferment at 62° F (17° C). When finished, carbonate the beer to approximately 2.5 to 3 volumes.

All-Grain Option

Replace the wheat extract with 5 lbs. (2.26kg) continental Pilsener malt and 10 lbs. (4.53kg) dark wheat malt. Replace the Munich extract with 2 lbs. (0.9kg) Munich malt. Mash at 152° F (67° C). Increase the pre-boil volume as needed to allow a 90-minute boil, which will help reduce DMS in the beer.

ROGGENBIER (GERMAN RYE BEER)

A dunkelweizen made with rye rather than wheat, with a fuller body. This is an advanced style that can only be brewed by partial mash or all-grain methods to convert the rye malt properly. Ferments at 62° F (17° C).

OG	FG	IBU	Color	Alcohol
1.046–1.056	1.010–1.014	10–20	14–19 SRM	4.5–6.0% ABV
(11.4–13.8 °P)	(2.6–3.6 °P)		28–37 EBC	3.6–4.7% ABW

Keys to Brewing Roggenbier:

Roggenbier is very similar to dunkelweizen, although it is made with rye malt instead of wheat. This beer has a rich, malty character like dunkelweizen, with some additional slightly spicy notes from the rye malt. About half of the base needs to be malted rye, which requires mashing. The rest of the grain bill is very much like a dunkelweizen.

The proper fermentation temperature creates a beautiful balance of fermentation flavors and helps keep some other unpleasant flavors in check. It is very important to follow the recommended fermentation temperature for this beer.

RECIPE: J.C.'S ROGGENBIER

I enjoy the occasional roggenbier whenever I come across one. Some are better than others, but none were really great until I tried my friend J.C.'s roggenbier. It was spectacular, with a fine rye note and a malty finish. I asked J.C. his secret, and he generously shared his recipe, as all great brewers are willing to do. The recipe below is a slightly simplified version of his and makes an excellent roggenbier.

OG: 1.054 (13.4 °P)
FG: 1.014 (3.6 °P)
ADF: 73%
IBU: 17
Color: 15 SRM (29 EBC)
Alcohol: 5.3% ABV (4.1% ABW)
Boil: 90 minutes
Pre-Boil Volume: 7.7 gallons (29.3L)

Pre-Boil Gravity: 1.042 (10.5 °P)

Extract	Weight	Percent
Munich LME (9 °L)	2.6 lbs. (1.18kg)	20.0

Partial Mash Grains		
Rye Malt (3.5 °L)	6.25 lbs. (2.83kg)	48.2
Pilsener (1.8 °L)	3.0 lbs. (1.36kg)	23.1
CaraMunich (60 °L)	1.0 lb. (0.45kg)	7.7
Carafa Special II (430 °L)	2.0 oz. (57g)	1.0

Hops		IBU
Tettnang 4% AA, 60 min.	1.0 oz. (28g)	16.1
Czech Saaz 3.5% AA, 15 min.	0.3 oz. (9g)	1.1

Yeast

White Labs WLP300 Hefeweizen Ale, Wyeast 3068 Weihenstephan Weizen

Fermentation and Conditioning

Use 2 liquid yeast packages or make an appropriate starter. Ferment at 62° F (17° C). When finished, carbonate the beer to approximately 2.5 to 3 volumes.

All-Grain Option

Replace the Munich extract with 3.5 lbs. (1.58kg) Munich malt. Mash at 154° F (68° C). Increase the pre-boil volume as needed to allow a 90-minute boil, which will help reduce DMS in the beer.

20 | BELGIAN AND FRENCH ALE

Belgian and French ales have a wide range of character. Perhaps the best way to describe this category is to say that most of them are very tasty beer styles that originated in Belgium or France in small, artisanal breweries.

WITBIER

A refreshing, elegant, moderate-strength wheat-based ale. This is an advanced style that can only be brewed by partial mash or all-grain methods to convert the oats and unmalted wheat properly. Ferments at 68 to 72° F (20 to 22° C).				
OG	FG	IBU	Color	Alcohol
1.044–1.052	1.008–1.012	10–20	2–4 SRM	4.5–5.5% ABV
(11–12.9 °P)	(2.1–3.1 °P)		4–8 EBC	3.6–4.3% ABW

Keys to Brewing Witbier:

Along with its light sweetness, zesty citrus, and low herbal character, witbier has a wonderfully soft, smooth, creamy feel to it. The key to that wonderful mouthfeel is a liberal dose of wheat and oats, which add a rich, luscious character to the beer.

One of the most common problems in brewing witbier is in balancing the various flavors; most amateur brewers either make them too bitter or too spicy. For the spice additions, the goal is to have a very subtle coriander seed (perfumy and peppery) character, a fairly prominent citrus note, and a subtle background herbal note. While there are some spicy notes from the yeast, the fermentation flavor is easy to control by pitching the proper amount of yeast and beginning fermentation at a restrained 68° F (20° C).

The coriander seed in the recipe should be gently crushed, until the seeds split into multiple pieces. The trick in using coriander seed is that the coriander available can vary from fresh and pungent to old and nearly flavorless. The amount in this recipe is for the coriander you can pick up at your local homebrew shop. It isn't right off the plant, but it isn't stale either. You might need to adjust the amount up or down based on the quality of coriander seed you can get. When you crush the coriander, it should have a fairly strong, spicy character. Crush a few seeds before brew day and see if you need to make any adjustments. Just keep in mind that the coriander note in the beer should be very subtle, not big and spicy.

Traditionally, brewers have added dried orange peel to witbier. This recipe uses fresh orange or tangerine zest, as it gives a fresher, more aromatic, and pleasant character to the beer. You want to find the best oranges or tangerines you can get. Often the best fruit can be found on a tree in someone's backyard or your local farmer's market. Fruit that gets a chance to ripen on the tree longer than the fruit you will typically find in the grocery store is usually better. That extra time on the tree improves the character of the fruit, and it tends to be more aromatic. Give a potential piece of fruit a light poke with a fingernail and do a sniff test. Try using a couple of different types of orange-skinned citrus fruit to create a nice complexity. Use only fruit with a fresh, bold citrus character, and use just the surface of the citrus skin. You don't want to dig deep into the white pith of the fruit, as it is bitter and lacks citrus character.

Chamomile adds a nice floral/herbal background note. You can use fresh or dried chamomile. The easiest source of dried chamomile is tea bags. Look for a chamomile tea that contains only chamomile flowers, since some contain other herbs. If you are using fresh chamomile, increase the amount by about 7 to 10 times to account for the water weight.

Add spices late in the boil, but use restraint. Start out with an amount you know will not be overwhelming. If it turns out the spicing wasn't enough, you can bump it up by boiling some spice in a little water and adding it to the beer.

RECIPE: WITTEBREW

OG: 1.050 (12.3 °P)
FG: 1.011 (2.9 °P)
ADF: 76%
IBU: 20
Color: 4 SRM (8 EBC)
Alcohol: 5.0% ABV (3.9% ABW)
Boil: 60 minutes
Pre-Boil Volume: 7 gallons (26.5L)
Pre-Boil Gravity: 1.042 (10.5 °P)

Extract	Weight	Percent
Wheat LME (4 °L)	6.75 lbs. (3.06kg)	74.0
Munich LME (9 °L)	0.25 lb. (113g)	2.7

Partial Mash Grains		
Flaked Oats (1 °L)	1.13 lbs. (0.51kg)	12.3
Pilsener Malt (1.6 °L)	1.0 lb. (0.45kg)	11.0

Hops		IBU
Hallertau 4% AA, 60 min.	1.2 oz. (34g)	19.7

Extras	
Fresh Citrus Zest, 5 min.	1.5 oz. (43g)
Crushed Coriander Seed, 5 min.	0.4 oz. (11g)
Dry Chamomile Flowers, 5 min.	0.03 oz. (1g)

Yeast
White Labs WLP400 Belgian Wit Ale, Wyeast 3944 Belgian Witbier, or Brewferm Blanche

Fermentation and Conditioning
Use 10 grams of properly rehydrated dry yeast, 2 liquid yeast packages, or make an appropriate starter. Begin fermentation at 68° F (20° C), slowly raising the temperature to 72° F (22° C) by the last third of fermentation. When finished, carbonate the beer to approximately 2 to 2.5 volumes.

All-Grain Option

Delete the 1 lb. (0.45kg) of Pilsener malt in the recipe. Replace the wheat extract and the Munich extract with 5.5 lbs. (2.49kg) continental Pilsener malt, 5 lbs. (2.26kg) flaked wheat, and 0.25 lb. (113g) Munich malt. Add 0.5 lb. (227g) of rice hulls or similar filtering aid. Mash at 122° F (50° C) for 15 minutes, then raise the temperature over the next 15 minutes to 154° F (68° C) and hold until conversion is complete. Increase the pre-boil volume as needed to allow a 90-minute boil, which will help reduce DMS in the beer.

BELGIAN PALE ALE

A moderately malty, fruity, somewhat spicy, easy-drinking, copper-colored ale. This is a beginner style that can be brewed by extract-with-grain or all-grain methods. Ferments at 66° F (19° C).

OG	FG	IBU	Color	Alcohol
1.048–1.054	1.010–1.014	20–30	8–14 SRM	4.8–5.5% ABV
(11.9–13.3 °P)	(2.6–3.6 °P)		16–28 EBC	3.8–4.3% ABW

Keys to Brewing Belgian Pale Ale:

This is a well-balanced beer. It is an easy-drinking, everyday beer, and it is important to brew it with that in mind. It is not uncommon for new brewers to turn this into a big, alcoholic, and very spicy beer.

This is not a sweet beer, either. Upon tasting, it might have an initial malt sweetness, but that shouldn't carry through to the finish. The Pilsener malt and the specialty grains will add enough malt character, and a proper fermentation will leave behind just the right touch of malt sweetness.

While pear and orange fruitiness can be fairly prominent, the spicy notes should not be more than moderate in strength; just a light spice note is best. Many poor examples of the style have too much of a spicy character and way too sweet a finish. Pitch enough clean, healthy yeast, and follow the recommended fermentation temperature to keep the yeast-derived flavors under control.

RECIPE: ANTWERP AFTERNOON

I once spent a day in Antwerp, Belgium, trying to find just the right gift for my wife. She really likes diamonds, which Antwerp is known for, but my budget prefers refrigerator magnets. I spent most of the day doing what I really hate, which is going from store to store trying to find the right piece of jewelry. As much as I tried, I couldn't find the right item at a price I could afford. By the afternoon I gave up and spent the rest of the day relaxing in a bar enjoying a popular Belgian pale ale that many locals drink. I brought my wife back a coaster from the bar. Hey, it's the thought that counts.

OG: 1.052 (12.9 °P)
FG: 1.012 (3.1 °P)
ADF: 76%
IBU: 26
Color: 8 SRM (16 EBC)
Alcohol: 5.3% ABV (4.1% ABW)
Boil: 60 minutes
Pre-Boil Volume: 7 gallons (26.5L)
Pre-Boil Gravity: 1.044 (11.1 °P)

Extract	Weight	Percent
Pilsener LME (2.3 °L)	8.3 lbs. (3.76kg)	89.2

Steeping Grains		
CaraMunich (60 °L)	0.75 lb. (340g)	8.1
Biscuit (25 °L)	0.25 lb. (113g)	2.7

Hops		IBU
Kent Goldings 5% AA, 60 min.	1.3 oz. (37g)	26.4
Kent Goldings 5% AA, 0 min.	0.3 oz. (9g)	0

Yeast
White Labs WLP515 Antwerp Ale or Wyeast 3655 Belgian Schelde

Fermentation and Conditioning
Use 10 grams of properly rehydrated dry yeast, 2 liquid yeast packages, or make an appropriate starter. Ferment at 66° F (19° C). When finished, carbonate the beer to approximately 2.5 volumes.

All-Grain Option
Replace the Pilsener extract with 11.2 lbs. (5.1kg) continental Pilsener malt. Mash at 152° F (67° C). Increase the pre-boil volume as needed to allow a 90-minute boil, which will help reduce DMS in the beer.

SAISON

| A medium to strong ale, usually pale orange in color, highly carbonated, well hopped, fruity and dry, with a quenching acidity. This is an intermediate style that can be brewed by extract-with-grain or all-grain methods. Ferments at 68 to 80° F (20 to 27° C). |

OG	FG	IBU	Color	Alcohol
1.048–1.065	1.002–1.012	20–35	5–14 SRM	5.0–7.0% ABV
(11.9–15.8 °P)	(0.5–3.1 °P)		10–28 EBC	4–5.5% ABW

Keys to Brewing Saison:

A great saison finishes very dry; the most common brewing mistake for this style is not getting a dry-enough finish. In order to get the beer to finish dry, the recipe must have a considerable amount of simple sugars. If you are brewing with extract, use the most fermentable Pilsener extract your homebrew shop carries. If it isn't very fermentable, don't be afraid to increase the amount of cane or corn sugar to improve fermentability, up to 20 percent of the total sugars. If you are an all-grain brewer, use a low mash temperature and some simple sugar.

Even with plenty of simple sugars and very warm fermentation temperatures, it is common for some saison yeasts to fail to attenuate enough, stopping at around 75 percent attenuation no matter what course of action you take. If the primary yeast doesn't finish low enough, your only course of action at that point is to add another yeast, such as dry champagne yeast, to get the beer to attenuate a little more.

RECIPE: RAISON D'SAISON

Contrary to what many people might think *raison* is not French for raisin. This beer has no raisins in it, but anyone who enjoys a good saison should find plenty of reasons, or *raisons*, to brew this beer. The BJCP Style Guidelines mention that the saison category spans a broad range of strengths. It labels the varying strengths as table, export, and strong versions. This recipe makes an export-strength saison, with an option to make a strong version.

OG: 1.060 (14.8 °P)
FG: 1.008 (2.0 °P)
ADF: 86%
IBU: 27
Color: 5 SRM (10 EBC)
Alcohol: 6.9% ABV (5.4% ABW)
Boil: 60 minutes
Pre-Boil Volume: 7 gallons (26.5L)
Pre-Boil Gravity: 1.051 (12.7 °P)

Extract	Weight	Percent
Pilsener LME (2.3 °L)	7.7 lbs. (3.49kg)	76.4
Cane Sugar (0 °L)	1.0 lb. (0.45kg)	9.9
Wheat LME (4 °L)	0.75 lb. (340g)	7.4
Munich LME (9 °L)	0.5 lb. (227g)	5.0

Steeping Grains		
CaraMunich (60 °L)	2.0 oz. (57g)	1.2

Hops		IBU
Hallertau 4% AA, 60 min.	1.7 oz. (48g)	26.5
Hallertau 4% AA, 0 min.	0.75 oz. (21g)	0

Yeast
White Labs WLP565 Saison Ale or Wyeast 3724 Belgian Saison

Fermentation and Conditioning
Use 2.5 liquid yeast packages or make an appropriate starter. Ferment at 68° F (20° C) to start, and then ramp up the temperature to 80° F (27° C) over the course of fermentation. If the beer fails to attenuate enough, add a secondary yeast (White Labs WLP001 California Ale, Wyeast 1056 American Ale, Fermentis Safale US-05, or a dry champagne yeast) to dry the beer out further. When finished, carbonate the beer to approximately 3 to 3.5 volumes.

All-Grain Option

Replace the Pilsener, wheat, and Munich extract with 10.5 lbs. (4.76kg) continental Pilsener malt, 0.75 lb. (340g) wheat malt, and 0.75 lb. (340g) Munich malt. Mash at 147° F (64° C). With the low mash temperature, you may need to lengthen the rest time to 90 minutes to get full conversion. Also increase the pre-boil volume as needed to allow a 90-minute boil, which will help reduce DMS in the beer.

Specialty Saison Option – Extract with Grains

Increase the Pilsener extract from 7.7 lbs. (3.49kg) to 9.3 lbs. (4.22kg). Increase the 60-minute hop addition from 1.7 oz. (48g) to 2.0 oz. (57g). The pre-boil gravity should be 1.059 (14.6 °P), and the OG should be 1.070 (17.0 °P). Use 3 liquid yeast packages or make an appropriate starter. The beer should attenuate down around 1.011 (2.7 °P).

Specialty Saison Option – All Grain

Increase the continental Pilsener malt to 12.5 lbs. (5.67kg) and increase the Munich malt to 1 lb. (0.45kg). Increase the 60-minute hop addition from 1.7 oz. (48g) to 2.0 oz. (57g). Increase the boil time to 90 minutes, which will help reduce DMS in the beer. The pre-boil gravity should be 1.054 (13.4 °P) and the OG should be 1.070 (17.0 °P). Use 3 liquid yeast packages or make an appropriate starter. The beer should attenuate down around 1.011 (2.7 °P).

BIÈRE DE GARDE

A fairly strong, malty, lagered, artisanal ale. Sweet and malty up front but dry in the finish. This is an intermediate style that can be brewed by extract-with-grain or all-grain methods. Ferments at 66 to 70° F (19 to 21° C).

OG	FG	IBU	Color	Alcohol
1.060–1.080	1.008–1.016	18–28	6–19 SRM	6.0–8.5% ABV
(14.7–19.3 °P)	(2.0–4.1 °P)		12–37 EBC	4.7–6.7% ABW

Keys to Brewing Bière de Garde:

Bière de garde often has an upfront sweetness in the aroma and the flavor, which can come through as either a malt sweetness or more like a candy sweetness, depending on the beer. However, bière de garde is a fairly dry beer. It has a high level of attenuation and a dryness to the finish that can be surprising, given the sweet character up front.

It is this sweet/dry aspect to the beer that many brewers find difficult to accomplish. It is important to use enough simple sugar and an easily fermentable extract or, for all-grain brewers, a low mash temperature. If you're an extract brewer and are having difficulties getting the proper level of attenuation, substitute some additional cane sugar or corn sugar for a portion of the malt extract or switch to a more attenuative yeast.

If you do switch yeasts, it is important to pick your yeast carefully. While you want a clean-fermenting ale or lager yeast, too clean and neutral of a yeast can make this beer seem more like an American pub ale. A subtle touch of esters helps fill out the character of the beer and keeps it from seeming bland. Most of the relatively clean European ale yeasts at a cool fermentation temperature do a nice job, or you can try a lager yeast fermented at ale temperatures.

Aging is a big part of this beer. An extended period of storage at cellar temperatures helps develop the bière de garde character. Make sure to set some aside for at least a year to see how it develops.

RECIPE: NO CULOTTES, NO PROBLÈME

OG: 1.075 (18.2 °P)
FG: 1.010 (2.6 °P)
ADF: 86%
IBU: 26
Color: 9 SRM (19 EBC)
Alcohol: 8.6% ABV (6.8% ABW)
Boil: 60 minutes
Pre-Boil Volume: 7 gallons (26.5L)
Pre-Boil Gravity: 1.064 (15.6 °P)

Extract	Weight	Percent
Pilsener LME (2.3 °L)	8.75 lbs. (3.97kg)	68.6
Munich LME (9 °L)	2.2 lbs. (1kg)	17.2
Cane Sugar (0 °L)	1.0 lb. (0.45kg)	7.8

Steeping Grains		
CaraVienna (20 °L)	0.75 lb. (340g)	5.9
Black Patent (525 °L)	1.0 oz. (28g)	0.5

Hops		IBU
Fuggle 5% AA, 60 min.	1.4 oz. (40g)	25.6

Yeast
White Labs WLP011 European Ale or Wyeast 1338 European Ale

Fermentation and Conditioning
Use 14 grams of properly rehydrated dry yeast, 3 liquid yeast packages, or make an appropriate starter. Begin fermentation at 66° F (19° C). As fermentation begins to slow, slowly raise the temperature 1° F (0.5° C) per day until reaching 70° F (21° C). When finished, carbonate the beer to approximately 2.5 to 3 volumes. Cellar the beer for at least 3 months to give it some age. Longer is better.

All-Grain Option
Replace the Pilsener extract with 11.5 lbs. (5.21kg) continental Pilsener malt. Replace the Munich extract with 3 lbs. (1.36kg) Munich malt.

Mash at 147° F (64° C). With the low mash temperature, you may need to lengthen the rest time to 90 minutes to get full conversion. Also increase the pre-boil volume as needed to allow a 90-minute boil, which will help reduce DMS in the beer.

BELGIAN SPECIALTY ALE

This style encompasses a wide range of Belgian ales produced by truly artisanal brewers more concerned with creating unique products than in increasing sales. The recipe below is an intermediate style that can be brewed by extract-with-grain or all-grain methods. It ferments at 66° F (19° C) and then 59° F (15° C). For this substyle, the OG, FG, IBUs, SRM, and ABV will vary from beer to beer.

Keys to Brewing Belgian Specialty Ale:

A wide array of beers might fall into this category. All of them have unique qualities that make them stand out from ordinary beers. For some brewers, it is a beer like this that got them interested in brewing in the first place. The recipe below is for a well-known beer that is wickedly effervescent and spritzy. It is refreshing with considerable citrus, spice, and even some earthy character. The flavors and character change over time, and it is going to be different depending on how old a bottle you try and how it has been handled since it was bottled. The character continues to change and develop new facets as the *Brettanomyces* works its magic over time. This beer will continue to develop for many years. Make sure to set some aside from each batch you brew, and every couple of years you can treat yourself to a little vertical tasting of the different vintages.

RECIPE: VAL D'OR

OG: 1.057 (14.0 °P)

FG: 1.011 (2.9 °P)

ADF: 79% (attenuation will increase past this with the addition of *Brettanomyces*)

IBU: 37

Color: 11 SRM (21 EBC)

Alcohol: 6.0% ABV (4.7% ABW)

Boil: 60 minutes

Pre-Boil Volume: 7 gallons (26.5L)

Pre-Boil Gravity: 1.048 (12.0 °P)

Extract	Weight	Percent
Pilsener LME (2.3 °L)	7.4 lbs. (3.35kg)	74.7
Cane Sugar (0 °L)	1.0 lb. (0.45kg)	10.1

Steeping Grains		
CaraMunich (60 °L)	1.5 lbs. (0.68kg)	15.2

Hops		IBU
Hallertau 4% AA, 60 min.	2.0 oz. (57g)	31.8
Styrian Goldings 5% AA, 15 min.	1.0 oz. (28g)	5.3
Styrian Goldings 5% AA, 0 min.	1.0 oz. (28g)	0
Styrian Goldings 5% AA, dry	2.0 oz. (57g)	0

Yeast

White Labs WLP510 Belgian Bastogne Ale or Wyeast 3522 Belgian Ardennes

White Labs WLP650 *Brettanomyces bruxellensis* or Wyeast 5112 *Brettanomyces bruxellensis*

Fermentation and Conditioning

Use 2 liquid yeast packages or make an appropriate starter. Ferment at 66° F (19° C). When finished, rack the beer to another fermentation vessel and add the *Brettanomyces bruxellensis* culture. Hold for 1 month around 59° F (15° C). Add dry hops during the final week. Carbonate the beer to approximately 3 volumes, and serve at 50 to 55° F (10 to 13° C).

All-Grain Option

Replace the Pilsener extract with 9.75 lbs. (4.42kg) continental Pilsener malt. Mash at 152° F (67° C). Increase the pre-boil volume as needed to allow a 90-minute boil, which will help reduce DMS in the beer.

21 | SOUR ALE

I am almost always a little surprised when people say they don't like sour beers. I used to think that it was just the unusual nature of the category that put some people off. After all, we brewers are told from day one that we should do everything we can to keep bacteria out of our beer. Sour flavors are supposed to be a flaw, right?

But then I realized sour beers are just like any other beer style: When people haven't had a chance to try a well-made example, they often declare that they don't like that style. With no knowledge of how the beer should really taste, they often assume a style is just nasty.

Sour beers may not be for every palate, but they are far from nasty. When well made they can be magically beautiful and supremely drinkable. They balance the sour and the funky with other aspects of the beer, making an intriguing and enjoyable combination. If you have had a less than ideal experience with sour beers, seek out the help of someone who really knows the style and can provide great examples. You will be glad you did.

BERLINER WEISSE

A very pale, sour, refreshing, low-alcohol wheat ale. This is an advanced style that can be brewed by extract or all-grain methods. Ferments at 67° F (19° C).

OG	FG	IBU	Color	Alcohol
1.028–1.032	1.003–1.006	3–8	2–3 SRM	2.8–3.8% ABV
(7.1–8.1 °P)	(0.8–1.6 °P)		4–6 EBC	2.2–3.0% ABW

Keys to Brewing Berliner Weisse:

Berliner weisse is a sharply sour beer, and there are several ways to get that sourness. Some folks like to avoid using any sort of bacteria in their breweries and instead add lactic acid to their beer. This method is quick and easy: You can control the amount of sourness in the beer, and the level of sourness won't change over time. However, the results are similar to microwaving a steak. It is faster and easier, but the taste and texture are just not the same as with grilling.

Another technique for souring the beer is inoculating the wort or mash with a handful of grain. Most grain has a population of *Lactobacillus* and other critters all over it. Tossing a handful into the mash or wort and letting it sit for a day or two at around 100° F (38° C) will produce a sour, aromatic soup. When you boil the wort, it stops the action of the various bugs, leaving a fixed amount of sourness. This technique is quite a bit more variable than dosing with lactic acid, but it adds a nice variety of flavors other than sour. If you are lucky, the beer can be fantastic. If you are not lucky, at least the snails seem to enjoy it.

My preferred technique for Berliner weisse is to add a commercial *Lactobacillus delbrueckii* culture. This is as simple as purchasing the product from your homebrew shop and tossing it into the beer along with your neutral ale yeast. While the main flavor characteristic of this bacterium is lactic sourness, it also produces other subtle flavors and aromas, resulting in a more intriguing beer than if you use lactic acid. And it is a much more reliable way to add sourness than tossing in a handful of grain.

If you are adventurous, split a batch of wort three ways, try all of the techniques, and see which you like best.

RECIPE: SAURES BIERGESICHT

OG: 1.032 (8.1 °P)
FG: 1.006 (1.5 °P)
ADF: 82%
IBU: 4
Color: 3 SRM (6 EBC)
Alcohol: 3.5% ABV (2.7% ABW)
Boil: 15 minutes
Pre-Boil Volume: 6.2 gallons (23.5L)
Pre-Boil Gravity: 1.031 (7.8 °P)

Extract	Weight	Percent
Pilsener LME (2.3 °L)	2.75 lbs. (1.24kg)	50.0
Wheat LME (4 °L)	2.75 lbs. (1.24kg)	50.0

Hops		IBU
Hallertau 4% AA, 15 min.	1.0 oz. (28g)	4.4

Yeast

White Labs WLP011 European Ale, Wyeast 1338 European Ale, or Fermentis Safale US-05
White Labs WLP677 *Lactobacillus* Bacteria, Wyeast 5335 *Lactobacillus delbrueckii*

Fermentation and Conditioning

Add 5 grams of properly rehydrated dry yeast, or 1 liquid yeast package, along with 1 package of *Lactobacillus*. Ferment at 67° F (19° C). When finished, carbonate the beer to approximately 3.5 to 4 volumes.

All-Grain Option

Replace the Pilsener extract with 4.2 lbs. (1.9kg) continental Pilsener malt. Replace the wheat extract with 3 lbs. (1.36kg) wheat malt. Mash at 149° F (65° C). With the low mash temperature, you may need to lengthen the rest time to 90 minutes to get full conversion.

FLANDERS RED ALE

A complex, sour ale with hints of red wine character. This is an advanced style that can be brewed by extract-with-grain or all-grain methods. Ferments at 65 to 70° F (18 to 21° C) and takes about 1 year to be ready.				
OG	FG	IBU	Color	Alcohol
1.048–1.057	1.002–1.012	10–25	10–16 SRM	4.6–6.5% ABV
(11.9–14.0 °P)	(0.5–3.1 °P)		20–31 EBC	3.6–5.1% ABW

Keys to Brewing Flanders Red Ale:

In some examples of Flanders red ale, the sourness is balanced with the residual sweetness; in other examples it is balanced much more sour and dry. Yet a Flanders red has a lot more going on than just the sourness. This style should have a lot of fruit character, some malt, often some oak, and other flavors and aromas that are almost wine-like. That being the case, the most important ingredient in a Flanders red is the blend of bacteria and yeast that produce many of the key flavors and aromas of the style.

A lot has been written lately about the process of fermenting sour beers. After all, it is the most critical part of what gives these beers so much character and makes them so special. I know people who go to great lengths culturing everything from the dregs of commercial beers to the critters on their kitchen sponges. Some people also have long, complex schedules of exactly when to dose each yeast or bacteria.

I will go out on a limb and say that I think going through all those steps is not really critical to brewing a great Flanders red ale, given the excellent products available from Wyeast and White Labs. For Flanders red ale, my preference is for Wyeast 3763 Roeselare Blend. This is a perfect blend of yeast and bacteria intended to produce the flavors of the classic Flanders red and brown beers. The results are spectacular and can produce exceptionally accurate reproductions of the best commercial Flanders red ales out there.

You can get excellent results by tossing a package of the Wyeast 3763 Roeselare Blend into your wort and letting it sit at ambient temperatures for a year or more. During that time the sour and other flavors develop, and a pellicle will form over the surface of the beer. At some point the pellicle will most likely fall from the surface, which is a good general indicator that the beer is done.

The conditions present affect how long this takes and will determine the character of the beer. Just like fermentation temperature affects a beer's character, temperature also affects the types of flavors and aromas the bacteria and yeast in the blend create. In general, the warmer the environment, the more sour the beer will become. I like to find a relatively cool and dark area of my home, where the temperature is somewhat steady throughout the day. A small temperature shift over the course of months with the changing seasons is not a problem. However, large daily swings can negatively affect the results, so try to find a spot that doesn't change dramatically. Any part of a building that gets hit by direct sun tends to have a larger temperature swing. I like a temperature around 65 to 70° F (18 to 21° C) for my sour Flanders beers. If you are impatient, you can go with a higher temperature of up to 80° F (27° C), and the beer will finish in as little as a few months, but the results will not be nearly as complex and tasty.

My preferred method for getting a controlled level of sourness is to preferment the beer with a neutral ale yeast before adding the Wyeast 3763 Roeselare Blend. This uses up most of the available sugars, and the alcohol helps suppress the activity of the bacteria and yeasts in the blend. However, if you use this method, be careful not to make too big of a beer. If there is too much alcohol present, the yeasts and bacteria in the blend will not get started, and it will never be sour enough.

The other factor that makes a difference in the outcome is the amount of oxygen the beer gets as the bacteria and yeasts work their magic. The sourness in a Flanders red is a combination of lactic and acetic acid (vinegar). The more oxygen present during fermentation, the more acetic acid, and the beer will have more vinegar-like character. You need enough acetic acid so that it is noticeable, more than in an oud bruin, but not so much that it tastes like salad dressing.

Traditionally, the Flanders brewers have put their beer in large oak barrels, which allows low levels of oxygen to reach it. As many brewers are aware, the plastic used for most bucket fermenters also allows oxygen to migrate through to the beer. However, as Raj Apte has calculated, the bucket's surface-area-to-beer ratio and the permeability of the plastic allows for far more oxygen to reach the beer than if you use a large oak barrel. Most of the time, this will result in way too much acetic character in the finished beer. If you use a sealed carboy, one with a stopper and airlock, it will not produce enough acetic acid. You can brew a batch in each and blend them at the end to get the right level of acetic acid, but Raj has an easier method.

Raj uses a glass carboy with a large oak peg inserted into the opening. The oak peg is tapered and acts both as a seal and as a way for a small amount of oxygen to reach the beer inside. He has determined that the surface area of the oak peg and its level of oxygen permeability result in almost exactly the same amount of oxygen in the beer as the barrels used in Flanders. This is a simple and very effective method.

RECIPE: ROUGE FLAMANDE

Locals once considered the area where I live a "cow town." Unfortunately, rapid growth has made it hard for any sort of cattle-based industry to survive in the area. To cattle people, the name "Flanders Red" is a breed of cattle, also known as *Rouge Flamande* or *Rouge du Nord*. This is my tribute to two industries where progress and development make it tough to keep traditional methods alive.

OG: 1.057 (14.0 °P)
FG: 1.008 (2.0 °P)
ADF: 86%
IBU: 16
Color: 13 SRM (25 EBC)
Alcohol: 6.5% ABV (5.1% ABW)
Boil: 60 minutes
Pre-Boil Volume: 7 gallons (26.5L)
Pre-Boil Gravity: 1.048 (12.0 °P)

Extract	Weight	Percent
Pilsener LME (2.3 °L)	5.75 lbs. (2.61kg)	56.1
Munich LME (9 °L)	2.5 lbs. (1.13kg)	24.4
Wheat LME (4 °L)	0.5 lb. (227g)	4.9

Steeping Grains

Aromatic (20 °L)	0.5 lb. (227g)	4.9
CaraMunich (60 °L)	0.5 lb. (227g)	4.9
Special "B" (120 °L)	0.5 lb. (227g)	4.9

Hops   **IBU**

Kent Goldings 5% AA, 60 min. 0.8 oz. (23g)   15.9

Extras

Oak Cubes, French Medium Toast 1.0 oz. (28g)

Yeast

Wyeast 3763 Roeselare Blend or White Labs WLP655 Belgian Sour Mix I

Fermentation and Conditioning

The oak cubes can be sanitized by adding them to the boil for the last couple of minutes, but you will need to make sure they get into the fermenter, as the flavor and aroma of the oak will be extracted over several months. My preferred method is to sanitize the oak cubes separately by immersing them in a cup of near-boiling water for 15 minutes, then adding them to the fermenter.

Oxygenate the wort, add the culture, and set in a cool dark place to ferment, around 65 to 70 °F (18 to 21 °C). A thick mat will form on the surface of the beer, called a pellicle. About a year later, the pellicle will fall back into the beer and it is ready for packaging. It is possible for the pellicle to remain intact much longer if the environment is very still and vibration free. If a sample tastes like it is ready, you can ignore the pellicle and bottle or keg your beer. This process makes a beer similar to Rodenbach Grand Cru, more on the sour end than the blended Rodenbach. If you prefer a less sour beer, you can ferment one batch with the blended culture and one batch with White Labs WLP001 or Wyeast 1056 and then blend them to taste.

Alternatively, use 1 package of White Labs WLP001 or Wyeast 1056 to ferment the beer at 65° F (18° C). When fermentation slows, rack it to a second vessel and add the blended culture. The culture will break down and consume the remaining sugars that the yeast did not or were unable to consume, adding sourness and character. The result will be a less sour beer than using the culture from the start.

When finished, carbonate the beer to approximately 2 to 2.5 volumes.

All-Grain Option

Replace the Pilsener extract, Munich extract, and wheat extract with 5.25 lbs. (2.38kg) continental Pilsener malt, 5.25 lbs. (2.38kg) Vienna malt, 0.5 lb. (227g) wheat malt, and 1 lb. (0.45kg) Munich malt. Mash at 154° F (68° C). Increase the pre-boil volume as needed to allow a 90-minute boil, which will help reduce DMS in the beer.

FLANDERS BROWN ALE/OUD BRUIN

A malty, fruity brown ale with touches of sourness and age. This is an advanced style that can be brewed by extract-with-grain or all-grain methods. Ferments at 65° F (18° C) and later at ambient temperatures. It takes about 1 year to be ready.

OG	FG	IBU	Color	Alcohol
1.040–1.074	1.008–1.012	20–25	15–22 SRM	4.0–8.0% ABV
(10–17.9 °P)	(2.0–3.1 °P)		30–43 EBC	3.2–6.3% ABW

Keys to Brewing Flanders Brown Ale/Oud Bruin:

Oud bruin is a bigger beer that has more malt character, more malt sweetness, and isn't nearly as sour as a Flanders red ale. Think English old ale with a definite sour character. Long aging periods can also introduce a touch of sherry character consistent with an aged beer. The trick with oud bruin is to get the right amount of souring, just enough to provide a counternote to the residual malt sweetness but less sour than Flanders red.

Although you can use a sour mash technique or a pure *Lactobacillus* culture to create the sourness in this beer, my preference is to use the same blend that I use for Flanders red ale.

It takes some management of the bacterial cultures to create a subtle, controlled sourness. Bacteria have a tendency to keep consuming sugars unless something in their environment stops them. Unless you are willing and able to pasteurize your beer, having the right amount of alcohol in an oud bruin is probably the easiest way to keep the sourness in check. The right amount of alcohol, sourness, and residual malt sweetness are the keys to an excellent oud bruin.

I prefer to initially ferment the beer using neutral ale yeast. Once it has mostly fermented, I add the souring culture. The timing of the addition can make a difference in the final beer. If you add the culture early and the conditions are right, it can end up a bit too sour for the style, more like Flanders red ale. If you add the culture late and the conditions aren't right for the organisms, the sourness will take a very long time to develop, or the sourness may never quite reach the level desired. Knowing the right moment to add the culture is something you will develop over several batches, with personal preference playing a big part in the timing. For me, the right time is when the beer is still fermenting but has slowed down considerably. I rack it to a second vessel, being careful to minimize oxygen pick-up, and then I add the souring culture. It is important to keep oxygen to a minimum, especially once there is alcohol in the beer. The more oxygen that gets in, the more acetic acid character it is likely to have. It will take some time for the sourness to become apparent. I like to keep it in a carboy with minimal headspace for about 1 month. At that point I rack to a keg, flush it with carbon dioxide, and store it around 65 to 70° F (18 to 21° C). I check the keg every few weeks, and when it is approaching the level of sourness I want, I move it to cold storage and force carbonate it.

RECIPE: FLANDERS BROWN ALE

OG: 1.070 (17.1 °P)
FG: 1.012 (3.1 °P)
ADF: 82%
IBU: 21
Color: 19 SRM (36 EBC)
Alcohol: 7.7% ABV (6.0% ABW)
Boil: 60 minutes
Pre-Boil Volume: 7 gallons (26.5L)
Pre-Boil Gravity: 1.060 (14.7 °P)

Extract	Weight	Percent
Pilsener LME (2.3 °L)	7.3 lbs. (3.31kg)	57.6
Munich LME (9 °L)	3.0 lbs. (1.36kg)	23.7
Wheat LME (4 °L)	0.5 lb. (227g)	3.9

Steeping Grains		
CaraMunich (60 °L)	0.75 lb. (340g)	5.9
Aromatic (20 °L)	0.5 lb. (227g)	3.9
Special "B" (120 °L)	0.5 lb. (227g)	3.9
Black Malt (600 °L)	2.0 oz. (57g)	1.0

Hops		IBU
Kent Goldings 5% AA, 60 min.	1.1 oz. (31g)	20.5

Yeast
White Labs WLP001 California Ale, Wyeast 1056 American Ale, or Fermentis Safale US-05
Wyeast 3763 Roeselare Blend or White Labs WLP655 Belgian Sour Mix I

Fermentation and Conditioning
Use 13 grams of properly rehydrated dry yeast, 3 liquid yeast packages, or make an appropriate starter. Ferment at 65° F (18° C). When fermentation begins to slow, rack beer to a second container and add the souring culture. The culture will break down and consume the remaining sugars that the yeast did not consume or was unable to consume, adding sourness and character to the beer. Store the beer around 65 to 70° F (18 to 21° C) until the sourness becomes noticeable, then move to cold storage to suppress further development. When finished, carbonate to approximately 2 to 2.5 volumes.

All-Grain Option
Replace the Pilsener extract with 9.75 lbs. (4.42kg) continental Pilsener malt. Replace the wheat extract with 0.5 lb. (227g) wheat malt. Replace the Munich extract with 4 lbs. (1.81kg) Munich malt. Mash at 152° F (67° C). Increase the pre-boil volume as needed to allow a 90-minute boil, which will help reduce DMS in the beer.

STRAIGHT (UNBLENDED) LAMBIC

Complex, sour/acidic, pale, wheat-based ale. This is an advanced style that can be brewed by extract or all-grain methods. Ferments at 68° F (20° C) over the course of 6 to 12 months.

OG	FG	IBU	Color	Alcohol
1.040–1.054	1.001–1.010	0–10	3–7 SRM	5.0–6.5% ABV
(10–13.3 °P)	(0.3–2.6 °P)		6–14 EBC	4–5.1% ABW

Keys to Brewing Lambic:

Make your first lambic on a day of the year you will easily remember. Then each year after that, make lambic on that same day. You want to make this beer every year, so you can make gueuze, and gueuze requires several batches of old and young lambic for blending.

The first time a friend showed me how to make lambic, it was a complex and involved process. The results were fairly good, but I was thinking it wasn't worth the extra trouble. What I found out later is that this is actually a fairly easy beer to brew, not nearly as complex as some folks think. To get good results, follow the example of Steve Piatz. Steve is an accomplished lambic brewer, winning a number of National Homebrew Competition medals for his sour beers. My impression is that he seems to keep everything simple by using liquid lambic cultures, a starter made from the dregs of commercial lambics, and malt extract instead of all grain.

There are three things to keep in mind when making lambic. The first is aged hops, the second is a good culture of yeasts and bacteria, and the third is patience.

Lambic brewers use aged hops for their preservative value. There shouldn't be any hop flavor, aroma or bittering in a lambic, and using aged hops reduces all three. I have heard several suppliers mention that they might start providing aged hops. If you are not able to find aged hops, it is pretty easy to age them yourself if you have enough time. Place whole hops loose in a paper bag and set it in a dry, warm location (an attic often works well). Wait 6 months to a couple of years, depending on temperature and humidity, and you've got aged hops. If the hops smell cheesy or rancid, then they are not done yet or have gone bad.

The liquid lambic cultures available from Wyeast and White Labs can make an excellent beer. Once the wort is inoculated, the conditions affect how long it takes to develop and help determine the beer's character. Just like fermentation temperature affects the character of an American pale ale, the temperature affects the types of flavors and aromas the bacteria and yeast create in a lambic. I like to find a relatively cool and dark area of my home with a steady temperature throughout the day. A temperature shift over time with the changing seasons is not a problem. However, large daily temperature swings will negatively affect the results, so try to find a spot that doesn't change too much throughout the day. I like a temperature around 65 to 70° F (18 to 21° C) for my lambic. If you're impatient, you can go with a higher temperature of up to 80° F (27° C), and the beer will finish in as little as a couple of months, but the results will usually be one-dimensional, heavily favoring one character of the culture over another. The taste will not be nearly as complex and interesting. As the beer sits, a pellicle will form over the surface. At some point the pellicle usually falls from the surface on its own, which is a good general indicator that the beer is done.

I have made lambic in plastic buckets, but the plastic can allow a little too much oxygen through to the beer. It is important to make sure it doesn't end up with an acetic (vinegar) character, which is inappropriate for this style. (See Flanders Red for controlling the rate of oxygen ingress.)

Probably the most important thing to keep in mind is to have patience. A great lambic can't be rushed. Once the beer is finished, it can be served as-is, uncarbonated. However, it will continue to develop for several years. The *Brettanomyces* character will gain a foothold and will create a beautiful complexity over time. If you brew at least one lambic per year, you'll soon have a selection to choose from for blending or making fruit lambic.

RECIPE: LAMBICUS PIATZII

While this recipe is loosely based on the methods of Steve Piatz, he does a few things differently. Steve prefers dry malt extract, because it is lighter in color than liquid extract. He also adds about 3.5 ounces (100g) of maltodextrin per batch, to ensure that there is something left for the *Brettanomyces* to slowly consume.

OG: 1.053 (13.1 °P)
FG: 1.006 (1.5 °P)
ADF: 89%
IBU: ~5
Color: 4 SRM (9 EBC)
Alcohol: 6.2% ABV (4.9% ABW)
Boil: 90 minutes
Pre-Boil Volume: 7.7 gallons (29.3L)
Pre-Boil Gravity: 1.041 (10.3 °P)

Extract	Weight	Percent
Wheat LME (4 °L)	5.0 lbs. (2.26kg)	54.9
Pilsener LME (2.3 °L)	4.1 lbs. (1.86kg)	45.1

Hops		IBU
Aged Hops, 90 min.	3.0 oz. (85g)	~5

Yeast
White Labs WLP001 California Ale, Wyeast 1056 American Ale, or Fermentis Safale US-05
White Labs WLP655 Belgian Sour Mix 1 or Wyeast 5278 Belgian Lambic Blend

Fermentation and Conditioning
Begin fermenting the wort with a small amount of neutral ale yeast around 68 °F (20 °C). Use 5 grams of dry yeast or 1 liquid yeast package without a starter. After a week add the liquid lambic culture from either Wyeast or White Labs and optionally, a starter made from the dregs of commercial lambic. Find an area where the temperatures aver-

age around 68 °F (20 °C) over the course of a year. A thick mat called a pellicle will form on the surface of the beer. Eventually the pellicle will fall back into the beer and it is ready for packaging. This will take about 6 months to 1 year. It is possible for the pellicle to remain intact much longer if the environment is very still and vibration free. If a sample tastes like it is ready, you can ignore the pellicle and bottle or keg your beer. In any case, don't rush the process. When finished, it is appropriate to serve the beer uncarbonated. If you wish to carbonate it, carbonation should be minimal, approximately 1 to 1.5 volumes.

All-Grain Option
Replace the Pilsener extract with 7.5 lbs. (3.4kg) continental Pilsener malt. Replace the wheat extract with 5 lbs. (2.26kg) flaked wheat. Dough in at 113° F (45° C) for 15 minutes. Perform a rest at 122° F (50° C) for 15 minutes, 149° F (65° C) for 45 minutes, and 158° F (70° C) for 30 minutes. Raise to a mashout temperature of 169° F (76° C) and then sparge with 190° F (88° C) water.

GUEUZE

Complex, pleasantly sour/acidic, balanced, pale, wheat-based ale. This is an advanced style that can be brewed by extract or all-grain methods. Ferments at 68° F (20° C) over the course of a year and requires multiple batches over the course of several years for blending.

OG	FG	IBU	Color	Alcohol
1.040–1.060	1.000–1.006	0–10	3–7 SRM	5.0–8.0% ABV
(10–14.7 °P)	(0–1.5 °P)		6–14 EBC	4–6.3% ABW

Keys to Brewing Gueuze:

Gueuze is a blended beer, made by mixing portions of young and old lambics to create the best complexity and balance of the individual beers. It is also highly carbonated, whereas lambic is uncarbonated. The blending process relies on skill to create that magical experience of flavors, aromas, and textures.

First you are going to need to brew at least one lambic a year for several years. Yes, this is a lot of work, but the results can be incredible. I like to brew lambics every year at the end of my "brewing season." Every so often, I pull out the lambics, young and old, and try some blending. The trick of crafting a great gueuze is a little trial and error and lots of patience.

Start by setting up your blending/tasting area. It should be free from distractions, strong aromas, and so forth. Make sure you have plenty of sample cups, accurate measuring instruments, water and unsalted crackers to cleanse your palate, and something for taking notes.

Taste each of the lambics, taking notes on all aspects of the beer. Note the intensity level of each flavor and aroma. Cleanse your palate between beers. Take your time. Once you have gone through all of the beers, decide on which one will be the "base" for your gueuze. I like to pick the beer with the softest, broadest flavors—one that isn't too prominent in any one area. Then from the remaining beers, decide which flavors and aromas will give the base beer some highlights in any bland areas. The idea is to create a complex, interesting beer without one character completely overwhelming the others.

Measure a given amount of the base beer (perhaps 100ml) and then add in measured doses of the other beers to enhance the desired character. The beer you add might be anywhere from 1ml to 100ml, depending on how prominent the flavor or aroma is that you're trying to introduce to the base beer. As you work, smell and taste the beer. If something goes wrong, start over. Don't try to fix it by dumping more beer into something that doesn't taste good.

Here is the most important tip: you cannot mask bad flavors or aromas. It just doesn't work. You need to start with good beers in the first place. Just like you can't take a beer that went bad and call it "Belgian," you can't blend bad lambics into a good gueuze.

Once you have the right measurements, step it up to the full size and taste again. If everything is good, add priming sugar and yeast to carbonate the beer to approximately 4 volumes. If you bottle it, use caution and champagne-type bottles that can handle the pressure. Exploding bottles can kill.

FRUIT LAMBIC

Complex, fruity, pleasantly sour/acidic, balanced, pale, wheat-based ale fermented by a variety of Belgian microbiota. This is a lambic with fruit, not just a fruit beer. This is an advanced style that can be brewed by extract or all-grain methods. Ferments at 68° F (20° C) over the course of several years.

OG	FG	IBU	Color	Alcohol
1.040–1.060	1.000–1.010	0–10	3–7 SRM	5.0–7.0% ABV
(10–14.7 °P)	(0–2.6 °P)		6–14 EBC	4–5.5% ABW

Keys to Brewing Fruit Lambic:

Even though there are some very sweet fruit lambics on the market, this shouldn't be a sweet beer. A great fruit lambic depends on a great base lambic. To make a fruit lambic, make a straight lambic or gueuze from the recipes in this book and add fruit to the beer after the primary sugars have been consumed. The yeast and bacteria will consume the sugars in the fruit. The decision about the type of fruit and how much fruit to add is best made after tasting the beer.

Traditional lambic fruits are tart cherries, raspberries, or Muscat grapes. However, it is possible to use other fruits, with tart, aromatic fruits the best candidates.

It is hard to put too much fruit in a fruit lambic. For your first one, try 5 lbs. (2.26kg) of raspberries per 2.5 gallons (9.5L) of base beer. Once you have added the fruit, let the beer sit on the fruit for 3 to 6 months, tasting along the way. You might need to do some blending to reach the right flavor (see Gueuze).

Once the fruit has been consumed, add priming sugar and yeast to carbonate the beer to approximately 4 volumes. If you bottle it, use caution and champagne-type bottles that can handle the pressure. Exploding bottles can kill.

22 | BELGIAN STRONG ALE

Similar to the Belgian and French ale category, Belgian strong ales have a wide range of character. Perhaps the best way to describe the styles in this category is to say that they are all higher-alcohol beers, with a level of Belgian spicy notes that range from very low to moderately high.

BELGIAN BLONDE ALE

A moderate-strength golden ale with a subtle Belgian complexity, slightly sweet flavor, and dry finish. This is an intermediate style that can be brewed by extract-with-grain or all-grain methods. Ferments from 64 to 68° F (18 to 20° C).

OG	FG	IBU	Color	Alcohol
1.062–1.075	1.008–1.018	15–30	4–7 SRM	6.0–7.5% ABV
(15.2–18.2 °P)	(2.1–4.6 °P)		8–14 EBC	4.7–5.9% ABW

Keys to Brewing Belgian Blonde Ale:
As Belgian strong beers go, Belgian blonde ale is a fairly low-key beer, with subtle spicy, earthy, and fruity notes. To keep the flavors restrained it is important to have good fermentation temperature control. The best results come from starting at a lower temperature, 64° F (18° C), and then letting the temperature rise slowly through the course of fermentation. It is important to let the temperature increase (or to increase it through heating) slowly throughout fermentation to ensure good attenuation and a dry-enough finish. If you are an extract brewer and are having difficulty getting sufficient attenuation, replace some of the Pilsener or wheat extract with sugar. All-grain brewers can increase the fermentability of the wort by lowering the mash temperature.

Since this beer doesn't have a lot of specialty malts to hide behind, it is important to use good-quality Pilsener malt extract. If you're an all-grain brewer, try to use Belgian Pilsener malt or at the very least use continental Pilsener malt. While it may seem like it isn't worth the trouble, for a beer like this, the source of the malt can make a big difference.

RECIPE: LEFTY BLOND

OG: 1.065 (15.8 °P)
FG: 1.012 (3.0 °P)
ADF: 81%
IBU: 25
Color: 5 SRM (9 EBC)
Alcohol: 7.0% ABV (5.5% ABW)
Boil: 60 minutes
Pre-Boil Volume: 7 gallons (26.5L)
Pre-Boil Gravity: 1.055 (13.6 °P)

Extract	Weight	Percent
Pilsener LME (2.3 °L)	7.75 lbs. (3.51kg)	72.1
Cane Sugar (0 °L)	1.5 lbs. (0.68kg)	14.0
Wheat LME (4 °L)	1.0 lb. (0.45kg)	9.3

Steeping Grains		
Aromatic (20 °L)	0.5 lb. (227g)	4.7

Hops		IBU
Hallertau 4% AA, 60 min.	1.6 oz. (45g)	24.5

Yeast
White Labs WLP500 Trappist Ale, Wyeast 1214 Belgian Ale, or Fermentis Safbrew T-58

Fermentation and Conditioning
Use 12 grams of properly rehydrated dry yeast, 2.5 liquid yeast packages, or make an appropriate starter. Pitch yeast at 64° F (18° C), and let the temperature rise slowly to 68° F (20° C) over the course of 1 week. When finished, carbonate the beer to approximately 3 to 4 volumes and

allow to lager for 1 month at 45 to 50° F (7 to 10° C)

All-Grain Option

Replace the Pilsener extract with 11 lbs. (5kg) continental Pilsener malt. Replace the wheat extract with 0.5 lb. (227g) wheat malt. Mash at 150° F (66° C). Increase the pre-boil volume as needed to allow a 90-minute boil, which will help reduce DMS in the beer.

BELGIAN DUBBEL

A deep reddish, moderately strong, malty, complex Belgian ale. This is an intermediate style that can be brewed by extract-with-grain or all-grain methods. Ferments from 64 to 70° F (18 to 21° C).

OG	FG	IBU	Color	Alcohol
1.062–1.075	1.008–1.018	15–25	10–17 SRM	6.0–7.6% ABV
(15.2–18.2 °P)	(2.0–4.6 °P)		20–33 EBC	4.7–6.0% ABW

Keys to Brewing Belgian Dubbel:

Well-made Belgian beers do not have a solvency, hot, or harsh alcohol character. The alcohol, no matter how big, should not taste like paint thinner. To keep the alcohol from being hot, it is important to have good fermentation temperature control, pitch the proper amount of yeast, and not over-oxygenate the wort. One addition of oxygen at pitching time is plenty, and there is no need to add additional oxygen later if the proper amount of yeast was pitched.

Good fermentation temperature control also produces the right kind of fruit esters for this style. The best results come from pitching the yeast at a lower temperature, in this case 64° F (18° C), and then letting the temperature rise slowly through the course of fermentation. It is important to let the temperature increase (or to increase it through heating) throughout fermentation to ensure good attenuation and a dry-enough finish. If you are an extract brewer and are having difficulty getting sufficient attenuation, replace a little more Pilsener extract with sugar. All-grain brewers can increase the fermentability of the wort by lowering the mash temperature.

While the recipe features several specialty malts, it is important to note the use of dark Belgian candi syrup. This is a byproduct of the Belgian candi sugarmaking process and has a more intense flavor and aroma than the Belgian dark rock candi you might find available. If you are unable to get the dark Belgian candi syrup, you can play around with the amount of Special "B" malt and perhaps add some molasses to compensate. However, it is worth the expense to get dark Belgian candi syrup, if you can find it.

RECIPE: BLACK SCAPULAR DUBBEL

OG: 1.064 (15.7 °P)
FG: 1.012 (3.0 °P)
ADF: 81%
IBU: 23
Color: 15 SRM (29 EBC)
Alcohol: 6.9% ABV (5.4% ABW)
Boil: 60 minutes
Pre-Boil Volume: 7 gallons (26.5L)
Pre-Boil Gravity: 1.054 (13.4 °P)

Extract	Weight	Percent
Pilsener LME (2.3 °L)	7.8 lbs. (3.53kg)	68.7
Munich LME (9 °L)	0.8 lb. (363g)	7.0
Dark Belgian Candi Syrup (~60 °L)	0.75 lb. (340g)	6.6
Cane Sugar (0 °L)	0.5 lb. (227g)	4.4

Steeping Grains		
Aromatic (20 °L)	0.5 lb. (227g)	4.4
CaraMunich (60 °L)	0.5 lb. (227g)	4.4
Special "B" (120 °L)	0.5 lb. (227g)	4.4

Hops		IBU
Tettnang 4% AA, 60 min.	1.5 oz. (43g)	23

Yeast
White Labs WLP530 Abbey Ale or Wyeast 3787 Trappist High Gravity

Fermentation and Conditioning
Use 12 grams of properly rehydrated dry yeast, 2.5 liquid yeast packages, or make an appropriate starter. Pitch yeast at 64° F (18° C) and let the temperature rise slowly to 70° F (21° C) over the course of 1 week. When finished, carbonate the beer to approximately 3 to 4 volumes and allow to lager for 1 month at 45 to 50° F (7 to 10° C)

All-Grain Option

Replace the Pilsener extract with 10.6 lbs. (4.81kg) continental Pilsener malt. Replace the Munich extract with 1 lb. (0.45kg) Munich malt. Mash at 149° F (65° C). With the low mash temperature, you may need to lengthen the rest time to 90 minutes to get full conversion. Also increase the pre-boil volume as needed to allow a 90-minute boil, which will help reduce DMS in the beer.

BELGIAN TRIPEL

A golden, complex, strong Belgian ale with a fuller body and finish than Belgian golden strong ale. This is an intermediate style that can be brewed by extract-with-grain or all-grain methods. Ferments from 64 to 70° F (18 to 21° C).

OG	FG	IBU	Color	Alcohol
1.075–1.085	1.008–1.014	20–40	4.5–7 SRM	7.5–9.5% ABV
(18.2–20.5 °P)	(2.0–3.6 °P)		9–14 EBC	5.9–7.5% ABW

Keys to Brewing Belgian Tripel:

You may have noticed that the grain bills and fermentation temperatures of the pale styles in this category are fairly similar. The biggest difference from beer to beer is mainly the starting gravity and yeast strain used. The brewing process has an effect, too, but fermentation is the most critical aspect for brewing many Belgian beers.

As with the other beers in this category, it is important to have good fermentation temperature control and to pitch the proper amount of yeast. Good temperature control will keep the alcohol from being solventy, it will control the spicy phenols and fruity esters, and it will help with the proper level of attenuation. The best results come from pitching the yeast at a lower temperature, in this case 64° F (18° C), and then letting the temperature rise slowly through the course of fermentation. It is important to let the temperature increase (or to increase it through heating) throughout fermentation to ensure good attenuation and a dry-enough finish. If you are an extract brewer and are having difficulty getting sufficient attenuation, replace a little more Pilsener extract with sugar. All-grain brewers can increase the fermentability of the wort by lowering the mash temperature.

As this beer doesn't have a lot of specialty malts to hide behind, it is also important to use good-quality Pilsener malt extract. If you're an all-grain brewer, try to use Belgian Pilsener malt or at the very least use continental Pilsener malt. While it may seem like it isn't worth the trouble, for a beer like this the source of the malt can make quite a difference.

RECIPE: STRICT OBSERVANCE TRIPEL

OG: 1.081 (19.5 °P)
FG: 1.012 (3.0 °P)
ADF: 85%
IBU: 34
Color: 4.5 SRM (9 EBC)
Alcohol: 9.2% ABV (7.2% ABW)
Boil: 60 minutes
Pre-Boil Volume: 7 gallons (26.5L)
Pre-Boil Gravity: 1.063 (15.4 °P)

Extract	Weight	Percent
Pilsener LME (2.3 °L)	10.4 lbs. (4.71kg)	79.1
Cane Sugar (0 °L)	2.5 lbs. (1.13kg)	19.0

Steeping Grains		
Aromatic (20 °L)	0.25 lb. (113g)	1.9

Hops		IBU
Tetnang 4% AA, 60 min.	2.3 oz. (65g)	32.7
Czech Saaz 3.5% AA, 10 min.	0.5 oz. (14g)	1.2

Yeast
White Labs WLP530 Abbey Ale, Wyeast 3787 Trappist High Gravity, or
Fermentis Safbrew T-58

Fermentation and Conditioning
Use 15 grams of properly rehydrated dry yeast, 3 liquid yeast packages,
or make an appropriate starter. Pitch yeast at 64° F (18° C), and let the
temperature rise slowly to 70° F (21° C) over the course of 1 week.
When finished, carbonate the beer to approximately 3 to 4 volumes and
allow to lager for 1 month at 45 to 50° F (7 to 10° C).

All-Grain Option
Replace the Pilsener extract with 14 lbs. (6.35kg) continental Pilsener
malt. Mash at 149° F (65° C). With the low mash temperature, you may
need to lengthen the rest time to 90 minutes to get full conversion. Also

increase the pre-boil volume as needed to allow a 90-minute boil, which will help reduce DMS in the beer.

BELGIAN GOLDEN STRONG ALE

A golden, complex, effervescent strong ale with a sweet start and a crisp, dry finish. This is an intermediate style that can be brewed by extract-with-grain or all-grain methods. Ferments from 64 to 82° F (18 to 28° C).

OG	FG	IBU	Color	Alcohol
1.070–1.095	1.005–1.016	22–35	3–6 SRM	7.5–10.5% ABV
(17.1–22.7 °P)	(1.3–4.1 °P)		6–12 EBC	5.9–8.3% ABW

Keys to Brewing Belgian Golden Strong Ale:

Perhaps the most important aspect of brewing this beer is getting a crisp, dry finish. While it may seem like there is a lot of plain sugar in the recipe, it is the right amount for this beer. Make sure you are using the yeast specified below, if you want to get the same pear notes that the classic beer of this style exhibits so well.

RECIPE: IT'S ALL IN THE DETAILS

As they say, the devil is in the details.

OG: 1.072 (17.5 °P)
FG: 1.007 (1.9 °P)
ADF: 89%
IBU: 32
Color: 3 SRM (6 EBC)
Alcohol: 8.5% ABV (6.7% ABW)
Boil: 90 minutes
Pre-Boil Volume: 7.7 gallons (29.3L)
Pre-Boil Gravity: 1.056 (13.8 °P)

Extract	Weight	Percent
Pilsener LME (2.3 °L)	8.4 lbs. (3.81kg)	73.7
Cane Sugar (0 °L)	3.0 lbs. (1.36kg)	26.3

Hops		IBU
Czech Saaz 3.5% AA, 90 min.	2.25 oz. (64g)	32.0

Yeast

White Labs WLP570 Belgian Golden Ale, Wyeast 1388 Belgian Strong Ale, or Fermentis Safbrew T-58

Fermentation and Conditioning

Use 14 grams of properly rehydrated dry yeast, 3 liquid yeast packages, or make an appropriate starter. Pitch yeast at 64° F (18° C), and let the temperature rise slowly to 82° F (28° C) over the course of 1 week. When finished, carbonate the beer to approximately 4 volumes and serve at 45 to 50° F (7 to 10° C).

All-Grain Option

Replace the Pilsener extract with 11 lbs. (5kg) continental Pilsener malt. Mash at 149° F (65° C). With the low mash temperature, you may need to lengthen the rest time to 90 minutes to get full conversion. Also increase the pre-boil volume as needed to allow a 90-minute boil, which will help reduce DMS in the beer.

BELGIAN DARK STRONG ALE

A dark, very rich, strong Belgian ale. It is complex, rich, smooth, and dangerous. This is an intermediate style that can be brewed by extract-with-grain or all-grain methods. Ferments from 68 to 72° F (20 to 22° C).

OG	FG	IBU	Color	Alcohol
1.075–1.110	1.010–1.024	20–35	12–22 SRM	8.0–11% ABV
(18.2–25.9 °P)	(2.6–6.1 °P)		24–43 EBC	6.3–8.7% ABW

Keys to Brewing Belgian Dark Strong Ale:

This is a rich, complex beer with a noticeable malty sweetness. As with other beers in this category, it is important to control fermentation temperatures. This keeps the alcohol from being solventy, hot, or harsh and it helps develop the proper profile of esters and phenols.

RECIPE: BREW LIKE A HOMEBREWER

This beer recently took first place in the final round of the National Homebrew Competition. I heard from several people that it came close to being the Best of Show beer also. I later received an email from Stan Hieronymus, author of the stellar book *Brew Like a Monk*. As a judge, Stan really seemed to have enjoyed the beer, but he was surprised to find out that the grain bill for this beer was quite complex. My early recipes, like those of many homebrewers, were overly complex. Overly complex recipes are often overwhelming, and the flavors are muddy. I learned over time to simplify many of my recipes, and they are much better for it.

Yet for some reason, there are a few early recipes that defy simplification. Any attempts to make them less complex produce unsatisfactory results, and I have to go back to the originals. This recipe is a good example of what I am talking about. It works well as-is, and changes seem to do nothing good for it. I am really glad I came up with this recipe when I did, or what I know today might have stopped me from adding that one extra grain.

OG: 1.103 (24.4 °P)
FG: 1.024 (6.0 °P)
ADF: 75%
IBU: 31
Color: 20 SRM (39 EBC)
Alcohol: 10.6% ABV (8.2% ABW)
Boil: 60 minutes
Pre-Boil Volume: 7 gallons (26.5L)
Pre-Boil Gravity: 1.087 (21.0 °P)

Extract	Weight	Percent
Pilsener LME (2.3 °L)	11.5 lbs. (5.21kg)	62.2
Munich LME (9 °L)	2.0 lbs. (0.90kg)	10.8
Cane Sugar (0 °L)	1.0 lb. (0.45kg)	5.4
Wheat LME (4 °L)	0.5 lb. (227g)	2.7

Steeping Grains		
Aromatic (20 °L)	1.0 lb. (0.45kg)	5.4
CaraMunich (60 °L)	1.0 lb. (0.45kg)	5.4
Special "B" (120 °L)	1.0 lb. (0.45kg)	5.4
Melanoidin (28 °L)	0.5 lb. (227g)	2.7

Hops		IBU
Hallertau 4% AA, 60 min.	2.42 oz. (69g)	31.4

Yeast
White Labs WLP530 Abbey Ale IV, Wyeast 1762 Belgian Abbey II, or
Fermentis Safbrew T-58

Fermentation and Conditioning
Use 19 grams of properly rehydrated dry yeast, 4 liquid yeast packages,
or make an appropriate starter. Begin fermentation at 68° F (20° C)
slowly raising the temperature to 72° F (22° C) by the last third of
fermentation. When finished, carbonate the beer to approximately 2.5 to
3 volumes.

All-Grain Option

Replace the Pilsener extract with 15 lbs. (6.8kg) continental Pilsener malt. Replace the Munich extract with 3 lbs. (1.36kg) Munich malt. Replace the wheat extract with 0.5 lb. (227g) wheat malt. Mash at 153° F (67° C). Increase the pre-boil volume as needed to allow a 90-minute boil, which will help reduce DMS in the beer.

23 | STRONG ALE

All of the styles in this category have two things in common: an elevated level of sweetness, and alcohol. These are considered big beers, something that you would sip by the fire on a cold winter night. They tend to age gracefully, and with a little knowledge, they are not that difficult to brew well.

OLD ALE

An ale of significant alcoholic strength, bigger than strong bitters and brown porters, although usually not as strong or rich as barley wine. It is usually tilted toward a sweeter, maltier balance. This is an intermediate style that can be brewed by extract-with-grain or all-grain methods. Ferments at 68° F (20° C).

OG	FG	IBU	Color	Alcohol
1.060–1.090	1.015–1.022	30–60	10–22 SRM	6.0–9.0% ABV
(14.7–21.6 °P)	(3.8–5.6 °P)		25–57 EBC	4.7–7.0% ABW

Keys to Brewing Old Ale:
I am a big fan of the smaller, drier, and more complex examples of this style, like Theakston Old Peculier or Greene King Olde Suffolk. Both have a wonderfully vinous quality underlying the beer along with some subtle sourness and other funky stuff going on. However, these beers are just one end of the style, and many people don't seem to think they are typical old ales. It seems the majority of folks like the bigger, sweeter beers that have far less character from aging. I like my old ales to have some beer in them that has been around for a few years. Many of the

commercial examples are never aged before being released to the public. As an amateur brewer, you have the option to do what you wish. Age your old ale, and let it develop some complexity with time.

A friend once told me that you could not make old ale without treacle. I must admit it adds a distinct flavor and aroma that is apparent in some of the commercial examples. While some people consider treacle to be just the British word for molasses, there are many products that are sold as treacle or molasses, and they are all slightly different. Treacle appropriate for brewing old ale is sometimes referred to as black treacle. It is dark, sweet, and full of highly caramelized notes. Some people say that blackstrap molasses is an acceptable substitute. My preference is for Lyle's Black Treacle. If your homebrew shop doesn't happen to carry it, you can find it at many English specialty shops. If you can't find it, you can omit it from the recipe below and add 0.5 lb. (227g) of crystal 150 °L malt instead. The beer won't be the same, but it won't be five dollars for a can of treacle, either.

While a number of examples of old ale can be on the sweeter side, the beer still needs a decent level of attenuation. Select an English yeast strain that is on the higher side of attenuation, or swap out a small amount of base malt with corn sugar to help reach the proper finishing gravity. And don't worry, it isn't a sin to have some adjuncts in a high-gravity English-type beer.

Once the beer is ready, it can be aged in bulk or by the bottle. While a slight bit of wood character from barrel aging is OK, too much wood character will make it a wood-aged beer. I like to age my old ale in a keg. If you want a wood character, add a small amount of oak cubes, perhaps 1 oz. (28g), for the first month or so to give it a subtle background wood character.

If you want to enter competitions with this beer style, I would advise against adding any lactic or *Brettanomyces* character, as most judges don't seem to expect it. It is possible to dose the beer with a pure culture, but the end result needs to be very subtle. This can be tricky, because once the alcohol goes over 8% ABV, the lactic acid bacteria generally won't work anymore. If you add the culture too early, the beer can end up a bit too sour. The best method is to set aside 2 quarts (~2L) of wort from the brew day and sour that separately. Once it obtains a nice strong sour or *Brettanomyces* character, pasteurize it by heating it to higher than 170° F (67° C) and adding a small portion to the old ale.

RECIPE: OLD TREACLE MINE

I don't think I really appreciated how wonderful real ale could be until I spent a week in Edinburgh, Scotland. I had found a pub with Theakston's Old Peculier on cask. This wonderfully complex ale is one of my all-time favorites. Each evening, after the conference sessions ended, I would walk over to the pub and have a pint or two. The beauty of cask ale is that it is a living thing, and it is slightly different at each pub that serves it. The temperature, the surrounding air, the handling all make a difference in real ale, and the cask of beer will change subtly over the day or two that it takes to finish it. This recipe doesn't make an Old Peculier clone, but it does make a nice, rich old ale.

OG: 1.093 (22.2 °P)
FG: 1.022 (5.7 °P)
ADF: 74%
IBU: 66
Color: 21 SRM (42 EBC)
Alcohol: 9.0% ABV (7.0% ABW)
Boil: 90 minutes
Pre-Boil Volume: 7.7 gallons (29.3L)
Pre-Boil Gravity: 1.072 (17.5 °P)

Extract	Weight	Percent
English Pale Ale LME (3.5 °L)	14.0 lbs. (6.35kg)	90.3
Black Treacle (100 °L)	0.5 lb. (227g)	3.2

Steeping Grains		
Crystal (80 °L)	0.75 lb. (340g)	4.8
Black Patent Malt (525 °L)	0.25 lb. (113g)	1.6

Hops		IBU
Horizon 13% AA, 60 min.	1.5 oz. (43g)	65.9

Yeast
White Labs WLP013 London Ale, Wyeast 1028 London Ale, or Danstar Nottingham

Fermentation and Conditioning
Use 17 grams of properly rehydrated dry yeast, 3.5 liquid yeast packages, or make an appropriate starter. Ferment at 68° F (20° C). When finished, carbonate the beer to approximately 2 volumes.

All-Grain Option
Replace the English extract with 19.5 lbs. (8.84kg) British pale ale malt. Mash at 152 °F (67° C). The mash volume for this beer, even at a thick 1 qt./lb. (2L/kg), will be almost 7 gallons (26 liters). If your brew system is unable to fit all of the base grain, feel free to replace up to half of the American two-row malt with light extract. The flavor difference is minimal in such a big-flavored beer, especially with the high-quality extracts available today.

ENGLISH BARLEY WINE

The richest and strongest of the English ales. A showcase of malty richness and complex, intense flavors. This is an intermediate style that can be brewed by extract-with-grain or all-grain methods. Ferments at 68 to 70° F (20 to 21° C).

OG	FG	IBU	Color	Alcohol
1.080–1.120	1.018–1.030	35–70	8–22 SRM	8.0–12% ABV
(19.3–28.1 °P)	(4.6–7.6 °P)		20–57 EBC	6.3–9.5% ABW

Keys to Brewing English Barley Wine:

As complex as some examples of this style can be, English barley wine is a very straightforward beer to make.

The recipe is simple, with the key factors being well-modified English pale ale malt for the backbone and some crystal malt for color and some sweetness. The hops need to be English as well, since other varieties, even for the bittering addition, can seem out of place.

If you want to develop more color and more melanoidin-based flavors and aromas, don't be afraid to start with a larger pre-boil volume so you can boil the wort for 2 hours or more. This develops a unique taste, which can't be had by grain additions alone. Just keep the hop addition times the same; don't make them longer.

The ingredient that needs the most attention is the yeast. Select an English yeast strain with plenty of character, but make sure it is one of the more attenuative yeasts. If not, you will need to use corn sugar in place of some base malt to help the beer reach the proper level of attenuation.

Once this beer is finished fermenting, a long aging period does wonderful things for it. Yes, you might be tempted to drink it just a couple of weeks after pitching the yeast, but try to set aside as much as you can, and enjoy it here and there over the years.

RECIPE: HARD AND HARDY

OG: 1.100 (23.8 °P)
FG: 1.024 (6.0 °P)
ADF: 75%
IBU: 63
Color: 15 SRM (29 EBC)
Alcohol: 10.2% ABV (7.9% ABW)
Boil: 60 minutes
Pre-Boil Volume: 7 gallons (26.5L)
Pre-Boil Gravity: 1.085 (20.5 °P)

Extract	Weight	Percent
English Pale Ale LME (3.5 °L)	15.5 lbs. (7.03kg)	92.5

Steeping Grains		
CaraMunich (60 °L)	10.0 oz. (284g)	3.7
Crystal (120 °L)	10.0 oz. (284g)	3.7

Hops		IBU
Horizon 13% AA, 60 min.	1.4 oz. (40g)	59.7
Kent Goldings 5% AA, 20 min.	0.6 oz. (17g)	3.3
Kent Goldings 5% AA, 0 min.	0.6 oz. (17g)	0

Yeast
White Labs WLP013 London Ale, Wyeast 1028 London Ale, or Danstar Nottingham

Fermentation and Conditioning
Use 18 grams of properly rehydrated dry yeast, 4 liquid yeast packages, or make an appropriate starter. Ferment at 68 ° F (20° C) to start, raising the temperature gradually to 70° F (21° C) for the last third of fermentation. When finished, carbonate the beer to approximately 1.5 to 2 volumes.

All-Grain Option
Replace the English extract with 21.5 lbs. (9.75kg) British pale ale malt. Mash at 150 °F (66 °C). The mash volume for this beer, even at a thick 1 qt./lb. (2 L/kg), will be about 7.5 gallons (29 liters). If your brew system is unable to fit

all of the base grain, feel free to replace up to half of the American two-row malt with light extract. The flavor difference is minimal in such a big-flavored beer, especially with the high-quality extracts available today. Increase the pre-boil volume as needed to allow a 90-minute boil.

AMERICAN BARLEY WINE

A well-hopped American interpretation of the richest and strongest of the English ales. This is an intermediate style that can be brewed by extract-with-grain or all-grain methods. Ferments at 68° F (20° C).

OG	FG	IBU	Color	Alcohol
1.080–1.120	1.016–1.030	50–120	10–19 SRM	8.0–12.0% ABV
(19.3–28.1 °P)	(4.1–7.6 °P)		25–49 EBC	6.3–9.5% ABW

Keys to Brewing American Barley Wine:
This is an American interpretation of the barley wine style. It is almost always bigger and hoppier than an English barley wine. Even though it is hoppier, it isn't crazy hoppy like an imperial IPA, and it has a lot more body and residual sweetness.

The key to making a good version of this style is avoiding the three most common pitfalls: not getting enough attenuation, ending up with a syrupy sweet beer; having solvency, hot, or harsh alcohol notes; and a total lack of balance.

While balance is taken care of mainly by the recipe and fermentation, the brewing process is also very important, especially for all-grain brewers. If your wort is in the kettle and you don't have the right pre-boil gravity, make sure to adjust with either some dried malt extract or some water. This is important, because the bittering level of the recipe is designed for the final gravity of the beer. Hop utilization will also change with the wort concentration, so there are multiple reasons to make certain you have the right gravity at both pre- and post-boil.

Controlling the character of the alcohols and getting sufficient attenuation is as easy as pitching enough clean, healthy yeast and proper fermentation temperature control. Make sure the temperature of the beer does not go significantly above or below the recommended temperature. Higher temperatures will result in a hot, solvency alcohol character. A significant drop in temperature can make the yeast stop fermenting, resulting in an underattenuated beer. Try to keep the temperature moderate and steady.

Once this beer is finished fermenting, a long aging period does wonderful things for it. You might be tempted to drink it just a couple of weeks after pitching the yeast, but don't. This beer requires a minimum of 6 months of aging before drinking. Two to 3 years is even better. Be sure to set aside as much as you can in a cool, dark place, and enjoy it slowly over the years.

RECIPE: OLD MONSTER

OG: 1.115 (27.0 °P)
FG: 1.022 (5.5 °P)
ADF: 80%
IBU: 99
Color: 17 SRM (33 EBC)
Alcohol: 12.5% ABV (9.7% ABW)
Boil: 60 minutes
Pre-Boil Volume: 7 gallons (26.5L)
Pre-Boil Gravity: 1.098 (23.3 °P)

Extract	Weight	Percent
Light LME (2.2 °L)	16.7 lbs. (7.57kg)	82.7
Corn Sugar (0 °L)	1.0 lb. (0.45kg)	5.0

Steeping Grains		
Crystal (15 °L)	1.0 lb. (0.45kg)	5.0
Crystal (80 °L)	1.0 lb. (0.45kg)	5.0
Pale Chocolate Malt (200 °L)	0.25 lb. (113g)	1.2
Special "B" (120 °L)	0.25 lb. (113g)	1.2

Hops		IBU
Magnum 13% AA, 60 min.	2.45 oz. (69g)	98.6
Chinook 13% AA, 0 min.	1.0 oz. (28g)	0
Centennial 9% AA, 0 min.	1.5 oz. (43g)	0
Amarillo 9% AA, 0 min.	1.5 oz. (43g)	0

Yeast

White Labs WLP001 California Ale, Wyeast 1056 American Ale, or Fermentis Safale US-05

Fermentation and Conditioning

Use 21 grams of properly rehydrated yeast, 4 liquid yeast packages, or make an appropriate starter. Ferment at 68° F (20° C). When finished, carbonate the beer to approximately 2 to 2.5 volumes.

All-Grain Option

Replace the light extract with 23.2 lbs. (10.52kg) American two-row malt. Mash at 149 °F (65 °C). With the low mash temperature, you may need to lengthen the rest time to 90 minutes to get full conversion.

The mash volume for this beer, even at a thick 1 qt./lb. (2L/kg), will be almost 8.5 gallons (32 liters). If your brew system is unable to fit all of the base grain, feel free to replace up to half of the American two-row malt with light extract. The flavor difference is minimal in such a big-flavored beer, especially with the high-quality extracts available today.

24 | FRUIT BEER

I find it interesting when I run into people who think a "fruit beer" is not a beer. Or they claim it isn't a beer for "real" beer drinkers. Well, that is silly, as there are some really wonderful fruit beers out there. Of course, there are some bad fruit beers, too, but just because you add fruit doesn't all of a sudden make it less of a beer.

FRUIT BEER

> A beer with the distinctive flavor and aroma of fruit well integrated with the beer character. The following recipes are intermediate level and can be brewed by extract-with-grain or all-grain methods. Ferments at 65 to 67° F (18 to 19° C). OG, FG, IBUs, SRM, and ABV will vary depending on the underlying base beer, but the fruit will often be reflected in the color.

Keys to Brewing Fruit Beer:
A lot of people think a fruit beer is a style for beginners to brew. While great fruit beers are not particularly difficult to make, they do require that the brewer make a great base beer first. If the base beer is no good, adding fruit will not make it better. It might help mask some off-flavor or add some character to a beer with little flavor to begin with, but you will never make a truly great fruit beer this way. Great fruit beers are not created by accident, they are carefully crafted with lots of trial and error.

When making a fruit beer, first think about what character (flavor, aroma, mouthfeel, and appearance) you are trying to achieve. I like to use foods that I enjoy to help me decide which fruits might go with different beers. Almost always the food for inspiration is a dessert of some kind—for instance, an apricot pie. What are the key flavors of an apricot pie? Apricots, certainly, but don't forget the pie crust. The crust is bready with some sweetness. What beer style is similar to those pie crust flavors? Perhaps American wheat beer might have some of those pie crust flavors?

Once you have decided which beer style to use and which fruit you want to add, you can use the recipes in this book as the base for your fruit beer. However, you will probably want to make some adjustments. If you are trying to create the impression of a sweet dessert, you will want to make the beer a little sweeter than the standard recipe. Generally, lowering the hop bittering in the beer by 10 to 20 percent will let just the right amount of sweetness come through. The more sour the fruit you use, the more you will want to reduce the bittering level. Keep in mind that if a given batch of fruit has a sweet/sour balance, the sweet is going to ferment out and the sour will be left behind. So pay attention to the amount of sourness, and target your recipe changes to balance it with the right level of malt sweetness. The other recipe adjustment you will want to make is to remove any late hop additions from the recipe. Although there might be some exceptions, the flavors and aromas of hops just don't seem to blend well with most fruits. The only hop additions for most fruit beers should be bittering additions.

The form of the fruit can make quite a difference in the final beer. The most common options are whole fruit (fresh or frozen), fruit purée, and fruit flavoring (extract). I can appreciate some folks' desire to use fresh whole fruit. If you happen to have a tree that produces a lot of great fruit, then this can be a good option. Personally, I find the results of most fresh fruit additions quite variable, often disappointing, and expensive if purchased at the grocery store. Fruit flavoring is convenient and inexpensive, but the flavor does seem a touch artificial in most cases. In side-by-side tests, everyone I have asked has been able to pick out the beer made with fruit flavoring. My preference is canned fruit purée. Many homebrew shops carry canned fruit purée. It is consistent, easy to use, and reasonably priced. The flavor of fruit purée compares well with fresh fruit and is far superior to fruit flavoring.

The amount of fruit needed is going to vary from beer to beer and fruit to fruit. In a beer with very little specialty malt, the fruit character comes through quite well, and usually less fruit is needed. In a beer with a lot of specialty malt or lots of dark malt flavors, it takes a lot more fruit to get the flavor to come through. Of course, the fruits are different, too. Some fruits, such as raspberries, have a very bold flavor and make a larger impact on the beer. Other fruits, like strawberries, have very little impact on a beer, and it takes a lot more for the flavor to be noticeable. A good starting point is about 0.5 lb. (227g) of fruit purée per gallon (3.8L) whether you are using a mild fruit in a mild beer or a bold fruit in a bold beer. If you are adding a milder fruit to a bold beer, using 2 to 4 times the amount of fruit is not unreasonable. If you are using a bold fruit in a mild beer, you might cut the amount of fruit in half. The key is to get a nice balance between the fruit and the beer. You want to be able to detect the fruit easily but not have it overwhelm the other beer flavors and aromas.

Do not add fruit to the boil. This tends to drive off much of the more delicate fruit character, gives the fruit a cooked flavor, and will often cause a pectin haze in the beer. I prefer to add fruit to the beer when the most active part of fermentation is beginning to slow. If you are using whole fruit, you might want to quickly parboil it to kill off any organisms and then freeze it to break down the cell walls. I add the fruit to another fermenter and transfer the beer onto it for a secondary fermentation. The longer the beer sits on the fruit, the more fruit flavor in the finished beer. If you are using purée or fruit flavoring extract, there is no concern over sanitation; you can add it directly to the secondary fermenter.

RECIPE: APRICOT WHEAT

OG: 1.050 (12.5 °P) / 1.052 (13.0 °P) with fruit
FG: 1.013 (3.3 °P)
ADF: 75%
IBU: 18
Color: 6 SRM (11 EBC)
Alcohol: 5.2% ABV (4.1% ABW)
Boil: 60 minutes
Pre-Boil Volume: 7 gallons (26.5L)
Pre-Boil Gravity: 1.043 (10.7 °P)

Extract	Weight	Percent
Wheat LME (4 °L)	8.3 lbs. (3.76kg)	94.3

Steeping Grains		
Crystal (15 °L)	0.5 lb. (227g)	5.7

Extras		
Apricot Purée	3.0 lbs. (1.36kg)	

Hops		IBU
Willamette 5% AA for 60 min.	0.85 oz. (24g)	18.2

Yeast

White Labs WLP320 American Hefeweizen, Wyeast 1010 American Wheat, or Fermentis Safale US-05

Fermentation and Conditioning

Use 10 grams of properly rehydrated dry yeast, 2 liquid yeast packages, or make an appropriate starter. Ferment at 65° F (18° C). When initial fermentation begins to slow, add apricot purée to a second fermenter and carefully rack the beer onto the fruit. Fermentation should pick up again as the yeast consumes the fructose in the fruit purée. Once fermentation finishes, carbonate the beer to approximately 2.5 to 3 volumes.

All-Grain Option

Replace the wheat extract with 5.6 lbs. (2.54kg) American two-row malt and 5.6 lbs. (2.54kg) wheat malt. Mash at 154° F (68° C).

RECIPE: RASPBERRY ROBUST PORTER

OG: 1.064 (15.7 °P) / 1.066 (16.2 °P) with fruit
FG: 1.017 (4.4 °P)
ADF: 73%
IBU: 31
Color: 35 SRM (69 EBC)
Alcohol: 6.5% ABV (5.0% ABW)
Boil: 60 minutes
Pre-Boil Volume: 7 gallons (26.5L)
Pre-Boil Gravity: 1.055 (13.5 °P)

Extract	Weight	Percent
Light LME (2.2 °L)	8.6 lbs. (3.9kg)	72.6
Munich LME (9 °L)	1.0 lb. (0.45kg)	8.4

Steeping Grains		
Crystal (40 °L)	1.0 lb. (0.45kg)	8.4
Chocolate Malt (350 °L)	0.75 lb. (340g)	6.3
Black Patent Malt (525 °L)	0.5 lb. (227g)	4.2

Extras		
Raspberry Purée	3.0 lbs. (1.36kg)	

Hops		IBU
Kent Goldings 5% AA, 60 min.	1.6 oz. (45g)	30.7

Yeast
White Labs WLP001 California Ale, Wyeast 1056 American Ale, or Fermentis Safale US-05

Fermentation and Conditioning
Use 12 grams of properly rehydrated dry yeast, 2.5 liquid yeast packages, or make an appropriate starter. Ferment at 67° F (19° C). When initial fermentation begins to slow, add raspberry purée to a second fermenter and carefully rack the beer onto the fruit. Fermentation should pick up again as the yeast consumes the fructose in the fruit purée. Once fermentation finishes, carbonate the beer to approximately 2 to 2.5 volumes.

All-Grain Option

Replace the light extract with 11.75 lbs. (5.33kg) American two-row malt. Replace the Munich extract with 1.5 lbs. (0.68kg) Munich malt. Mash at 154° F (68° C).

25 | SPICE, HERB, OR VEGETABLE BEER

The most common examples of this category are seasonal or holiday-type beers, like pumpkin ale or Christmas spiced beer. However, you might find a chile beer, a coffee beer, or something completely extraordinary, because spice, herb, and vegetable beers are only limited by a brewer's imagination.

SPICE, HERB, OR VEGETABLE BEER

A beer with the distinctive flavor and aroma of the spice, herb, or vegetable well integrated with the character of the beer. The recipes below are intermediate level and can be brewed by extract-with-grain or all-grain methods. Ferments at 67° F (19° C). OG, FG, IBUs, SRM, and ABV will vary depending on the underlying base beer.

Keys to Brewing Spice, Herb, or Vegetable Beer:
You can take almost any recipe in this book and turn it into a spice, herb, or vegetable beer. The trick to using them in beer is similar to using fruit in beer (see Chapter 24). Think about how the special ingredients are going to interact with the character of the beer. Look to your favorite foods to find complementary flavor combinations, and try to imagine how those flavors will either blend or contrast with the base beer.

Generally, you need to lower the IBUs and remove the late hop additions from a recipe in order to let the spice, herb, or vegetable flavors shine. If you're going for a dessert-like impression, go with a bigger and sweeter beer. If you want a spicy food impression, use something drier and less sweet. Beers with a light character, such as blonde ale or Kölsch, are better bases for delicate flavors. If you want to use a bolder, more flavorful beer as the base, you will need a heavier hand with spices, herbs, and vegetables, especially if they are delicately flavored.

When using spices, herbs, and vegetables, don't overdo the number of ingredients. Five spices might be great for a Vietnamese chicken dish, but it can be very hard to balance all those flavors in a beer. It is better to go with fewer flavors or aromas and do them well instead of tossing in the entire spice cabinet and hoping for the best.

One thing to keep in mind when making any beer is that first and foremost, the character of the beer must be there. The beer should still taste like a beer. The spice, herb, or vegetable should be noticeable but in harmony with the rest of the beer, and it should not overwhelm the beer character.

You can add most spices, herbs, and vegetables to the boil with good results. Usually, you will want to add them during the last few minutes to retain as much of the volatile aromatics as possible. You can use many spices and herbs after fermentation, but sanitation can be an issue. The solution is to make a tea of the spices. Steeping spices in near-boiling water can kill off the majority of organisms that will spoil your beer. Boil a cup or two of water, turn off the heat, and add your spices. Let them sit until adequately cooled, and you can add the entire volume, including the spices, to the beer.

In some cases, a good alternative is an extract of the spice, herb, or vegetable. Many of the extracts you find in the grocery store are actually pretty good substitutes and have the benefit of being completely sanitary. I like to get some character from using the ingredient itself in the boil and then adjusting the flavor and aroma of the final beer with an extract. The benefit is a slightly more complex flavor and aroma than just using the extract by itself.

If you can't find an extract of the spice, herb, or vegetable you want, it is possible to make your own. Place the spice, herb, or vegetable in a few ounces of vodka in a well-sealed jar, and let it sit for a week or more. The alcohol and water in the vodka will extract the oils and other compounds from the ingredient. Once the vodka has a nice bold flavor from the ingredient, you can use it to dose the beer to taste.

RECIPE: CHOCOLATE HAZELNUT PORTER

I began entering competitions to get objective feedback on my beers. Winning a medal was nice but not nearly as valuable as getting solid feedback on my brewing process. But I must admit, the first time one of my beers won Best of Show, I was elated. This recipe is the first Best of Show beer I ever brewed. If I were to create the recipe from scratch today, I would eliminate the later hop additions and only go with the boiling hops.

It is important to use a low-fat, unsweetened cocoa powder. Add it at the end of the boil to sanitize it and to help it mix thoroughly in the wort. In the fermenter it will look like chocolate sludge, but that is OK. The longer you can let the beer sit on that chocolate sludge, the more chocolate flavor and aroma you will extract. Try to give it at least 10 days, but feel free to adjust the time based on taste.

Hazelnut is not an extract you should make yourself. You should be able to find it at your local homebrew shop or grocery store. Add the hazelnut extract at bottling or kegging time. Typically, it takes about 0.5 oz. (15ml) of hazelnut extract for 5 gallons (19L) of porter, but start with half that amount and see how it comes across before adding the full amount. Each brand of hazelnut extract has a different level of intensity, so you will need to taste the beer before you add the entire amount.

OG: 1.066 (16.1 °P)
FG: 1.019 (4.8 °P)
ADF: 70%
IBU: 36
Color: 38 SRM (75 EBC)
Alcohol: 6.2% ABV (4.8% ABW)
Boil: 60 minutes
Pre-Boil Volume: 7 gallons (26.5L)
Pre-Boil Gravity: 1.056 (13.8 °P)

Extract	Weight	Percent
English Pale LME (3.5 °L)	7.8 lbs. (3.53kg)	64.7
Munich LME (9 °L)	1.0 lb. (0.45kg)	8.3

Steeping Grains

Crystal (40 °L)	1.0 lb. (0.45kg)	8.3
Crystal (80 °L)	1.0 lb. (0.45kg)	8.3
Chocolate Malt (350 °L)	0.75 lb. (340g)	6.2
Black Patent Malt (525 °L)	0.5 lb. (227g)	4.1

Extras

Cocoa Powder (unsweetened), 0 min.	0.5 lb. (227g)
Hazelnut Extract, at bottling	0.5 oz. (15ml)

Hops

		IBU
Kent Goldings 5% AA, 60 min.	1.25 oz. (35g)	23.7
Willamette 5% AA, 30 min.	0.8 oz. (23g)	7.8
Willamette 5% AA, 15 min.	0.8 oz. (23g)	4.1
Kent Goldings 5% AA, 0 min.	0.4 oz. (11g)	0
Willamette 5% AA, 0 min.	0.4 oz. (11g)	0

Yeast

White Labs WLP001 California Ale, Wyeast 1056 American Ale, or Fermentis Safale US-05

Fermentation and Conditioning

Use 13 grams of properly rehydrated dry yeast, 2.5 liquid yeast packages, or make an appropriate starter. Ferment at 67° F (19° C). When finished, carbonate the beer to approximately 2 to 2.5 volumes.

All-Grain Option

Replace the light extract with 11.4 lbs. (5.17kg) American two-row malt. Replace the Munich extract with 1.5 lbs. (0.68kg) Munich malt. Mash at 156° F (69° C).

RECIPE: PUMPKIN SPICE ALE

I am not one for drinking a lot of spiced beers, but around Halloween I get a thirst for pumpkin beer that lasts through New Year's Day. The trickiest part of brewing a great holiday spiced beer is being able to brew a great beer and then enhancing it with spice, versus ruining it with spice. For pumpkin spice ale, you want a firm spice flavor and aroma, similar to a pumpkin pie, but not overdone.

While you can just dump pumpkin pie spice mix into the boil, you are not going to have a lot of control over the final flavor. I prefer to create my own spice mix and then add about two-thirds of the amount that I think will be the right spice level during the last few minutes of the boil. Once the beer is past primary fermentation, I check the taste and add the last third, more or less. I add the spices loose to the fermenter, and they sink to the bottom within a couple of days. Regular taste tests let me know when the beer has just the right spice level. At that point I keg or bottle it, leaving the spices behind. This process gives you more control over the spice level in the beer and adds a fresher spice flavor and aroma than an all-boiled spice addition. If you do happen to add too much spice, letting the beer sit in cold storage for a few months will usually reduce the overall spice character enough to make it palatable.

People say that pumpkin adds very little flavor to a pumpkin beer, that it is the pumpkin spice mix that people identify as the pumpkin flavor. I can't argue with that. I think if you made this beer without pumpkin but told someone there was pumpkin in it, they would believe you. So, if you're not an all-grain brewer or don't want the hassle of working with pumpkin, feel free to omit the pumpkin and toss in a little more base grain.

However, one of the best pumpkin beers I have ever had is Wild Goose Pumpkin Patch Ale, and Head Brewer Tim Deutsch tells me a key ingredient to such a good pumpkin beer is the use of pumpkin pulp from a local farm. If you would like to use pumpkins, fresh pulp is better than canned pumpkin. If you want to use whole pumpkins, use medium-sized pie pumpkins, quarter them, and place them cut side down on a cookie sheet in a 330° F (166° C) oven until they become soft, sweet, and the juices have caramelized a bit on the pan. You can scrape out the pulp or just break up the pumpkins with a potato masher. Mix the whole mess, including the caramelized juices, into your mash, and work as normal from there. You might need to add some rice hulls to prevent a stuck sparge, but I have never needed to do so.

If you have a favorite pumpkin spice mix or a family recipe, feel free to substitute that for the spices listed in the recipe.

OG: 1.056 (13.7 °P)
FG: 1.016 (4.2 °P)
ADF: 69%
IBU: 24
Color: 12 SRM (24 EBC)
Alcohol: 5.2% ABV (4.0% ABW)
Boil: 60 minutes
Pre-Boil Volume: 7 gallons (26.5L)
Pre-Boil Gravity: 1.047 (11.8°P)

Extract	Weight	Percent
English Pale Ale Extract (2.3 °L)	7.9 lbs. (3.58kg)	81.9

Steeping Grains		
Aromatic (20 °L)	0.5 lb. (227g)	5.2
Crystal (40 °L)	0.5 lb. (227g)	5.2
Crystal (120 °L)	0.5 lb. (227g)	5.2
Special Roast (50 °L)	0.25 lb. (113g)	2.6

Hops		IBU
Kent Goldings 5% AA, 60 min.	1.2 oz. (34g)	23.9

Extras	
Cinnamon (ground, dry), 1 min.	1/2 tsp.
Ginger (ground, dry), 1 min.	1/4 tsp.
Nutmeg (ground, dry), 1 min.	1/8 tsp.
Allspice (ground, dry), 1 min.	1/8 tsp.

Yeast

White Labs WLP002 English Ale, Wyeast 1968 London ESB, or Fermentis Safale S-04

Fermentation and Conditioning

Use 11 grams of properly rehydrated dry yeast, 2 liquid yeast packages, or make an appropriate starter. Ferment at 68° F (20° C). When finished, carbonate the beer to approximately 2 to 2.5 volumes.

All-Grain Option

Replace the English pale ale extract with 11 lbs. (5kg) British pale ale malt. Mash at 154° F (68° C). If you want to include real pumpkin in the beer, reduce base malt by 2 lbs. (0.9kg) and add 5 lbs. (2.26kg) baked pumpkin pulp and 0.5 lb. (227g) rice hulls to the mash. In order to make sure the pumpkin converts completely, you may need to lengthen the rest time to 90 minutes.

RECIPE: VANILLA ROBUST PORTER

OG: 1.064 (15.7 °P)
FG: 1.015 (3.8 °P)
ADF: 76%
IBU: 31
Color: 35 SRM (69 EBC)
Alcohol: 6.5% ABV (5.1% ABW)
Boil: 60 minutes
Pre-Boil Volume: 7 gallons (26.5L)
Pre-Boil Gravity: 1.055 (13.5 °P)

Extract	Weight	Percent
Light LME (2.2 °L)	8.6 lbs. (3.90kg)	72.6
Munich LME (9 °L)	1.0 lb. (0.45kg)	8.4

Steeping Grains		
Crystal (40 °L)	1.0 lb. (0.45kg)	8.4
Chocolate Malt (350 °L)	0.75 lb. (340g)	6.3
Black Patent Malt (525 °L)	0.5 lb. (227g)	4.2

Hops		IBU
Kent Goldings 5% AA, 60 min.	1.6 oz. (45g)	30.7

Extras

Vanilla Bean	1 whole bean, last 5 min. of boil
Vanilla Extract	to taste at bottling

Yeast

White Labs WLP001 California Ale, Wyeast 1056 American Ale, or Fermentis Safale US-05

Fermentation and Conditioning

Use 12 grams of properly rehydrated dry yeast, 2.5 liquid yeast packages, or make an appropriate starter. Ferment at 67° F (19° C). Once fermentation finishes, just before bottling, adjust the vanilla flavor and aroma to taste, using the vanilla extract. Carbonate the beer to approximately 2 to 2.5 volumes.

All-Grain Option

Replace the light extract with 11.75 lbs. (5.33kg) American two-row malt. Replace the Munich extract with 1.5 lbs. (0.68kg) Munich malt. Mash at 153° F (67° C).

CHRISTMAS/WINTER SPECIALTY SPICED BEER

A stronger, darker, spiced beer that often has a rich body and warming finish good for the cold winter season. This is an intermediate style that can be brewed by extract-with-grain or all-grain methods. Ferments at 68° F (20° C). OG, FG, IBUs, SRM, and ABV will vary depending on the underlying base beer. ABV is generally above 6%, and most examples are somewhat dark in color.

Keys to Brewing Christmas Spiced Beer:
The most commonly appreciated examples of the style usually are rich, slightly sweet, with some warming alcohol and Christmas holiday spices in the background. The base beer in the recipe below is similar to the English old ale recipe in this book, and the spice additions are the same as the pumpkin ale recipe. The tips for brewing those styles apply to this beer as well.

RECIPE: OL' YULE LOGGY

On a cold winter's night, build a fire and pour a half pint of this beer to make a memorable beer moment. I don't drink a lot of spiced beers, but I certainly get in a holiday mood a lot faster after a spiced beer or two.

OG: 1.090 (21.6 °P)
FG: 1.022 (5.6 °P)
ADF: 74%
IBU: 45
Color: 19 SRM (37 EBC)
Alcohol: 9.0% ABV (7.0% ABW)
Boil: 90 minutes
Pre-Boil Volume: 7.7 gallons (29.3L)
Pre-Boil Gravity: 1.070 (17.0 °P)

Extract	Weight	Percent
English Pale Ale LME (3.5 °L)	14 lbs. (6.35kg)	93.3

Steeping Grains

Crystal (80 °L)	0.75 lb. (340g)	5.0
Black Patent Malt (525 °L)	0.25 lb. (113g)	1.7

Hops

		IBU
Horizon 13% AA, 60 min.	1.0 oz. (28g)	44.5

Extras

Cinnamon (ground, dry), 1 min.	1/2 tsp.
Ginger (ground, dry), 1 min.	1/4 tsp.
Nutmeg (ground, dry), 1 min.	1/8 tsp.
Allspice (ground, dry), 1 min.	1/8 tsp.

Yeast

White Labs WLP013 London Ale, Wyeast 1028 London Ale, or Danstar Nottingham

Fermentation and Conditioning

Use 17 grams of properly rehydrated dry yeast, 3.5 liquid yeast packages, or make an appropriate starter. Ferment at 68° F (20° C). When finished, carbonate the beer to approximately 2 volumes.

All-Grain Option

Replace the English extract with 19.5 lbs. (8.84kg) British pale ale malt. Mash at 152° F (67° C).

26 | SMOKE-FLAVORED & WOOD-AGED BEER

The thing I love about smoke-flavored and wood-aged beers is how rustic they seem. I used to do a lot of camping and backpacking back in the day when it was common to have a wood fire at night, and these beers almost always remind me of those good times.

CLASSIC RAUCHBIER

A malty-rich lager with lots of smooth, complex malt character and a sweet, smoky aroma and flavor. This is an advanced style that can be brewed by extract- with-grain but is best brewed by partial-mash or all-grain methods, unless *rauch* malt extract can be obtained. Ferments at 50° F (10° C).

OG	FG	IBU	Color	Alcohol
1.050–1.057	1.012–1.016	20–30	12–22 SRM	4.8–6.0% ABV
(12.4–14.0 °P)	(3.1–4.1 °P)		24–43 EBC	3.8–4.7% ABW

Keys to Brewing Classic Rauchbier:
Brewing a good rauchbier requires the same level of skill as brewing a good Oktoberfest. You need to be able to brew a nice, clean, malty lager. While there are several differences between most classic rauchbiers and most Oktoberfest beers, the key difference is in the use of beechwood-smoked malt. The level of smoke flavor and aroma can vary from relatively low to intensely high, but it shouldn't be harsh or ash-like. The worst smoked beers I have ever had were all made with smoke flavoring. Smoke flavoring in beer tastes like flavoring: bad bacon, an ashtray, charcoal, or worse. Don't do it, no matter how tempted you might be.

Unfortunately, at the time of this writing, it is difficult to find *rauch* malt extract in homebrew shops. Brewers have steeped *rauch* malt in the past, and some of them think they get decent results. The problem is that the starch in *rauch* malt needs to be converted, and with the percentage required for a nice, strong smoke flavor, steeping it just won't work. Unless you can get some *rauch* malt extract, this is going to be a partial mash or all-grain recipe only. The good news is that rauch malt does have enough diastatic power to convert itself, so a partial mash is actually pretty simple for this beer. You need to hold the *rauch* malt in water at the appropriate mash temperature for only an hour or so, and it will convert the starches to sugar.

You can adjust smoke intensity in the recipe below by varying the *rauch* malt anywhere from 20 to 100 percent. Personally I prefer about 50 percent *rauch* malt, but most people seem to think the beer is plenty smoky at 33 percent, so I keep it around that level for everyone else. Brew it at least once as it is below, but after that feel free to dial it up or down as your preference dictates.

RECIPE: RAUCH ME GENTLY

OG: 1.056 (13.8 °P)
FG: 1.014 (3.5 °P)
ADF: 75%
IBU: 27
Color: 16 SRM (32 EBC)
Alcohol: 5.6% ABV (4.4% ABW)
Boil: 60 minutes
Pre-Boil Volume: 7 gallons (26.5L)
Pre-Boil Gravity: 1.048 (11.8 °P)

Extract	Weight	Percent
Pilsener LME (2.2 °L)	4.25 lbs. (1.92kg)	42.6
Rauch LME (14 °L)	3.3 lbs. (1.49kg)	33.1
Munich LME (9 °L)	1.3 lbs. (0.59kg)	13.0

Steeping Grains

CaraMunich (60 °L)	0.75 lb. (227g)	7.5
Melanoidin (28 °L)	0.25 lb. (113g)	2.5
Black Malt (600 °L)	2.0 oz. (57g)	1.3

Hops		**IBU**
Hallertau 4% AA, 60 min.	1.5 oz. (43g)	23.9
Hallertau 4% AA, 10 min.	0.5 oz. (14g)	2.7

Yeast

White Labs WLP830 German Lager, Wyeast 2124 Bohemian Lager, or Fermentis Saflager S-23

Fermentation and Conditioning

Use 21 grams of properly rehydrated dry yeast, 4.5 liquid yeast packages, or make an appropriate starter. Ferment at 50° F (10° C). Allow the beer to lager for at least 4 weeks before bottling or serving. When finished, carbonate the beer from 2 to 2.5 volumes.

Partial-Mash Option

Replace the *rauch* extract with 4.5 lbs. (2.04kg) German beechwood-smoked *rauch* malt. Do not use peat-smoked malt under any circumstances. Follow the partial-mash instructions in the Appendix.

All-Grain Option

Replace the Pilsener extract with 5.6 lbs. (2.54kg) continental Pilsener malt. Replace the Munich extract with 1.75 lbs. (0.79kg) Munich malt. Replace the rauch extract with 4.5 lbs. (2.04kg) German beechwood-smoked *rauch* malt. Do not use peat-smoked malt under any circumstances. Mash at 154° F (68° C). Increase the pre-boil volume as needed to allow a 90-minute boil, which will help reduce DMS in the beer.

OTHER SMOKED BEER

This is any beer that is exhibiting smoke as a principal flavor and aroma characteristic other than the Bamberg-style rauchbier. The better examples of this style exhibit a balance in the use of smoke, hops, and malt character. This is an advanced style that can be brewed by extract-with-grain but is best brewed by partial-mash or all-grain methods, unless *rauch* malt extract can be obtained. This recipe ferments at 67° F (19° C).

Keys to Brewing Other Smoked Beer:

Like any beer style, Other Smoked Beers are all about balance. You want a harmony between the character of the beer and the smoke character. If you are brewing smoked cream ale, you will need a very light level of smoke, because the beer doesn't have any bold flavors to balance a lot of smoke. Conversely, if you're brewing a smoked Russian imperial stout, you need a lot more smoke if you hope to have it show up against the bold flavors of that beer. It is also important to think of how the beer will age. Smoke character tends to mellow over time, so if you expect the beer to age well, you will want to bump up the level of smoke to compensate.

You can use almost any smoked malt for Other Smoked Beers, but there are certain things that just don't work well. The worst smoked beers I have ever tried were all made with smoke flavoring or peat-smoked malt. I recommend never using either, no matter how tempted you might be.

The recipe below uses about 20 percent smoked malt for the right level of intensity. You can adjust it up or down as preference dictates, but less than 20 percent results in a very weak smoke flavor if you keep the beer for a couple of years.

RECIPE: SMOKED ROBUST PORTER

Of all the awards I have ever won for my beers, one of the medals I am most proud of is the second-place that I received for this beer in the final round of the National Homebrew Competition. The judges were Ray Daniels, Geoff Larson, and Harold Gulbransen, three people for whom I have the utmost respect in all things beery. Geoff and Ray actually wrote the book on smoked beers. Geoff and Alaskan Brewing Company pretty much defined the style with their smoked porter. And Harold brews some of the most fantastically well-balanced smoked beers I have ever tasted. Bamberg is his favorite town in Germany. To have those three deem this smoked porter as worthy of a medal was quite an honor. Alaskan Brewing keeps a stash of its smoked porter from each year. The differences between vintages are amazing and complex. This is a great beer to brew every year and then store in the cellar for several years. As it ages, the flavors merge, change, and become ever more intriguing.

OG: 1.065 (15.9 °P)
FG: 1.016 (4.0 °P)
ADF: 75%
IBU: 35
Color: 39 SRM (77 EBC)
Alcohol: 6.5% ABV (5.1% ABW)
Boil: 60 minutes
Pre-Boil Volume: 7 gallons (26.5L)
Pre-Boil Gravity: 1.055 (13.6 °P)

Extract	Weight	Percent
English Pale Ale LME (3.5 °L)	5.75 lbs. (2.61kg)	47.9
Rauch LME (14 °L)	2.25 lbs. (1.02kg)	18.8
Munich LME (9 °L)	0.75 lb. (340g)	6.3

Steeping Grains		
Crystal (40 °L)	1.0 lb. (0.45kg)	8.3
Crystal (80 °L)	1.0 lb. (0.45kg)	8.3
Chocolate Malt (350 °L)	0.75 lb. (340g)	6.3
Black Patent Malt (525 °L)	0.5 lb. (227g)	4.2

Hops		IBU
Kent Goldings 5% AA, 60 min.	1.25 oz. (35g)	23.9
Willamette 5% AA, 30 min.	0.75 oz. (21g)	7.3
Willamette 5% AA, 15 min.	0.75 oz. (21g)	3.8
Kent Goldings 5% AA, 0 min.	0.4 oz. (11g)	0
Willamette 5% AA, 0 min.	0.4 oz. (11g)	0

Yeast

White Labs WLP001 California Ale, Wyeast 1056 American Ale, or Fermentis Safale US-05

Fermentation and Conditioning

Use 12 grams of properly rehydrated dry yeast, 2.5 liquid yeast packages, or make an appropriate starter. Ferment at 67° F (19° C). When finished, carbonate the beer to approximately 2 to 2.5 volumes.

Partial-Mash Option

Replace the *rauch* extract with 3 lbs. (1.36kg) German beechwood-smoked *rauch* malt. Do not use peat-smoked malt under any circumstances. Follow the partial-mash instructions in the Appendix.

All-Grain Option

Replace the English extract with 8.5 lbs. (3.85kg) British pale ale malt. Replace the Munich extract with 1 lb. (0.45kg) Munich malt. Replace the *rauch* extract with 3 lbs. (1.36kg) German beechwood-smoked *rauch* malt. Mash at 154° F (68° C).

WOOD-AGED BEER

> A harmonious blend of the base beer style with characteristics from aging in contact with wood. The best examples will be smooth, flavorful, well balanced, and well aged. OG, FG, IBU, SRM, and ABV will vary depending on the underlying base beer style.

Keys to Brewing Wood-Aged Beer:
Almost any recipe in this book can be aged in wood, but some beers are better suited to wood aging than others. Historically, people would only age bigger, higher-alcohol beers, because they would not spoil as easily. The higher alcohol content kept most bacteria that might be in the barrel from spoiling the beer. The same is true today, but today it is easier to use cubes or chips to get the flavor of wood, and they are much easier to sanitize than an entire barrel. However, the idea of using big beers, or more special beers, for barrel aging persists, so a high-alcohol style is still a good choice. Just remember that you can try wood aging with any beer style.

Aging beer in an unlined wood barrel produces several effects. Obviously, you will get some wood flavor and aroma. The flavors and aromas can range all over, including vanilla, caramel, toffee, toast, tea, coconut, or even cocoa notes. Less obvious is the slight oxidation that will occur, as oxygen makes its way through the wood and into the beer. Other flavors can develop from any organisms present that sour beer or create other complex flavors. However, not all of these flavors are necessary or desired for every beer style. In fact, many of these flavors and aromas would be considered flaws in most beers. So while some of these non-wood flavors and aromas from barrel aging can add complexity and are worth experimenting with, the only real requirement for a great wood-aged beer is wood flavor and aroma.

Luckily, you don't need a barrel to make a wood-aged beer. You can create wood character in your beer with wood cubes, chips, or sawdust. Your homebrew shop will likely carry some wood products for this, usually French, American, or Hungarian oak, in different levels of toast. The type of oak and the level of toast determine the flavor it will impart. I put oak cubes in Mason jars and sterilize them in a pressure cooker before use, but a 15-minute soak in a little bit of near-boiling water will sanitize them well enough. Either way, there is very little risk of contamination.

As with fruits and spices, the bolder the base beer flavor, the more wood character it will take before it will become evident to the drinker. You don't want the beer to taste like gnawing on a tree, but you do want enough presence for it to be an enjoyable accompaniment to the beer. A good all-around oak choice is French medium-toast cubes. Depending on the base beer, I like to start with 1 to 2 oz. (28 to 57g) in 5 gallons (19L) for 4 to 12 weeks. The more oak you add and the finer the size of the pieces (cubes, chips, shavings, sawdust), the more rapid the release of wood flavor and aroma into the beer. The less oak you use, the longer it takes to get the wood notes into your beer, but it imparts a more complex and pleasing wood character. Using a lot of wood for a shorter time results in a more one-dimensional oak character. It is important to taste the beer every so often to see how the flavor is developing. Once it seems right to you, rack it to another container, leaving the wood behind.

Aging beer in bourbon or whiskey barrels has become popular for a number of breweries, and a bourbon-barrel barley wine can be a wonderful beer experience. Unfortunately, this is something that is too easily overdone, and the resulting beer is lost in a sea of bourbon flavor. Don't forget that any non-beer flavors need to integrate well into the overall drinking experience. There should be a harmony and balance between these types of flavors and the beer. If you do want to add some bourbon or whiskey flavor, you don't have to age the beer in a bourbon barrel. An easy and effective method is to wood-age it using oak cubes first, and then add some bourbon or whiskey directly to the beer after aging is complete. Use restraint and taste it as you add the flavoring.

27 | SPECIALTY BEER

This category is a catchall for beers that don't fit into any of the other categories. This might include historical beers, clones of commercial beers that don't fit other styles, or beers made with unusual techniques or ingredients that prevent them from fitting into the fruit or the spice, herb, vegetable categories.

SPECIALTY BEER

This style includes a very wide range of beers. The following recipe is an intermediate style that can be brewed by extract-with-grain or all-grain methods. Ferments at 67° F (19° C). OG, FG, IBUs, SRM, and ABV for this style will vary depending on the underlying base beer style.

Keys to Brewing Specialty Beer:
The most important thing to keep in mind when designing a specialty beer is that the character of the beer must be there. That is not as much of a problem if you are making an example of an historical beer. Just make sure it is an accurate representation of that beer. If you are making something with a whole bunch of fruits, spices, and other flavorings combined, then the beer character can easily get lost if you are not careful.

For example, if you are making a chocolate cherry stout, the person drinking it should always be able to taste a very good stout, with chocolate and cherry character expertly entwined with the character of the beer. If the character of a stout isn't there, then it isn't a great specialty beer. This is why the specialty category is not as easy as some brewers think. You must be able to brew a good example of the base beer before you can make a good specialty beer from that base style.

When adding non-traditional ingredients, think about how those ingredients are going to interact with the character of the beer, such as you would when designing a fruit beer or a spice, herb, or vegetable beer. Take inspiration from your favorite foods to find great flavor combinations, but don't overdo the number of ingredients. Simpler is usually better, and it will be easier to create a balanced beer.

RECIPE: BLACK FOREST STOUT

This beer has a lot of chocolate and cherry flavors, like a luscious Black Forest cake.

It is important to use a low-fat, unsweetened cocoa powder in this beer. Add it at the end of the boil to sanitize it and to help it mix thoroughly in the wort. In the fermenter it will look like chocolate sludge, but that is OK. The longer you can let the beer sit on the chocolate sludge, the more chocolate flavor and aroma you will extract. It is best to add the cherries once the bulk of fermentation has passed. When initial fermentation begins to slow, add cherry purée to a second fermenter and carefully rack the beer onto the fruit. Try to bring along a good portion of the cocoa to continue extracting chocolate flavors.

Cherries will vary from season to season, and sometimes you will need to enhance the cherry character of the beer. If the final beer seems to lack a fresh cherry character, you can try adding a very small amount of acid blend to taste. Don't go overboard, but a little bit of additional acidity can brighten the fruit character. If your beer is very low in cherry character, you can try adding a small amount of cherry extract. However, cherry extract tastes like cough syrup, so use it sparingly to support natural cherry flavors and only as a last resort.

OG: 1.071 (17.2 °P) / 1.075 (18.1 °P) with fruit
FG: 1.018 (4.5 °P)
ADF: 75%
IBU: 38
Color: 39 SRM (77 EBC)
Alcohol: 7.6% ABV (5.9% ABW)
Boil: 60 minutes
Pre-Boil Volume: 7 gallons (26.5L)
Pre-Boil Gravity: 1.060 (14.8 °P)

Extract	Weight	Percent
English Pale Ale LME (3.5 °L)	10.0 lbs. (4.53kg)	80.0

Steeping Grains		
Black Roasted Barley (500 °L)	0.75 lb. (340g)	6.0
Crystal (40 °L)	10.0 oz. (284g)	5.0
Crystal (80 °L)	10.0 oz. (284g)	5.0
Chocolate Malt (420 °L)	0.5 lb. (227g)	4.0

Extras	
Cocoa Powder (unsweetened), 0 min.	0.5 lb. (227g)
Cherry Purée, secondary	6.0 lbs. (2.72kg)

Hops		IBU
Kent Goldings 5% AA, 60 min.	2.1 oz. (60g)	38.4

Yeast

White Labs WLP013 London Ale, Wyeast 1028 London Ale, or Danstar Nottingham

Fermentation and Conditioning

Use 13 grams of properly rehydrated dry yeast, 3 liquid yeast packages, or make an appropriate starter. Ferment at 67° F (19° C). When initial fermentation begins to slow, add cherry purée to a second fermenter and carefully rack the beer onto the fruit. Fermentation should pick up again as the yeast consumes the fructose in the fruit purée. When finished, carbonate the beer to approximately 2 to 2.5 volumes.

All-Grain Option

Replace the English extract with 13.9 lbs. (6.3kg) British pale ale malt. Mash at 152° F (67° C).

A | YEAST PITCHING RATES AND STARTERS

Proper fermentation is what sets great beers apart from just OK beers. One fundamental aspect of proper fermentation is having the right amount of clean, healthy yeast to ferment your wort. A starter is a small volume of wort that yeast use to refresh themselves and multiply in preparation for fermenting a full batch of beer.

The liquid yeast products from Wyeast and White Labs are excellent, but employing a starter can reduce the number of yeast packages needed and can often improve the performance of older or poorly handled yeast. You should always make a starter if you suspect the viability (overall health) of your yeast might be low. If the yeast package is nearing its best-by date, or the yeast has been left out warm for an extended period of time (i.e., in shipping for several days), make a starter.

You generally don't want to make a starter for dry yeast. It is usually cheaper and easier to buy more dry yeast than it would be to make a starter. For dry yeasts, just do a proper rehydration in tap water; do not make a starter.

Making a Starter

A starter is easy to make. It is like a mini-batch of beer, with the focus being yeast growth and health, not drinkability. One of the most important aspects of making a starter is keeping everything sanitary. Pay strict attention to sanitization and handling of the starter wort and yeast. When adding yeast to the starter, work in a draft-free area, and try to keep the containers covered as much as possible.

You will need a clean, sanitized container that is able to hold the starter plus some head space, aluminum foil, dried malt extract (DME), yeast nutrients, and water. It is important to use malt-based sugars for your starters. Do not use table sugar, corn sugar, or honey, as they will cause the yeast to quickly lose the ability to ferment maltose, the main sugar in making beer.

When making starter wort, keep the starting gravity between 1.030 and 1.040 (7 to 10 °P). You do not want to make a high-gravity starter

to grow yeast. As a ballpark measurement, use about 6 ounces (by weight) DME to 2 quarts of water. If you are working in metric units, it couldn't be easier. Use a 10 to 1 ratio. Add 1 gram of DME for every 10ml of final volume. (If you're making a 2-liter starter, add water to 200 grams of DME until you have 2 liters total.) Add 1/4 teaspoon of yeast nutrient, boil 15 minutes, cool, and add yeast. Cover the top of the flask or jar with aluminum foil, wrapping it down over the edge, but don't seal it with a rubber band. You want the carbon dioxide to be able to vent, and oxygen to be able to diffuse in. Don't worry, airborne bacteria cannot navigate this covering.

Adding oxygen to the starter will promote more growth and better yeast health. There are several ways to add oxygen: intermittent shaking, a stir plate, pure oxygen, or an air pump with a sterile filter. While it may not seem the most high-tech solution, shaking the starter is quite effective. Shaking the starter as often as possible makes a large difference in the amount of yeast growth and health. With enough attention and good air exchange, shaking can be almost as effective as a stir plate.

Keep starters between 65° F (18° C) and 75° F (24° C). A temperature around the low 70s (72° F, 22° C) strikes the best balance for the propagation of yeasts. Lager yeast starters can be kept a few degrees cooler, and ale yeasts can be kept a few degrees warmer, but this temperature strikes a good balance of yeast health and efficient propagation for both types of yeast.

A 2-liter starter made with healthy yeast will reach its maximum cell density within 12 to 18 hours. If you are starting with a very small amount of yeast or low-viability yeast, it can take 24 hours or more to reach maximum cell density. Once that point is reached, you can pitch the entire starter into your wort.

Of course, if you have a large starter volume in relation to your batch of beer, or a starter that was continuously aerated, then you probably don't want to pitch the entire thing into your wort. Adding a large starter or a heavily oxidized starter to your wort can alter the flavor of the finished beer. In this case, put the starter in the refrigerator for a day or two, and let the yeast settle to the bottom. Decant most of the spent wort off the top, swirl the remaining liquid to re-suspend the yeast, and then pitch that into your wort.

How much yeast, or how big a starter, do I need?

According to both White Labs and Wyeast, a White Labs Pitchable Yeast vial and a Wyeast Activator 125 XL Smack Pack both contain an average of 100 billion cells and are enough to pitch directly into 5 U.S. gallons (18.9 liters) of an ale wort at 1.048 SG (12 °P). This is a pitching rate of 5.3 million cells per milliliter, which can work well with a fresh package of yeast. This is because the yeast when fresh from the supplier is in tiptop shape. However, if the yeast is not at its freshest or has been mishandled, you will need to make a starter.

Higher-gravity worts require more yeast, and lower-gravity worts require less. For an ale, you want to pitch approximately 0.75 million cells of viable yeast for every milliliter of wort for every degree Plato. You should pitch twice that amount, 1.5 million, for a lager. Here is the simple math to calculate the number of cells needed.

(0.75 million) X (milliliters of wort) X (degrees Plato of the wort)

There are about 3,785 milliliters in a gallon. There are about 21,000 milliliters in 5.5 U.S. gallons.

One degree Plato is close to 1.004 of specific gravity (SG). Just divide the decimal portion of the SG by 4 to get the approximate degrees Plato (e.g., 1.060 is 15 °P).

The proper amount of yeast for 5.5 U.S. gallons of 1.060 wort would be around 236 billion cells if pitching 0.75 million per milliliter.

$$(750,000) \times (21,000) \times (15) = 236,000,000,000$$

With each vial or pack having about 100 billion cells, you would need two vials or packs (approximately 200 billion cells) to get close to that rate, if you didn't want to make a starter.

In general, a 2-liter starter doubles the amount of yeast in a single vial or pack. For the above example, you would only need 1 package of yeast if you made a 2-liter starter. The chart at the end of this chapter makes it easy to figure out how large a starter you will need to replace multiple packages of liquid yeast. There are also free calculators on the Internet that can determine exactly how much yeast you need for a given wort.

You might ask, why not pitch as much yeast as possible? There is also an upper limit to how much yeast you should add. Overpitching can cause other problems with beer flavor, such as a lack of esters, yeasty off-flavors, and poor head retention. Changes in the flavor profile are noticeable when the pitch rates are as little as 20 percent over the recommended amount.

Besides the popular 125ml Activator Smack Pack, Wyeast sells the Propagator 50ml Smack Pack, which contains about one-fourth the amount of yeast as their Activator product. If you make a 2-liter starter with the Propagator, the resulting yeast is about the same as a 125ml Activator Smack Pack.

Table 5—Yeast Pack Quantities

Liquid Yeast Packs Needed Without a Starter

0	1	2	3	4	5	6	7	8	9	10	11	12	13	14	15	16	17	18	19	20	25	28	32
1.0	1																						
1.5		1																					
2.0			1																				
2.5					1																		
3.0		2																					
3.5			2																				
4.0				2						1													
4.5			3		2								1										
5.0				3													1				1		
5.5					3																		
6.0				4	4	3																	
6.5							2	2		2													
7.0						4						2		2		2							
7.5						5	3																
8.0							4	3		3	3								2	2			
8.5							5	4					3									2	
9.0								5	4	4				3									2
9.5									5		4					3							
10.0								6		5			4						3				2

The numbers in the grid represent the number of liquid yeast packages to add to the starter. For example, if the recipe calls for 4 liquid yeast packages, you can make a 4-liter starter using 2 packages or a 9-liter starter using 1 package. Either will result in the same amount of yeast as found in 4 packages.

B | STEEPING SPECIALTY GRAINS

Steeping specialty grains adds characteristic flavors for a recipe that pale, amber, and/or dark malt extract alone cannot provide. You want to extract the fermentable and non-fermentable character of these grains without extracting astringency from the grain husks. After steeping, you will add the malt extract to the pot and begin the boil.

1. Heat 1 gallon (3.8 liters) of water in the brewpot until it reaches 160° F (71° C) ± 10° F (6° C).
2. Immerse the grain bag in the pot for 30 minutes. The grain bag

may be dunked and swirled like a teabag during this time to make sure that all of the grain is wetted. Moving it around will help improve the yield, but don't squeeze and wring it, because that encourages bitter tannin extraction. Maintaining the temperature during the steep is not important.

3. After 30 minutes, remove the grain bag from the pot, and let it drain. Do not wring out every drop of wort.

4. Now you can add the malt extract and any additional water to the boiling pot to bring it up to the boiling volume.

Tips: For best flavor results, the ratio of steeping water to grain should be less than 1 gallon (3.8 liters) per pound. This will help keep the pH below 6 and minimize tannin extraction in alkaline water. If you are steeping very dark malts such as roasted barley or black patent malt, you may want to steep them in cooler water for longer periods of time, or even overnight in cold water, to reduce the acridness that can result from steeping a lot of dark malt in soft water.

C | STOVETOP PARTIAL MASHING

Conduct a mini-mash in a 3-gallon (11L) stockpot using a 5-gallon (19L), nylon mesh paint strainer bag from the hardware and paint store.

1. Crush the grain and put it in the mesh bag.

2. Heat water to 165° F (74° C) at a water/grist ratio of 1.5 quarts/pound (3L/kg), and immerse the grain bag. Gently stir the grain to make sure it is thoroughly wetted and then check the temperature. The mash temperature of the grain and water should now be about 150 to 155° F (65 to 68° C). Let the mash sit for 30 minutes.

3. Add heat from the stove while stirring to get the temperature back up to 155° F (68° C). Let mash sit for another 30 minutes.

4. Place 2 gallons (7.5L) water in your boiling pot and heat this water to 165° F (74° C) also.

5. Lift bag out of the first pot and let the bag drain for a minute before transferring the grain bag to the other pot. Swirl the bag in the pot to rewet the grain, and let it sit for 10 minutes.

6. Lift the grain bag, let it drain, and discard. Add the wort from the first pot and any malt extract the recipe requires to the boiling pot, and begin your boil.

D | PRIMING RATES AND CO₂ VOLUMES

The carbonation levels for the recipes in this book are given in "volumes of CO_2," which means that there is "X" liters of carbon dioxide gas dissolved into 1 liter of solution (beer). To convert volumes of CO_2 to a weight of priming sugar for bottling, use the nomograph on p. 298. To convert volumes of CO_2 to a forced-carbonation pressure for kegging, use the chart on p. 299.

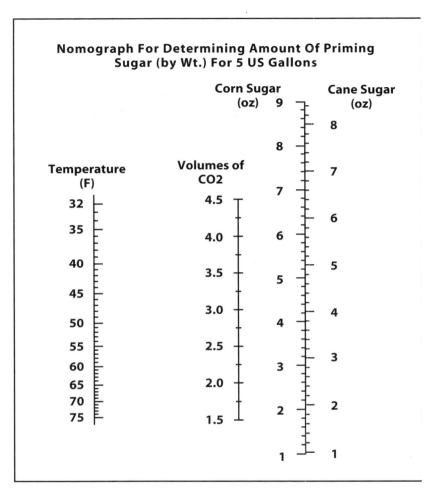

Nomograph for determining more precise amounts of priming sugar. To use the nomograph, draw a line from the temperature of your beer through the volumes of CO2 that you want, to the scale for sugar. The temperature is not the serving temperature, it is the temperature of the beer when primed, and quantifies how much CO_2 is already present. The intersection of your line and the sugar scale gives the weight in ounces (either glucose or sucrose) to be added to 5 gallons of beer to achieve the desired carbonation level. If you are priming more (e.g. 6 gallons) then the amount of priming sugar can be determined by ratio (e.g. 6/5) to the 5 gallon amount.

°F	°C	5 psi 34.5 kPa	10 psi 69 kPa	15 psi 103 kPa	20 psi 138 kPa	25 psi 172 kPa	30 psi 207 kPa	35 psi 241 kPa	40 psi 276 kPa
30	-1	2.3	2.8	3.4	4.0	4.5	5.1	5.7	6.3
35	2	2.0	2.5	3.0	3.6	4.1	4.6	5.1	5.6
40	4	1.8	2.3	2.7	3.2	3.7	4.1	4.6	5.1
45	7	1.7	2.1	2.5	2.9	3.4	3.8	4.2	4.6
50	10	1.5	1.9	2.3	2.7	3.1	3.5	3.9	4.3
55	13	1.4	1.8	2.1	2.5	2.9	3.2	3.6	3.9
60	16	1.3	1.7	2.0	2.3	2.7	3.0	3.3	3.7
65	18	1.2	1.5	1.9	2.2	2.5	2.8	3.1	3.4
70	21	1.2	1.5	1.7	2.0	2.3	2.6	2.9	3.2
75	24	1.1	1.4	1.6	1.9	2.2	2.5	2.8	3.0
80	27	1.0	1.3	1.6	1.8	2.1	2.3	2.6	2.9
85	29	1.0	1.2	1.5	1.7	2.0	2.2	2.5	2.7

This chart is based on Henry's Law and calculates the equilibrium volumes of CO_2 achieved when force-carbonating a beer at a specified temperature in a keg. The pressure is the regulator pressure (psi and kPa) and the temperature is the temperature of the beer.

GLOSSARY

acetic acid (CH₃COOH). A pungent, colorless liquid commonly known as vinegar, it is the product of the oxidation of alcohol by a variety of bacteria and certain types of yeast. Naturally occurring in a variety of fruits and other foods.

Acetobacter. A genus of aerobic, rod-shaped bacteria that grows in the presence of alcohol and secures energy by oxidizing organic compounds to organic acids i.e. alcohol to acetic acid.

acidic. Having a sour taste/aftertaste.

adjunct. Any unmalted grain or other fermentable ingredient added to the mash.

aeration. The action of introducing air to the wort at various stages of the brewing process. Proper aeration before primary fermentation is vital to a vigorous ferment.

aerobic. Requiring the presence of oxygen to survive and reproduce (aerobic bacteria).

airlock. See fermentation lock.

airspace. See ullage.

alcohol by volume (v/v). The volume percentage of alcohol in beer. To calculate the approximate volumetric alcohol content, subtract the final gravity from the original gravity and divide the result by 0.0075. For example: $1.050 - 1.012 = 0.038 \div 0.0075 = 5\%$ v/v.

alcohol by weight (w/v). The percentage of alcohol in beer based on the weight of the alcohol. To calculate the approximate alcohol content by weight, subtract the final gravity from the original gravity and multiply by 105. For example: $1.050 - 1.0212 = 0.038 \times 105 = 4\%$ w/v.

ale. 1. Historically, an unhopped malt beverage. 2. Now, a generic term for hopped beers produced by top fermentation, as opposed to lagers, which are produced by bottom fermentation.

all-extract beer. A beer made with only malt extract as opposed to one made from barley or a combination of malt extract and barley.

all-grain beer. A beer made with only malted barley as opposed to one made from malt extract or from malt extract and malted barley.

all-malt beer. A beer made with only barley malt with no adjuncts nor refined sugars.

alpha acid. A soft resin in hop cones. When boiled, alpha acids are converted to iso-alpha-acids, which account for 60 percent of a beer's bitterness.

alpha-acid unit. A measurement of the potential bitterness of hops, expressed by their percentage of alpha acid. Low is 2–4 percent; medium is 5–7 percent; high is 8–12 percent. Abbreviation is AAU.

anerobic. The inability to survive and reproduce in the presence of oxygen (aerobic bacteria).

antioxidant. A reducing agent that delays oxidation and prolongs useful life of an organic product.

attenuation. The reduction in the wort's specific gravity caused by the transformation of sugars into alcohol and carbon dioxide.

astringent. A drying, tannic aftertaste.

autolysis. A process in which yeast feed on each other, producing a rubbery odor. To avoid this, rack beer to remove excess yeast as soon after fermentation as possible.

bacteria. Unicellular microorganisms that may typically infect wort and beer.

beer engine. Device used to draw beer from a cask by the use of suction created by pulling a handle. Also called a handpump.

beta acid. Hop resin essentially insoluble in liquid, unless oxidized, and cannot be isomerized by boiling. Exhibit a powerful antibacterial effect against the growth of thermophilic gram-positive lactic acid-producing bacteria.

bitter. A sharp taste and aftertaste associated with hops, malt and yeast.

Bitterness Units (BU). A measurement of the American Society for Brewing Chemists for bittering substances in beer, primarily iso-alpha-acids, but also including oxidized beta acids. See also International Bitterness Units.

blending. The mixing together of different batches of beer to form a final composite intended for bottling

blow-by (blow-off). A single-stage homebrewing fermentation method in which a plastic tube is fitted into the mouth of a carboy, and the other end is submerged in a pail of sterile water. Unwanted residues and carbon dioxide are expelled through the tube, while air is prevented from coming into contact with the fermenting beer, thus avoiding contamination.

bottle-conditioned. A beer where carbonation is the result of the fermentation of sugar by yeast in the bottle.

Brettanomyces. A yeast common in the fermentation of wild beers and often resident in the equipment and vessels of breweries which make such beers. Produces very distinctive acid and ester profiles.

calcium carbonate ($CaCO_3$). Also known as chalk. Added during brewing to increase calcium and carbonate content.

calcium sulfate ($CaSO_4 \cdot 2H_2O$). Also known as gypsum. Added during brewing to increase calcium and sulfate content.

carbohydrates. A group of organic compounds including sugars and starches, many suitable as food for yeast and bacteria.

carbonation. The process of introducing carbon dioxide into a liquid by: (1) injecting the finished beer with carbon dioxide; (2) adding young fermenting beer to finished beer for a renewed fermentation (kraeusening); (3) priming (adding sugar) to fermented wort prior to bottling, creating a secondary fermentation in the bottle.

carboy. A large glass, plastic, or earthenware bottle.

catalyst. A substance, such as an enzyme, which promotes a chemical reaction.

chill haze. Haziness caused by protein and tannin during the secondary fermentation.

cold break. The flocculation of proteins and tannins during wort cooling.

coolship. A large, shallow tank historically used to cool and settle freshly boiled wort. Also used to expose wort to yeast and bacteria for spontaneous fermentation.

***Cuvee* (Flemish).** A special product produced by a brewery.

decoction. A method of mashing that raises the temperature of the wash by removing a portion, boiling it, and returning it to the mash tun.

diacetyl. A compound contributing an objectionable butterscotch character.

dimethyl sulphide. A naturally occurring beer constituent which originates in malt. While it contributes to favorable beer flavors at low levels, in increased concentrations DMS contributes an objectionable corn-like or cooked vegetable character.

dry-hopping. The addition of hops to the primary fermenter, the secondary fermenter, or to casked beer to add aroma and hop character to the finished beer without adding significant bitterness.

dry malt. Malt extract in powdered form.

European Brewery Convention (EBC). The scientific body which establishes measurement standards and test methods for use in brewing in Europe. Also, see Standard Reference Method.

Enterobacter. Any of various gram-negative rod-shaped bacteria of the family *Enterobacteriaceae* that includes some pathogens including salmonella.

esters. A group of compounds in beer, which impart fruity flavors and aromas.

ethanol. Ethyl alcohol: the colorless, odorless, alcohol of beer , wine and spirits.

extract. The amount of dissolved materials in the wort after mashing and lautering malted barley and/or malt adjuncts such as corn and rice.

fermentation lock. A one-way valve, which allows carbon dioxide to escape from the fermenter while excluding contaminants.

filter (to). To extract solids, generally yeast and protein, from beer

final gravity. The specific gravity of a beer when fermentation is complete.

fining. The process of adding clarifying agents to beer during secondary fermentation to precipitate suspended matter.

flocculant yeast. Yeast cells that form large colonies and tend to come out of suspension before the end of fermentation.

flocculation. The behavior of yeast cells joining into masses and settling out toward the end of fermentation.

framboise **(French).** A beer fermented with raspberries.

fusel alcohol. High molecular weight alcohol, which results from excessively high fermentation temperatures. Fusel alcohol can impart harsh bitter flavors to beer as well as contribute to hangovers.

gelatin. A fining agent added during secondary fermentation, clarifying the beer.

genus. A taxonomic category ranking below a family and above a species, generally consisting of a group of species exhibiting similar characteristics

glucose ($C_6H_{12}O_6$). An easily fermentable sugar used in brewing, sometimes contributing a cidery character in higher quantities.

grist. The milled malt and adjuncts prior to mashing.

gueuze. A blend of different batches and ages of lambic beer, which undergo an additional fermentation in the bottle due to the presence of yeast and fermentable sugar.

hedgehog. Small, prickly mammal found primarily in European countries.

Homebrew Bittering Units. A formula invented by the American Homebrewers Association to measure bitterness of beer. Calculate bittering units by multiplying the percent alpha acid in the hops by the number of ounces. Example: if 1.5 ounces of 10 percent alpha acid hops were used in a 5-gallon batch, the total homebrew bittering units would be 15: 1.5 x 10 = 15 HBU per 5 gallons.

hop pellets. Finely powdered hop cones compressed into tablets. Hop pellets are 20–30 percent more bitter by weight than the same variety in loose form.

horny tank. Tank employed after the coolship and before a fermenter at a time when the yeast and bacteria are jumping and ready to go.

humulone. Synonym for alpha acids.

hydrometer. A glass instrument used to measure the specific gravity of liquids as compared to water, consisting of a graduated stem resting on a weighed float.

infusion mash. See step infusion.

inoculation. Introduction of microorganisms to wort for the purpose of fermentation or acidification.

IBU (International Bitterness Units). The measurement of the European Brewing Convention for the concentration of iso-alpha-acids in 34 milligrams per liter (parts per million) in wort and beer. See also Bitterness Units.

infection. Growth of microorganisms in wort or beer detrimental to flavor or aroma.

Irish moss. Copper or lead "finings" that help precipitate proteins in the kettle. See also cold break.

isinglass. A gelatinous substance made from the swim bladder of certain fish and added to beer as a fining agent.

isomerization. The extraction (inversion) of hop alpha acids by boiling in wort.

kilning. The final stage in the malting process where malt is exposed to high temperatures to halt modification and increase color and character.

kraeusen. n. The rocky head of foam which appears on the surface of the wort during fermentation. v.. To add fermenting wort to fermented beer to induce carbonation through a secondary fermentation.

kriek **(Flemish).** A beer fermented with cherries.

lactic acid ($C_3H_6O_3$). A clear, odorless acid found in beer, sour milk and fruit.

Lactobacillus. Any of various rod-shaped, aerobic bacteria of the genus *Lactobacillus* that ferment lactic acid (and often others) from sugars.

lager. n. A generic term for any bottom-fermented beer. Lager brewing is now the predominant brewing method worldwide except in Britain where top-fermented ales dominate. v. To store beer at near-zero temperatures in order to precipitate yeast cells and proteins and improve taste.

lambic. A spontaneously fermented beer produced with a portion of unmalted wheat, generally containing specific characteristics due to various acids and esters. Also used to describe the unblended form of the beer – as opposed to gueuze – commonly served young on draft or old in bottles.

lauter tun. A vessel in which the mash settles and the grains are removed from the sweet wort through a straining process. It has a false slotted bottom and spigot.

liquefaction. The process by which alpha-amylase enzymes degrade soluble starch into dextrin.

liquor. Water intended for brewing.

Lovibond (°L). The scale used to measure beer color. See also Standard Reference Method.

lupulone. Synonym for beta-acid.

malt. Barley that has been steeped in water, germinated, then dried in kilns. This process converts insoluble starches to soluble substances and sugars.

malt extract. A thick syrup or dry powder prepared from malt.

mashing. Mixing crushed malt with water to extract the fermentables, degrade haze-forming proteins, and convert grain starches to fermentable sugars and nonfermentable carbohydrates.

Method Champenoise. A blend of wine or beer, refermented in the bottle to produce a sparkling, effervescent product.

microorganism. An organism of microscopic or submicroscopic size, such as a bacterium.

mixed fermentation. Use of both a culture and microorganisms that grow in a wooden barrel for fermentation.

modification. 1. The physical and chemical changes in barley as a result of malting. 2. The degree to which these changes have occurred, as determined by the growth of the acrospire.

moldy. An objectionable earthly aftertaste often caused by damp, unsanitary conditions during the fermentation or aging of beer.

nitrogen content. The amount of nitrogen in malt as a percentage of weight.

oaky. Exhibiting the characteristics commonly associated with oak i.e. vanilla, tannic.

old beer. Beer that has undergone sufficient fermentation and aging as to be considered of a mature flavor and aroma profile.

original gravity. The specific gravity of wort previous to fermentation. A measure of the total amount of dissolved solids in wort.

oxidation. A chemical reaction involving oxygen, detrimental to beer.

pasteurization. Exposure to heat to destroy and microorganisms present in beer (or other food product susceptible to infection).

Pediococcus. A genus of gram-positive, facultative anaerobic bacteria whose growth is dependent on the presence of a fermentable carbohydrate.

pH. A measure of acidity or alkalinity of a solution, usually on a scale of 1 to 14, where 7 is neutral.

phenols. Volatile compounds in beer contributing a pleasant spicy character or objectionable plastic or medicinal character.

pitching. The process of adding yeast to the cooled wort.

Plato. A saccharometer that expresses specific gravity as extract weight in a 100-gram solution at 68 °F (20 °C). A revised, more accurate version of Balling, developed by Dr. Plato.

polyphenols. An antioxidant phytochemical that tends to prevent or neutralize the damaging effects of oxygen and free radicals.

primary fermentation. The first stage of fermentation, during which most fermentable sugars are converted to ethyl alcohol and carbon dioxide.

priming sugar. A small amount of corn, malt, or cane sugar added to bulk beer prior to racking or at bottling to induce a new fermentation and create carbonation.

racking. The process of transferring beer from one container to another, especially into the final package (bottles, kegs).

recirculation. Clarifying the wort before it moves from the lauter tun into the kettle by recirculating it through the wash bed.

reduction. A reaction by which oxygen is removed from a compound.

refermentation. An additional fermentation, generally in the bottle, with the intention of producing carbonation as well as additional alcohol.

saccharification. The naturally occurring process in which malt starch is converted into fermentable sugars, primarily maltose.

saccharometer. An instrument that determines the sugar concentration of a solution by measuring the specific gravity.

Saccharomyces. Any of several single-celled yeasts belonging to the genus *Saccharomyces,* many of which ferment sugar. Yeasts of the genus Saccharomyces cerevisiae are the most common in brewing.

secondary fermentation. 1. The second slower stage of fermentation, lasting from a few weeks to many months depending on the type of beer. 2. A fermentation occurring in bottles or casks and initiated by priming or by adding yeast.

solventy. An objectionable aroma and flavor of higher (fusel) alcohols, reminiscent of acetone.

sour. A sharp, acidic taste and aftertaste.

sparging. Spraying the spent grains in the mash with hot water to retrieve the remaining malt sugar.

species. A fundamental category of taxonomic classification, ranking below a genus, consisting of related organisms capable of interbreeding.

specific gravity. A measure of a substance's density as compared to that of water, which is given the value of 1.000 at 39.2 °F (4 °C). Specific gravity has no accompanying units because it is expressed as a ratio.

spontaneous fermentation. A method of fermentation by which all microorganisms necessary for fermentation are naturally occurring in the brewery; the brewer adds no cultures of microorganisms.

Standard Reference Method (SRM) and European Brewery Convention (EBC). Notations used to indicated two different analytical methods for color. Degrees SRM, approximately equivalent to degrees Lovibond, are used by the American Society of Brewing Chemists (ASBC) while degrees EBC are European units. Both methods are based on spectrophotometer readings at the same wavelength and conversion between the two is calculated by this equation: (°EBC) = 1.97 x °Lovibond

starter. A batch of fermenting yeast, added to the wort to initiate fermentation.

step infusion. A method of mashing whereby the temperature of the mash is raised by adding very hot water, and then stirring and stabilizing the mash at the target step temperature.

strain. A group of microorganisms of the same species, having distinctive characteristics but not usually considered a separate species.

strike temperature. The initial temperature of the water when the malted barley is added to it to create the mash.

style. Characteristics, generally flavor and aroma, by which beers are categorized.

superattenuation. Achieving a final apparent extract as low or lower than 0.1 Plato, nearly 1.000 SG, attributed to fermentation by the highly attenuative *Brettanomyces* yeasts in the presence of the other organisms.

sweet. Having the taste of sugar or resembling sugar.

tannin. Various soluble, astringent, phenolic substances, often present in yeast, malt and wood.

terroir. A unique combination of environmental conditions, present in every place where alcoholic beverages are produced, largely contributing to the character of wild beer and wine.

tertiary fermentation. An additional period of aging when beer if left to fully mature due to the presence of various microorganisms.

torrefied wheat. Wheat which has been heated quickly at high temperature, causing it to puff up, which renders it easily mashed.

trub. Suspended particles resulting from the precipitation of proteins, hop oils, and tannins during boiling and cooling stages of brewing.

tun. Any open tank or vessel.

turbid mash. A method of mashing involving the boiling of liquid from a mash consisting of a portion of unmalted grain resulting in a highly dextrinous wort.

ullage. 1. The empty space between a liquid and the top of its container. Also called airspace or headspace. 2. Waste beer, often leftover from handpumps or the bottom of casks.

viscous. Having a glutinous consistency and the quality of sticking or adhering

v/v. See alcohol by volume.

vorlauf. To recirculate the wort from one mash tun through the grain bed to clarify.

w/v. See alcohol by weight.

water hardness. The degree of dissolved minerals in water.

whirlpool. A method of bringing cold break material to the center of the kettle by stirring the wort until a vortex is formed.

wild beer. Any beer fermented of matured with yeast and/or bacteria other than those belonging to the genus Saccharomyces.

wort. The mixture that results from mashing the malt and boiling the hops, before it is fermented into beer.

yeast. Any of various unicellular fungi of the genus *Saccharomyces,* especially *S. cerevisiae,* reproducing by budding, capable of fermenting carbohydrates.

young beer. Beer that has not undergone sufficient fermentation and aging as to be considered of a mature flavor and aroma profile. Usually contains significant concentrations of viable microorganisms and sugars.

INDEX

Entries in **boldface** refer to illustrations